Your Mission:

Get Ready! Get Set!

GO!

Your Mission:

Get Ready! Get Set!

GO!

Dr. Bruce Steffes
and
Michelle Steffes

Companion volume to
Medical Missions: Get Ready, Get Set, GO!

www.s3ministries.com

Discounts for bulk orders and special printing runs in large volume, are available for church, mission and humanitarian non-profit groups. Please go to www.s3ministries.com to request information on them.

YOUR MISSION: GET READY, GET SET, GO!
Copyright © 2002, 2009, 2010 by Dr. Bruce Steffes
Linden, North Carolina 28356
Much of the material in this book has been updated and revised from the *Handbook for Short-term Medical Missionaries (ABWE, 2002)*. There is duplication of some material found in the companion volume *Medical Missions: Get Ready, Get Set, GO! (S3 Ministries, 2009)*

Notice: Unless otherwise indicated, all scripture is taken from the HOLY BIBLE, NEW INTERNATIONAL VERSION.
Copyright © 1973, 1978, 1984 International Bible Society

Library of Congress Cataloging-in-Publications Data
(Application pending)

Steffes, Bruce and Michelle Steffes

Missions, Non-fiction
ISBN-10: 0615348653
ISBN-13:9780615348650

Printed and bound in the United States of America

DEDICATION

We would like to dedicate this book to all those outstanding men and women who have heard the call of the Lord of the Harvest and who have responded as career missionaries, as short-term missionaries, or as logistical support to missionaries. We pray that this work will encourage still more to join God in doing His work. Most of all, we fervently hope and pray that this book will bring glory and honor to Jesus Christ.

"The harvest is plentiful, but the workers are few. Ask the Lord of the harvest, therefore, to send out workers into his harvest field." Luke 10:2 (NIV)

—BRUCE AND MICKY STEFFES

TABLE OF CONTENTS

FOREWORD

When we first went on the mission field, we didn't prepare well. We made all sorts of mistakes. Having survived most of them, we looked for the answers to all that had befuddled us, not so much for the benefit of others, but for our own survival in case we ran into them again. The birth of a boy and subsequent travel with him provided new experiences that broadened our horizons by allowing us to make a whole new set of mistakes. After a few years, we were urged to share with others the information we had collected. Although our first book, the *Handbook for Short-Term Medical Missions* (ABWE Publishing, 2002), had only limited print run and distribution, we were encouraged and gratified by the response to it. Certainly, the same things which had blind-sided us and caused us to write the book in hopes of helping others are still major stress factors for both short-term and career missionaries. When it became obvious that the material needed to be updated and republished, we decided to divide the previous single large book into two companion volumes, expanding where necessary and updating any material that was no longer accurate. We also decided to make it smaller in physical size so each would fit into one's jacket pocket or purse. That decision had the unintended but delightful benefit of allowing you to have more information at a lower price, even if you buy both books.

Medical Missions: Get Ready, Get Set, GO! (published in March 2009) and this one, *Your Mission: Get Ready, Get Set, GO!* are designed to be stand-alone books. That meant that some chapters are largely replicated in both books because we felt the material was vital to both medical and non-medical missionaries. Non-medical missionaries may well find the book they are now holding to be sufficient for their needs, but medical missionaries probably need both books to be fully prepared. And these books are not just for short-termers. Even career missionaries with years of experience have found the information to be of great interest to them, covering facts and tidbits about activities of daily living that they missed in their preparation to serve.

Despite being jam-packed with details, hints and advice, this book has no plot. It is not really intended to be read from cover to cover, although we admire those who do are disciplined enough to do it. Each chapter or appendix can be read as a separate topic at various times and points along your journey—some chapters will be most appropriate when you are trying to decide whether and how to go, some when you are packing and traveling, some on the field, some on return and some when you are debriefing. We actually had more information than we could put in the book and that information (expanded chapters, check-lists and articles on various topics) can be downloaded from www.S3Ministries.com and are distributed for free.

Since this book was partly written by a surgeon and has more health information in it than most such books, we must make the standard disclaimer—the information in these chapters should not take the place of personal advice from your healthcare provider. It has been provided so that you may be a more informed patient. Most family physicians do not have a familiarity with travel medicine or tropical diseases and the material has been provided so that you can ask the right questions and make sure you get the best care for your family and yourself. The information in this book, although as accurate as we could make it at the time of publication, is not intended to take the place of a timely visit to an informed healthcare provider who is able to do a complete history and physical and order appropriate tests.

You are being invited by the Lord God, the Omniscient, Omnipotent, Omnipresent One, to join Him in His work of redemption. If you accept it with an open heart, your life will never be the same! We wish you a blessed and joyous journey of discovery.

CHAPTER 1

WHAT HAVE I GOTTEN MYSELF IN FOR?

"The harvest is plentiful, but the workers are few. Ask the Lord of the harvest, therefore, to send out workers into his harvest field."

Luke 10:2 (NIV)

It is still true—there is a great harvest and too few workers. If you are reading this, you are probably interested in exploring what God would have you do as a short-term or career missionary. You have decided to answer God's call on your life. It may be the greatest adventure you ever have. It may change your life forever. But questions and second-thoughts always arise. What will actually happen on this great adventure? What will I actually accomplish? Am I going to get sick, fail at my task or otherwise embarrass myself? Why do I think I can be a missionary at all, even a short-term one? Am I really "spiritual" enough?

That is a pretty normal reaction. If you start to make a list of what you don't know and of your uncertainties, the list gets longer and longer and looks scarier and scarier. We sympathize—it happened to us as well. We looked and looked for some book or resource that would give us the answers to our concerns and a book[1] grew out of an effort to find those answers. Caveat Emptor! We will be honest—we don't have all of the answers yet. Probably never will. With the benefit of hindsight derived by twelve years of frequent mission trips, we now truly know that God can make up any deficit. Not only that, the journey will often show you more about yourself and your relationship with God than about anything else you planned to do. The purpose of this book is to help you avoid many of the problems that can hinder you from concentrating on the truly important things. The problems of living overseas or in another culture can get so overwhelming that you

---

[1] The first handbook was the "Handbook for Short-Term Medical Missionaries" (ABWE Publishing, 2002). It has been revised and updated as two companion volumes, this one and one entitled "Medical Missions: Get Ready, Get Set, GO! (2009)

1

can't focus on the real issues—the meaning of your life, the reality of Jesus in your life and the outworking of that deepened understanding.

Why are you going on a short-term mission trip and will it do any good? The role of short-term missions in the greater world of the Christian missionary effort is being argued hotly by missiologists (people who study the role of missions). What is not arguable is that short-term mission involvement is a phenomenon which blossomed in the late twentieth century and the movement shows no signs of abating early in the twenty-first century. Despite debates over the desirability of short-term missionaries (defined here in this book as people serving less than two years and often only a few weeks), it remains a fact that many present-day missionary efforts are deeply indebted to these people. The career missionaries and mission enterprises are thankful for the relief provided by short-termers, without which their orphanages, ministries and hospitals might not remain open or might not move to the next level of effectiveness. Despite our daydreams to the contrary, a short-term volunteer, who does not know the language, culture, national diet or native diseases, will rarely have a major impact on the indigenous culture or regional health statistics, but he or she can be a blessed sight to the staff who needs a break for personal, ministerial, family or educational reasons. There are many benefits to all concerned—to the career missionary, to the short-term missionary and to the short-term missionary's church and support team at home. We have listed some of the reasons in the table at the end of the chapter, admitting that the list can be much longer.

However, honesty compels us to admit that there are significant challenges in serving for short terms overseas. Many of these challenges are also present for career missionaries facing the field for the first time, but the very brevity of a short-term experience may serve to magnify the effects. Some of those challenges are unique to medical

---

[2] Many references will be made to medical missions throughout this book. That is because this book is designed to be a companion to the book entitled "Medical Missions: Get Ready, Get Set, GO!" (2009) and because we know medical missions better than we know anything else. Medical missionaries have some unique stressors, but there are many similarities between the experiences of a medical missionary and those who are not medical missionaries.

missions but most are experienced by all missionaries.[2] Failure to recognize what is happening to you as a short-term missionary (including the very real effect of culture shock both going and coming back) can make the experience miserable for you and your hosts, souring the experience for everyone. The report of an unfavorable experience will have a definite negative impact upon those back home who are considering similar trips. It does strangely satisfy those at home who predicted doom and gloom though—and you will have some of those! How then do we avoid a bad experience?

The first question must be, "What is the role of missions?" and the second that follows is "Why do I want to be involved in this mission trip?" We submit to you that the true mission of the church is to bring honor and glory to God in all that the church does. Our church building, social work, community health, education, medical care and all the other things we do in the name of missions are just steps we use to accomplish that goal. We will leave the provision of a complete answer to that first question to the rest of the book, your meditation, your prayers and your study of the Bible. But the second question remains: Why should God's church (that means *you*) be involved with short-term missions?

There are many good reasons why you personally should get involved in short-term missions and many benefits that accrue to you when you do so. There are many jobs on the mission field that you can do. You can bring new expertise to your chosen area of service. Your family can experience a new closeness with God and with each other. You can introduce your family to your career in a way you cannot do at home. You can serve to help make missions a reality to your church. The list goes on and on. A word of caution: Please do not undertake a short-term mission just for "the experience" of missions. There is a rising interest in our society in "eco-tourism". Please don't just become a "missio-tourist", collecting countries, ministries and souvenirs like a Boy Scout collects merit badges ("Ah yes, I have that country ribbon along with a cannibal cluster!") A short-term mission trip should be taken only when you are certain that God has called you to go and you are going for the "right" reasons—because God has told you to go and because you want to become closer to Him through your obedience. Harry Blackaby and Claude King state in their "Experiencing God" workbook, *"God is far more interested in your having an experience with Him, than He is interested in getting a job done. You can complete a job and never experience God at all. He is not interested just in getting a job done. He can get the job done any time He wants. What is He interested in? You and the world—knowing Him and experiencing Him."*[3]

You are probably familiar with these verses: *"'Everyone who calls on the name of the Lord will be saved. 'How, then, can they call on the one they have not believed in? And how can they believe in the one of whom they have not heard? And how can they hear without someone preaching to them? And how can they preach unless they are sent?* (Romans 10:13–15a). Although this passage is often used to recruit missionaries, we do not wish to lay a false guilt trip on those who are not called to be career missionaries. Not all people are called to be Go-ers, i.e. called to be involved in the front-lines of missions. The majority of people in the Christian Church are legitimately Senders. Both Going and Sending are a true calling and demand a clear and active response. Let's clarify them a bit.

The Go-er
• Has a burden for people to come to the Lord
• Has a desire to take the message to those people
• May feel inadequate to the task and struggle with the necessary sacrifices
• Has a driving desire for God to receive the full glory due Him from all the nations and for all the peoples to have the opportunity to hear the gospel (*"...There before me was a great multitude that no one could count, from every nation, tribe, people and language, standing before the throne and in front of the Lamb...",* Rev 7:9)
• Has heard the statistics of how many are lost and going to Hell—and has brought that need to the Lord in prayer

---

[3] Blackaby, Henry T. and Claude V. King, *Experience God: Knowing and Doing the Will of God.* Nashville: Lifeway Press, 1990, page 118.

• In asking for a solution, a Go-er becomes the answer to his or her own prayer

The Sender
• Is just as sure of his or her call as the Go-er!
• Has a burden for peoples of the world to come to the Lord—but knows his or her role in advancing the kingdom is to send
• Also has a call that demands counter-cultural living
• The sender refutes our culture's call to live for self, choosing rather to live for the glory of God and the advancement of His Kingdom
• A Sender is NOT a washed-up missionary or a Go-er who never made it!
• You may be called to be a Sender at one time in your life and a Go-er in another

Both roles in God's army are active, not passive, roles. Too many people feel that if God has not called them to be a Go-er, they are (must be) a Sender by default. They say to themselves, "Since I am not going, I must be a sender because that is all that is left." That is not true. With no desire to be unkind, a strong case can be made that if you are not actively going and not actively sending, you actually belong in a third category, the Uncommitted (or the Disobedient). Being uncommitted or disobedient is not the same thing as being a Sender.

In the modern army, the soldiers on the front lines get most of the attention. They are critical to the success of the army—but they actually make up a relatively small percentage of it. Ask the paratrooper who is about to parachute out of a (perfectly good) airplane if the fellow who packed his parachute is important to him. Ask him if the medic on the ground who will help him if he gets injured is important to him. Ask him if the people who provided the ammo, the food, and all the other support are important to him. The front lines must have logistical support. In the modern army, 85% of the army functions to provide logistical support.

In the Christian army, we must have both front-line troops and logistics as well. Any mission is a team effort. Like any tripod, it takes all three legs for stability: God, Goers and Senders

If, after this experience with short-term missions, you discover that God calls you to be a career missionary, then we praise the Lord with you. But if you find that He has called you to be "just" a Sender, don't feel second-rate (I Cor 12:12–31). Don't bother to explain to the Goers why you should stay when they go—show them why by being the very best sender you can be for God's glory. Live a counter-cultural life for the glory of God among the nations—seek the high ground for HIS glory! Your calendar and your checkbook will reveal your priorities. You will devote yourself to doing whatever you can to see the great commission completed in other lands. You will intentionally develop relationships and connections with missionaries. You will commit to pray for missionaries and their work. You will seek to go on short-term trips to assist those on the field and the people they are serving so you can gain a greater heart for the ministry and communicate it more effectively to those around you. You will take personal responsibility and carry a burden for the people groups God has led you to be involved with. You will cry out to God on their behalf and boldly declare that these people belong to God and He will have an inheritance among them. You will say, "I am not called to go, but I'm going to do everything within my power to see the name of Jesus proclaimed and honored among the nations." You will revel in the fact that the Lord has called you to be in His army and that you have a vital role. You will keep your weapon ready! You know that all in the service of the Lord must always know how to be on the front lines even here at home, sharing the Gospel of Jesus Christ at the slightest provocation, for we live in, with and among those who are dying and going to hell.

You may be protesting that God hasn't let you know yet which group you are in. All you know is that you have been led to go on this mission. That is great—and that is sufficient! If you have prayerfully asked "Is this where God wants me?" and received an affirmative answer, the rest will follow. Come along and let's complete your mission! The Lord God Almighty, Creator of the Universe, is leading us onward to where He is already working and He is eager to have you come along.

SOME REASONS TO GO ON SHORT-TERM MISSIONS TRIPS

1. **God has told you to go**
2. **Service to the missionaries**
   - Giving them time for furlough, continuing medical education, personal time, or a break from call
     - Teaching them new techniques and skills
     - Bringing needed supplies, medications, and equipment
     - Fellowship, laughter, and friendship
     - Continued prayer and advocacy upon your return
3. **Service to the nationals**
   - Biblical teaching
   - Teaching of other skills
   - Fellowship, laughter, and friendship
   - A sense that your church and country care about them and their struggles
   - A lifelong commitment to pray for your newfound friends and a renewed sense of the field "white unto harvest"
   - Medical care
   - Medical teaching
4. **Personal growth**
   - New cultures and new experiences
   - Expanded worldview
   - A deeper awareness of the role of God in your workplace
   - A deeper awareness of the need to trust God for daily life
   - A reordering of your priorities
   - A deeper awareness of the need to understand that a medical cure is for a lifetime but a spiritual cure is for eternity
   - A renewal of the enthusiasm you had when you went into medicine
5. **Family growth**
   - A chance to have quality time together
   - New cultures and new experiences encountered together
   - Introduce or reinforce a set of values and a worldview to your children
   - Introduce your children to missions as a possible career option
   - Let your children experience medicine and career in a first-hand manner not often possible at home
6. **Service to your church upon your return**
   - Bring a new sense of the reality of missions and vibrancy to your church's mission program
   - Act as an advocate and prayer warrior for the mission field you are most familiar with
   - Act as a resource person for others interested in missions
7. **For those of you in medicine**
   - New medical experiences and learning
   - Pick up new skills and newfound confidence in old skills and training that stand you in good stead
   - Experience with new diseases and treatments
   - Diseases you haven't seen before or heard of since your training
   - Use your experiences as a way to talk to your medical colleagues of your faith
8. **Introduce yourself to the possibility of a career in missions**

CHAPTER 2

EENY, MEENY, MINY, MO: PICKING AN ORGANIZATION AND PLANNING YOUR TRIP

Okay! You are willing to consider going, but what you really want to know is about the snakes, the food, sleeping in the mud huts, malaria, personal safety, disgusting parasitic disease, ad infinitum. There are lots of books that cover that stuff (including this one).

A better first question is:

With Whom Should You Travel?

Answer: The group that offers an experience that best fits your desires and needs. Now to the next question:

What! Wait a Minute...

Well, we certainly do not know all the answers that are right for you, but if you insist, we will share some of the questions you must ask yourself to help you determine what might work best for you. None of these questions have "right" or "wrong" answers except where they are "right" or "wrong" for you.

What Group and Kind of Mission Experience Is Right for You?

Answer: A good question, but in order to answer that question, you really need to answer this question first:

What Do I Really Hope to Gain from This Experience?

Answer: Usually, any single type of trip can neither give you all possible types of experience, nor meet all possible permutations of your desired conditions. For example, the experience in a mission hospital is different from that of a trip emphasizing "black bag evangelism." An experience emphasizing prayer walking and construction may not be heavy on the "getting to know the people" side. In other words, make sure that you know the trip agenda and that it is acceptable to you.

However, most of us cannot easily give specific answers to the question of what we hope to gain. We struggle to give answers such as: "I want to do good for people," "I want to see God at work," "I want to get a real grasp of the reality of mission life," or "I want to share the good news of Jesus Christ." All are laudable answers and probably true, but they don't help much with the specifics. You can be effective in situations where the answers may not be entirely in line with your preferences. As the Apostle Paul pointed out in Philippians 4:13, "I can do everything through Him who gives me strength." Short-term missions is a great way to find out how much this is true in your own life, but in the beginning, as you learn to apply this principle, you will minimize some of the potential stress if you stick to the areas where you know you have personal strengths, gifts and talents. Answers to the questions below may shed some light on this for you. They do not all need to be answered affirmatively, but the process of answering them will help you through the thought process.

When and Where Should I Go?

▶ When can they use me and when do they really need me? Some times of year are more popular with short-term missionaries. Can go at a different time?

▶ Are there local climate conditions (altitude, rainy season versus dry, allergies, extremes of temperature or humidity) that I need to take into account?

▶ Are the living conditions ones to which I can adapt?

▶ Do I have personal medical needs that can only be met in certain places?

▶ When can I get free from my usual commitments here at home?

▶ If I want to take my family, when can they get free from their usual commitments of schooling, work, and other activities?

▶ Does the purpose and format of this trip match my skills and interests (or alternatively, am I willing to stretch enough to fit the bill)?

▶ Can my skill in another language be used to good effect there or is my lack of language skills something that is not going to be a problem?

▶ Does the work I am going to visit match well enough with my philosophical and doctrinal positions that they will accept me and I them? Can I continue to support them, at least in prayer, when I come home?

▶ If I am practicing my profession, is there enough available professional supervision and experience in the type of work that we will be doing to make me feel reasonably comfortable? After reviewing the work format for this trip, am I willing to accept the possibility that the usual infrastructure that I use to do my work may be limited?

▶ Can my family go with me?

▶ Will my family be able to effectively serve?

▶ Is there flexibility enough to allow my family and me to do things we want to do apart from the scheduled group activities, either before, during, or after the fulfillment of our planned work?

▶ Do I know missionaries on the field there or do we have some point of mutual interest that can be used to advantage?

What Is My Budget, Both of Money and Time?

▶ Do I have enough time left between now and my planned departure time to allow me to get all of my needed vaccinations, passport, visas, tickets, and make my reservations?

▶ Do I have enough time available to take in account travel to and from the location (as well as get over jet lag) and still be effective?

▶ You will be funding most of these trips either personally or through your own fund-raising (see Chapter 3). Realizing that faith will always be required, can you reasonably expect to raise the required funds?

Am I the Adventurous Type or Do I Want to Have the Details Taken Care of for Me?

▶ If I travel alone (outside of a group), am I willing to attend to the large number of details that such a trip entails?

▶ If I travel alone (outside of a group), are my language, travel and adaptation skills enough for me to handle problems that might arise?

Should I Work With a Group on This Trip or Look for an Experience Where I Might be Largely by Myself?

▶ Am I willing to exchange the security of a group situation and a strong leader for being told what to do and having to conform to the schedule of the group?

▶ Am I able to be flexible enough to conform to, or at least tolerate with grace, the doctrinal, religious, and philosophical nature of the group with which I will be working?

▶ Is fellowship with fellow believers and professional colleagues an important part of the experience for me?

▶ If I go as a member of a group, am I willing to accept the possibility that I might have less one-on-one time with the missionaries and nationals with whom I come in contact?

"I have found out that there ain't no surer way to find out whether you like people or hate them than to travel with them."

—Mark Twain

Most people who are going on their first few mission experiences will opt to go with a group or organization that has done something like this before. It is not absolutely necessary to do so, but it often helps to have a safety net as you learn how to function in a new environment.

What Questions Do I Ask to Find a Credible Organization?

▶ Have they adequate experience in planning and facilitating such trips?

▶ Can they give adequate support before and during the trip if I run into difficulties?

▶ Are the team leaders experienced?

▶ Does the organization have financial integrity?

▶ Do they have a good grasp of the culture and politics of the local environment and do they have sensitivity to special needs where you will serve?

▶ Are they detail-oriented, both when they brief you about the trip and in attention to (and assistance with) the myriad of details involved with your trip?

▶ Are their trips the sort of trips that fit your plans, hopes and limitations?

▶ Is evangelism the ultimate role of your trip and are you going to be working with some organization that will be able to follow-up with any people who come to know Christ as a result of your trip?

There is a new organization which is trying to give some standardization to the short-term missionary experience. You can read more about this effort, the kinds of questions they (and you should) ask and the organizations which have already received their Standards of Excellence award—at www.stmstandards.org.

There are many good organizations that provide short or long-term opportunities for serving overseas. Word of mouth, trips planned by your church or sister churches, organizational or denominational publications, and the Internet are all ways to find trips and groups that might be suitable for you.

CHAPTER 3

RAISING SUPPORT AND
BUILDING A SUPPORT TEAM

"Why, I'd rather eat a live mamba than ask for support!"
"Perhaps I can go the ultra-devout route—I won't ask for money and
if the Lord wants me to go, He will provide it!"
"I won't be able to take a safari with my own funds if I ask for
support for our ministry."
"I don't want to feel like I am begging."
"I am not sure it is biblical to ask for support."
"I don't want it to appear that I think I am more spiritual than others,
trying to live by faith."

Do any of those statements sound familiar? We have used them all and with any thought at all, you too can come up with at least ten more. Sometimes God really does want you to pay for your trip entirely by yourself. But it must also be admitted that sometimes paying for everything yourself is just an excuse to cover your pride and embarrassment at asking. You may have a self-sufficient personality that causes you to want to pay your own way rather than being dependent on others or asking anyone for money. If you are a professional or a businessman, you may make a good income, but you are also aware of the high ongoing overhead expenses for your equipment, staff salaries, building payments, and insurance. As you go overseas, these expenses continue while the resultant dip in your income may make it difficult to cover them in addition to paying for your trip. You should not be embarrassed to share your call to ministry and ask for support if necessary. Indeed, you may be robbing someone of a true blessing if you do not share the opportunity. There is a sound biblical rationale behind the practice of allowing others to help with your ministry. Once you have an understanding of it, you will be able to share the blessings you will receive by allowing them to share in your support. Don't be selfish!

Adequate support for your trip consists of two parts. The first is financial support and perhaps the hardest for which to ask. The second is prayer support and that is sometimes the hardest to actually get in a consistent fashion despite the glib promises you may receive before you go. We will try to help with ideas for both.

Examples of Financial Support for God's Ministers

▶ Levites: In the Old Testament economy, Levites were the "professional" ministers. They were to rely on God for their income and financial stability. It was provided by the tithes and offerings of their fellow Israelites. They gave so that the Levites could dedicate time and effort to serving God in a way that their compatriots could not do.

▶ Nehemiah, the Old Testament prophet: He used financial support even from unbelievers. His approach in Nehemiah 2:1–8 is a good model. He prayed before he asked. In fact, he prayed about it for 3 months before he acted! He asked the king for specific items, and he thought carefully about those things he would request.

▶ Jesus was supported by others: He didn't do tent-making as Paul was to do later, although as a trained carpenter, He certainly could have done so. The Son of the God who owns the cattle on the thousand hills had financial supporters. He relied on people such as Joanna and Susanna who helped ". . . support Him out of their own means" (Luke 8:3).

• Jesus instructed His followers in Matthew 10:7–10 to minister and trust Him for their physical provisions: "*As you go, preach this message: 'The kingdom of heaven is near.' Heal the sick, raise the dead, cleanse those who have leprosy, drive out demons. Freely you have received, freely give. Do not take along any gold or silver or copper in your belts; take no bag for the journey, or extra tunic, or sandals or a staff; for the worker is worth his keep.*"

• Jesus instructed His disciples to heal people physically, spiritually and to trust to the goodness of others to provide for their need.

▶ The apostle Paul was supported by others: we are so used to the truth that Paul had a tent-making career in Corinth that we forget that Christians other than those in Corinth helped him financially and in other ways. Paul chose to make his own living in Corinth despite his assertion that he had the right to be supported by them, because he didn't want anyone to misjudge his motives. He did receive assistance from other individuals and churches. In Romans 15:24, the original language was clear that he was talking about money when he wrote and asked for support, *"...when I go to Spain. I hope to visit you while passing through and to have you assist me on my journey there...."*

▶ The Apostle John wrote referring to the need for God's people to back their own (3 John 1:7–8), *"It was for the sake of the Name that they went out, receiving no help from the pagans. We ought therefore to show hospitality to such men so that we may work together for the truth."*

There Really are Good Reasons to Ask for Support

▶ It is a chance for you to see what God can and will do in your life. It will enlarge your faith and increase your confidence in God and in what the two of you can do. No matter what your personal resources are, there is always a God-sized project that your resources are inadequate to handle. The needs on the mission field are great and the resources of the national churches are limited. Maybe this is how God is going to show you what He is capable of doing. If you have sensed God's call to go on this mission trip and you are in need of partial or total financial help in order to go, just remember that this does not come as a surprise to the Lord. He is always aware of your need, and He has prepared a way to meet this need. Remember, "The One who calls you is faithful and He will do it" (I Thessalonians 5:24).

▶ It stimulates and encourages a missionary vision in the body of Christ. You can serve as a model for others who are considering involvement with missions. You can mobilize others to serve Christ. You can act as an advocate and champion for missions, facilitating the communication between the missionary (and his or her mission agency) and your church and your sphere of influence.

▶ Don't rob others of a chance to be blessed. If someone does not know of an opportunity to be part of God's work, he can't be blessed by being part of it. Many people take seriously their spiritual gift of giving, or perhaps have a particular interest in the ministry that you are joining, or in the ministry in a particular part of the world. Your trip might just be the thing they are looking for and for which God has primed them. Don't be selfish and rob them of the chance to be part of your ministry.

▶ People who give financially may also be some of your strongest prayer warriors. They have demonstrated their willingness to be involved by literally putting their money where their mouth will be. The money you may be able to do without; the prayers you cannot.

▶ God has sanctioned this method of support. It can teach you humility and dependence on others and on God. It can increase your awareness of your inadequacy for the job, a prerequisite for recognizing the adequacy of God. We are instructed in Romans 12:2 not to conform to the world. By going against our culture's reluctance to depend on others, we are more closely following God's economy. In this sense, raising support is a matter of obedience to God's word and calling, by not following your feelings of self-sufficiency that may be rooted in (perhaps sinful) pride. All Christians need to live by faith (2 Corinthians 5:7, Hebrews 11:6) regardless of how they receive their paychecks or how big they are. If God had laid this on your heart and you need financial support, then He will provide everything you need to fulfill your ministry, including emotional strength and perseverance (Philippians 4:19; 1 Thes-

YOU DON'T KNOW ANYONE TO ASK? CONSIDER THIS LIST OF PEOPLE YOU MAY HAVE CONTACT WITH ON A DAILY BASIS:

advertising agencies
apartment manager
Avon lady
baker
bank presidents
banker
barber
beautician
Bible bookstore
brothers & sisters
butcher
Chambers of Commerce
Christian business groups
church directories
church members
church missions committees
church-related news ads
civic clubs
coach
college friends
community leaders
dentist
doctor
editor of local newspaper
eye doctor
family attorney
fellow workers

(cont'd on p. 17)

salonians 5:24). For further study and consideration, see Numbers 1:47–54; Deuteronomy 18:1–6; Jeremiah 29:11; Matthew 16:25; Luke 6:38, 8:1–3; 1 Corinthians Chapter 9; and John 15:16.

▶ Raising support does not make you holier or less holy than other Christians. There's nothing you can do or fail to do that will alter your eternal position in Christ (see Ephesians 1:3–4, Romans 6:5–9). It does help to develop you as a person, increases your people skills, and teaches you flexibility, patience and the sense of being an alien in a strange land. And it does increase your understanding of living by faith.

▶ It opens opportunities to witness. Unselfish acts are uncommon enough in our society that they are remarkable. Fund-raising may give you the chance to tell others why you are doing what you are doing and about the God whose love compels you (1 Corinthians 5:14, 15).

Even if you are now persuaded that there is nothing wrong in receiving support, it is still very difficult to ask, especially if you have never done anything like that before. The first thing to do as you plan your finances for mission ministry is to deal frankly with your feelings. Your role model should always be Christ, but remember that during His ministry, He was unemployed, homeless, and dependent on His friends for

(cont'd from p. 16)

florist
former college professors
former customers
former employees
former high school teachers
foundations
friends
friends of relatives
grocery store clerks
high school friends
exercise class
insurance agent
Kiwanis Club
local businesses
local radio stations
mailman
military personnel
milkman
missionary societies
neighbors (current & former)
office building directory
parents
parents' work associates
pastor
printers
retired people
Rotary Club
service station manager
Sunday school classes
teammates
telephone directory
veterinarian
wedding lists
youth group

lodging and support. The key to success in missionary service, how-ever, is to "take on the characteristics of a servant and humble your-self."[1] Humility and a "servanthood" mentality will let God use you for His Kingdom. The best place to begin this quest is in the area of your own finances. Make a commitment to trust God for the money you need. Step out in faith and make a commitment to go; then eagerly antic-ipate how God will open the doors for you to do so. Here are some steps you can follow that may help: 1. Pray. 2. Keep a biblical per-spective. 3. Spread the news of your trip and your need. 4. Pack. If the Lord is in it, it will happen!

Prayer is the most important foundation of this entire trip. Throughout this entire book, you will be reminded to pray so that you will make the right decisions and so that the Lord will bless your work. Pray that God will provide and He will tell you how best to do the fundraising. Many people immediately are attracted to George Mueller's approach to fund-raising—pray but tell no one of your need and make no solicitations. Somehow, that seems more spiritual to many of us and avoids the embarrassment. However, it may not be right for you. Remember, that other great men of God used other means. Hudson Taylor prayed mightily, kept people informed but made no solicitations. Dwight L. Moody prayed, kept people informed, and actively solicited for the Lord's work. The Apostle Paul blatantly asked, "What would the Lord have you do?"[2] All prayed and all trusted God for His provision.

Keep in mind the biblical perspective. The verses above and the pattern that God has established for the support of those who are obey-ing his commands are clear. These verses may also help:

"Every animal of the forest is mine, and the cattle on a thousand hills. ...The world is mine, and all that is in it" (Psalm 50:10, 12).

"And my God will meet all your needs according to his glorious riches in Christ Jesus" (Philippians 4:19).

---

[1] See Philippians 2:7,8
[2] See 2 Corinthians Chapters 8 & 9

Obtain a commission from your church. In Acts 13:1–3, we read that Paul and Barnabas were selected by the church leaders through the direction of the Holy Spirit. They were called out, commissioned and sent by the local church. They later returned to this church to serve and were accountable to them. If at all possible, seek the support and blessing of your church. You should be sent by your church. It is the Biblical pattern and it has a built-in accountability program: you are accountable to them and they are accountable to you. Starting first with your pastor, then with your church mission committee, give them the trip brochure or some other literature that fully explains the nature of the organization with which you are traveling and the particulars of your trip. Be sure to explain the purpose of the trip and share your testimony, your calling to go, and your vision of what might be accomplished. Ask for their spiritual blessing on your proposed trip. Ask them to pray with you, for you, and to keep you accountable. Once they have approved you, they may be able to assist you with finances from the organization and may also be able to assist you with your personal fund-raising.

How Do I Spread the News of My Trip?

▶ Ask if the pastor or any of the other people in your church would like to go with you. Ask if they can, on your behalf, challenge others to help. It is always easier to raise money for someone else, and they are in the position and have the platform to do it. Explain to your pastor or the group what the total cost of the trip is and what part of the total price you are able to cover yourself. Explain that you will need to raise funds for the rest. Emphasize that while you may be writing or asking some of the people in the church, you have no expectations that the church or the church members will be responsible for any or all of the needed money. Remember to be sensitive to any restrictions that your church places on your fundraising.

▶ Keep in mind that some churches have part of their budget set aside to help people on trips such as the one you are taking. Perhaps your trip would be eligible for such help. If the organization with which you are traveling does not provide the service, consider asking your pastor if your church could be the organization that oversees the financial aspect of your trip. As a volunteer serving in an overseas ministry under the auspices of a recognized charitable organization, you may be able to claim your out-of-pocket expenses related to the ministry as deductions for U.S. tax purposes. This includes transportation to and from the field, as well as food and lodging while performing your volunteer duties. Please refer to IRS Publication 526 and consult your tax adviser for specific information. This arrangement has the advantage of providing (and requiring) financial accountability for yourself and allows a tax-deductible receipt for those who give gifts to your ministry. If your proposed ministry is in line with things that are part of the church's vision, the pastor and church may be willing to act as your financial agency. However, be aware that because of increasing IRS scrutiny of the charitable nature of church funding, the pastor and leadership council of your church may decline to allow that.

▶ Call or write your friends and family. At first blush, it is often hard to come up with very many names, but review your Christmas card list, your parent's Christmas card list, your relatives, the list of people in your Bible study, your cell group or Sunday School class, your schoolmates, your teachers, your coworkers, Christian business men's and women's clubs, and so on. Hint: Perhaps the third grade class picture from forty years ago is overdoing it just a bit!

▶ Spend some time writing a straightforward one-page letter that gives the nature of the trip, that explains why you feel you should go and what the reader can do to help. ALWAYS personalize it. NEVER write a form letter, addressed to "Dear Friend or Relative" or "Dear Coworker". You probably would not write a check in response to such a letter. Not surprisingly, neither will they. Suggest an amount or a range of amounts that might be appropriate for them to give. Make sure the date of the deadline for contributions is clearly spelled out. Sign it and add a brief personal note as a postscript. We have written a sample letter that contains all the essential elements (see Appendix B or download it from www.S3Ministries.com). Feel free to copy it, modify it, and make it sound like you wrote it. Just make sure all the critical elements are included: who, what, where, when, why and how much. If you need to have them send the money to a third party, be sure to spell out the particulars (including the account number or any other identifying information). Caution—many groups do NOT want donors to include the person's name (on whose behalf the check is being donated) written on the check itself. Rather, the donor may need to write the name and any identifying information on a separate piece of paper and include it with the check. Improper handling of this detail may result in the loss of the giver's ability to deduct the donation for tax purposes.

▶ Send it out. Be sure to enclose a self-addressed (or one addressed to the proper organization) and stamped envelope for their convenience.

▶ After giving enough time for the letter to be delivered and for the recipient to think about your request, follow up your letter with a phone call. Many more people will give you a positive response if you follow up with a personal call. We know of many people who make it a rule to NEVER send a check in response to a letter appeal, feeling that if the person asking does not care enough to call or see them personally, then neither do they care enough to write a check.

▶ Look for groups that you can personally address. In your presentation to the group, share everything you wrote about in your letter (who, what, where, when, why and how much), especially remembering to share why and how you feel you are called to go. The best way to relate to an adult audience is through an illustration. Share a story from the place where you will serve or from your reading of a missionary book. Remember to keep it short and to the point. Offer mission trip brochures and invite others to go with you. Communicate your financial and prayer needs. Distribute self-addressed (or properly addressed) envelopes for them to use. Make sure you are touching them as individuals. A challenge to everyone is often interpreted as a challenge to no one! Perhaps you may close your talk by saying you need "investors in your ministry." Just like someone would invest in the stock market to get dividends, you need people whom God leads to invest in your "company" that will pay "eternal dividends." Communicate your deadline. Pass a sign-up sheet around the group. Be sure to follow-up with a call or personalized letter thanking them for the opportunity to speak to them and to present your vision. You can communicate with them from the field and again when you get back from the trip.

▶ If your children are going with you, encourage them to share about their trip in school and with their friends. Suggest to your children that they need to think of ways they can minister while they are on the trip and then use those ideas to challenge their friends to contribute toward a project, e.g. the purchase of a sound recorder and some Christian music tapes for the pediatric ward at the hospital, or Christian children's books, or balloons, or puppets, or candy or toys or . . . you get the idea. Let your children talk to children's groups or use their ideas when you talk to children's groups.

▶ If you are a professional or a businessman, you have a built-in constituency of people who think favorably of you—your clients and customers. Make a flyer. Make copies of your picture on an 8" x 10" piece of paper and give a short description of what you will be doing. Post them in your office, at the front desk and on the bulletin board. The flyer should answer the questions of who, what, when, where, and how much is needed. Consider putting an advertisement next to the cashier's window stating that you are donating a certain percentage of each bill paid that month to enable you to serve overseas. State that if a customer would like to contribute something more toward a need at your place of service or your direct costs, they can add that amount to their bill or place it in mission box provided. This is also a great way to get your staff involved.

If you work as an employee, ask your boss to give you paid time off as their contribution to your trip. It may help to point out that this can be a great public relations move for them, demonstrating that the company is caring for their employees and their employees care for the needs of the world.

▶ Write a short news release for your paper. Include the "who, what, where, when, why and how" of good journalism and include a picture of those who are going. Contact the editor personally. He might be interested in a human-interest story on you and your trip. Offer to help them with background information, pictures or other information they may need.

Other Methods of Fund-raising:

Here are some other examples of special programs:

► Employee Matching Fund Programs: some organizations have programs to match gifts given by their employees to non-profit organizations. If the funds used for your travel are all channeled through a recognized 501(c)(3) charity, the money you send in for your trip could qualify for a matching gift.

► Your church mission committee, local foundations in your community, and your local Christian Medical and Dental Associations chapter (if you are a physician or dentist) are other options.

One last consideration for fund-raising involves planning ahead and using Christ-honoring principles in your own personal financial plan. You plan for your retirement, house payments, and much more, so plan for your future mission trips. Consider setting up a charitable remainder trust or similar instrument. See if your mission agency will let you set up an account in your name for future use by you. With either of these options, it is possible to set aside money each month for the charitable remainder trust or mission fund. Gifts from the charitable remainder trust can be used as contributions to a mission agency to cover your travel expenses. Regular giving promotes steady growth, and the funds are then available when you decide to serve. This will also balance your tax deductions over several years.

This next item would seem to go without saying, but it will not. Write thank you notes for each gift as soon as you get it. There is no doubt that you are busy and have many things on your mind and your schedule, but there is no acceptable substitute for a personalized thank you. They deserve the thanks and your mother will be proud.

The Care and Feeding of a Support Team:

This may sound like an extreme statement, but this is the best bit of advice contained in this book: If you are leaving on a short-term mission trip without having prayed about it thoroughly, without having prepared spiritually for what you are going to face and without a bevy of Christians praying for you, don't go. It is that simple. It is that critical. This is a team effort. Your preparation by prayer and Bible study is your responsibility (see Chapter 5). Your team's responsibility is to pray faithfully. God is responsible for preparation and the outcome (Ephesians 2:10). Fortunately, the only prerequisite to join your team of prayer warriors is a willingness to pray for you faithfully while you are gone, so the list of potential recruiting prospects is great. Your obligation to them is to give them the information they need so they can pray knowledgeably and wisely.

Earlier in this chapter, the statement was made that it was often easier to get someone to contribute money to the effort than it was to get consistent, effective prayer on your behalf. The reasons behind this are many. Some make the promise glibly, figuring it is a way to sound spiritual. For some, it is the cheaper alternative to their pocketbook. For most, it is a matter of good intentions gone awry. Virtually all of us have promised to pray for something and then guiltily realized at a later time that it had slipped our mind. We meant to do it, we were vitally interested but it just didn't happen. It is your job to help them remember.

There are many ways to do this effectively. The steps that should be covered are:

10 WAYS YOUR CHURCH, FAMILY, AND FRIENDS CAN SUPPORT YOU

1. Provide for some of your personal expenses
2. Provide supplies for your trip
3. Form a prayer support team (hospital ID band idea)
4. Hold a commissioning service to bless and encourage you before the trip
5. Write notes of encouragement which you will open each day of your trip
6. Go with you to the airport to see you off
7. Give a short prayer outside the terminal or at the edges of the ticket area before you check in
8. Give you a small package filled with items of encouragement—bookmarks, tapes, poems, notes, special Scriptures, etc.
9. Welcome you home with banners and signs when you arrive at the airport
10. Allow you to share your experience

Taken from the *VIM International (IMB) Preparation Guide*

▶ Make the recruitment and sign-up process memorable.

▶ Educate your team.

▶ Use some memory device to help remind them of their promise.

▶ If at all possible, keep up a flow of timely information from the field.

▶ Give it a memorable wrap-up upon your return.

Make the recruitment and sign-up process memorable so that it sticks in their mind. Recruitment of your team is of considerable import and should be given appropriate attention. Do not just limit the list of possible candidates to those who have given money or other tangible forms of support. Some of the most staunch prayer warriors are those who are the aged, or in nursing homes, or in tight financial straights, but they have had a track record stretching back fifty, sixty or seventy years of talking with God on an intimate basis. They are often the ones with both experience and the freedom to uphold you before God in their prayers. As you talk to various individuals and groups to inform them about your trip, present your need for financial support but also present your need for prayer support. Tell them that you are looking for a serious commitment of prayer. Ask them to make a written commitment by signing up on a list or by asking them if you may put their name down on your list of names for your prayer team. In a few days, communicate again with them by personal visit, telephone call, snail mail or e-mail, thanking them for agreeing to pray for you.

Educate your team. Send them progress reports of your readiness to go. Send summaries of the basic geographic, social, economic and religious climate of the country you are visiting. Look up the country you will visit in the encyclopedia, the Internet (e.g., http://prayer-cast.com/ or www.operationworld.org) or in Patrick Johnstone's *Operation World* or *Operation World Prayer Calendar.*[3] This suggestion is especially valid for countries with which they might not have familiarity. Send brochures about the group you are traveling with. Send photocopies of newspaper articles of interest pertaining to the trip. Forward e-mails and newsletters from the field that tell them what

---

[3] Johnstone, Patrick and Jason Mandryk *Operation World Prayer Calendar*: Authentic, 2001. ISBN 978-1884543593. It is somewhat dated and has not been updated, but it still has great material in it.

is happening where you will soon be. See if someone has professional or amateur videos about the work or previous trips. Send them brief biographies about the people and missionaries with whom you will work.

Use some sort of memory device or reminder to help them remember on a daily basis. This is where your imagination can have full run. Prayer cards are the old standby and still have their place. Most missionaries have had printed up postcard-sized pictures of themselves, their families and contact information. You can do something similar. Computers and graphic art programs can make this easy, fun and affordable. The trick is then to get them to look at it. Be imaginative in how it can be displayed.

▶ Refrigerator magnets are not just for the refrigerator—they can stick on their desk, their dashboard, and their bathroom mirror. One easy way is to use your computer (or your friend's computer if you are not computer literate) is to print your own business card sized reminders and use the self-adhesive flexible magnets designed for business cards.

▶ Give some small gift that can be easily displayed that will remind them of the country where you are –miniature flags, pins (including the make-your-own kind), postage stamps, maps and other memorabilia.

▶ One particularly effective tool, especially for the men, is to give them a small piece of currency from the country (if you can get it ahead of time) and ask them to put it in their wallet—each time they pay for something, they will see it and will remember you and what you are doing. Since they will probably keep it, it is a good long-time reminder to continue praying for that country.

▶ Ask them to tie a string around a wrist or finger as an unobtrusive way to be reminded many times a day to pray for you. The plastic patient identification bracelets used in hospitals is another way to accomplish the same end. They can write your name and country on it and wear it the entire time you are gone. It is a great opening to witness to their friends and co-workers. To give you an unasked-for opinion, tattoos are probably a bit too much to ask—but might still be effective!

▶ Magazines (especial in-flight magazines), the Internet and the like give many options for inexpensive items (pins, buttons, T-shirts, etc.) that can be personalized in a way that would provide an effective reminder for prayer.

Other suggestions are highly effective but can be a little more labor-intensive. Some have created a "prayer calendar" and people have committed to sign up to pray for a certain portion (hour, day or week) of their trip. Some have appointed someone willing to be a prayer coordinator and that person has been responsible for frequently reminding—by personal call, phone, mail or e-mail—people to pray for you. If a special prayer need comes up, having such a person has the advantage of giving you someone you can contact quickly and consistently while on the trip.

Ongoing communication with your prayer team is very important. They have invested in your ministry. You would not like it if you invested in a mutual fund and received no information about what was happening with your investment. Your investors will not either. One great idea is to send a postcard detailing answers to prayer and new prayer requests a week after you arrive in country. An acceptable alternative is e-mail, especially with the occasional digital picture attached. E-mail is a real blessing to missionaries, both long and short-term. If you have appointed a prayer coordinator as described above, it also gives you the added advantage of having a person who will be responsible for getting any other communication to the team as well. Remember that not everyone has e-mail if that is how you choose to communicate and this system will facilitate the transfer of information from you to your team. Communication with those at home is a very effective tool. Whether that is by e-mail newsletter and digital pictures or by regular letters and postcards, regular communication is a must. It does not have to be a polished piece of prose but should reflect what you have experienced and how it affects your mind and heart. Suffice it to say, that if you have built a close relationship with your support team before you leave, you may have some items of deeper sensitivity that you can share with them about your struggles that you might not be able to share with a more general reading audience.

Follow-up when you get home is very important. All good military commanders insist on an after-action report and it is highly recommended that you put your thoughts down on paper. Analyze what the Lord has done, what was done well and what might be done better next time. As vivid as your memories are when you get back, and it seems that you will never forget, you will forget. Share your report with your supporters, both the financial benefactors and the prayer warriors and be certain to thank them for their help. A small souvenir (including such things as a coin, a flag, a postcard, or a bookmark) is often much appreciated, especially if personally presented with a word of thanks. As your mother told you—and she is usually right—the thought here is the important thing, not the size of the gift. A tract in the local language along with a note that reminds them they have sent the Gospel; a letter opener to remind them with every use that they have helped open the hearts of others; a piece of currency to put in their wallet to help remind them of their newfound financial priorities; a calendar from that country to remind them to pray daily for the missionaries there and the people you have left behind.

Conduct a "Shareholders' Meeting." Invite those that have had a "share" in your ministry over to your house for a report night. Show your good slides, your best video or PowerPoint presentation and have everyone that went give a report. Keep it short and leave time for questions. Share your frustrations, failures, and triumphs. They will want to know more about your reactions than hearing a travelogue. Lace the evening with humorous anecdotes. If you can, bring something home from the country you visited, e.g., tea, coffee, candy, etc., to serve at this meeting. Close the evening with a short time of prayer for the place where you served.

Don't forget to give a report to your church if possible. Express your appreciation for their support and prayers; share briefly the impact of your ministry on yourself and the people you served, emphasizing the spiritual aspects. Let them know your trip and their prayers and support have reaped a spiritual harvest.

In summary, missionaries overseas desperately need you to help them hold up their end in remote locations under trying circumstances.

Don't let money stand in your way. Trust the Lord that when he says, "Go!" He will always provide the way. As Abraham went "by faith," believe that God will also honor your commitment to serve Him to the ends of the earth. Dillon writes, "As you raise support, God will increase your faith in miraculous ways. He will lead you to new friends and through new experiences. When an effective strategy is followed, support-raising, rather than being a nightmare, becomes an exciting journey of spiritual growth. And if that is God's will for you, it is a process you won't want to miss."[4]

---

[4] William P. Dillon. People Raising—A Practical Guide to Raising Support. Chicago: Moody Press, 1993, Page 245.

CHAPTER 4

GETTING READY TO GO: TRAVEL DOCUMENTS

If you have only traveled in North America, you are spoiled. When you leave the ground on the first leg of the international flight, the same rights, privileges and ways of thinking that you have taken for granted no longer protect you. Getting ready is not difficult but must be done in a timely fashion (read "as soon as possible") and correctly.

PASSPORTS

Effective January, 2007, United States citizens must have a passport or passport card to get back into the U.S. Passport cards are valid only for land or sea travel from Canada, Mexico, Bermuda and the Caribbean. They are not good for international travel. You can find out more about them at http://travel.state.gov/passport/ppt_card/ppt_card_3926.html. Most of you will require a passport. Your passport MUST be valid for six months after you return in order for many countries to accept it. Therefore, check your passport now. If it is not valid for six months after the scheduled date of your return, or if you can't find it or you never had one, get one. If your children are traveling with you, they will each need a passport. Any adult, including your spouse, traveling with you will also need one. Additionally, you must have a passport BEFORE you get any visas if they are necessary to visit the country you are entering. Each of those visas can take up to a month (and sometimes even more—up to six months) to process. Start early!

Obtaining a passport is simple but you should allow at least one month and preferably two months to obtain one. If you have procrastinated, shame on you, but don't despair. There are still options. There are also 13 regional passport agencies, and one Gateway City Agency, which serve customers who are traveling within two weeks (14 days), or who need foreign visas for travel. Appointments are required in such cases. Please go to http://travel.state.gov/passport/get/first/first_ 832.html for instructions and to determine the fee for expediting the processing of your request. There you will also find the list of regional agencies if you need one. Also, there are many companies who will expedite the service for passports and visas for you and can usually deliver the passport in three business days. Ask your travel agent for the name of one they use. It will usually require paying for overnight mail delivery in both directions and an additional fee to the company above and beyond the passport fee (usually about $30–$50 or more).

If this is your first passport, you will need to apply in person. The steps are as follows:

▶ Before you go, make sure you have passport photographs taken. They must be identical, two-inches square and be a full-face view. You must provide pictures taken within six months of your application. Get additional copies made for the visa, for the mission board application, for your International Driver's License, and get a few extra to take with you in case you need to apply for another visa or replacement passport. Many drugstores, one-hour photo-processing stores and department stores have this service for a lower price than a professional photographer. Digital cameras and processing often make this an immediate service.

▶ Go to the nearest passport agency. They are usually located in courthouses and/or some post offices. Your travel agent can usually tell you where the nearest passport office is located and the information is available at the URL above.

▶ Present a proof of identity. In addition to the original of your proof of identity, you will need to provide an 8.5" x 11" photocopy of the document which must contain your photo and signature, such as a valid driver's license, naturalization certificate, a state-issued ID card, student ID, military ID, etc.

▶ Present proof of U.S. citizenship. An old passport, certified birth certificate or naturalization papers are needed.

▶ Fill out the passport application and pay the fee. The form and list of required information is obtainable from the Clerk or Deputy Clerk of a Federal Court of Record, passport office, certain post offices and the Internet (http://travel.state.gov/passport/get/first/first_830.html). The fee is $95 + a $25 executive fee for first-time adults (the passport is good for ten years) and $82 plus the $25 executive fee if under 18 years of age (the passport is good for 15 years). It will take three to four weeks to receive your passport in the mail. Renewal is $70 + a $25 execution fee and the fee is $60 if expediting the process.

▶ If you are filing a passport application for a child, BOTH parents must sign the application form in the presence of the agent.

▶ You should make an appointment to be seen at one of the Regional Passport Agencies only if the passport is needed within less fourteen days for international travel and/or the U.S. passport is needed within four weeks to obtain a foreign visa.

If you are renewing your passport (or if you have a valid passport but it is getting filled with stamps from previous trips so that supplemental pages are needed), you can get the appropriate form from your local passport office or the Internet. Send in the form, the photos, a check for the appropriate fee, and your old passport. Allow four weeks for processing.

Important tip! As soon as you get your passport, make three photocopies of the first two pages of your passport. Put one in a safe place in your home. Put the second copy with the information you are leaving for your family or friends. Put the third copy with two extra passport pictures in your luggage. Keep them separate from your passport itself (either in a separate body wallet or suitcase). In case your passport is lost or stolen, having these pictures and information with you is a wise idea and makes replacement much easier.

A variation on that tip! Scan the first two pages of your passport and then use your computer to shrink the picture until it is twice the size of a wallet card (~3.25' x 4.25'). Print it, fold it so that it is the size of the credit card (3.25" x 2.12") and then laminate it to keep in your wallet.

A third variation on that tip! If you have a web-based e-mail, send the scanned passport (as well as any other important papers) to yourself in a series of e-mails and keep them stored on the Internet so you can download them from anywhere in the world if the need arises.

VISAS

WARNING! This can take months! Allow enough time!

Many countries require a separate visa (and of course a fee to go along with it) in order to let you visit their country. Sometimes they are available at the airport when you land but this seems to invariably require American currency (never credit cards), a long wait at a time when you are already exhausted and usually you can only get single-entry visas. As a general rule, it is probably wiser to get the visa in your home country before you leave. This is especially true if you want a multi-entry visa or some specialized sort of visa.

Your mission agency or travel agent can tell you what forms or other special documents are needed (e.g. a letter of invitation from your hosts to visit the country is needed to get a visa in many countries). These forms are available from your travel agent, your passport/visa expediting service, the embassy of the country you are visiting, and usually from the Internet (use a search engine to check for the embassy web page). They are usually self-explanatory but be sure to check with your mission agency or board before filling them out. They can guide you as to whether it is wiser to check "tourist" or "business" or "work", whether you want "single" or "multiple entries" and give you clues about how to fill in any questionable areas. If in doubt, ask! The wrong answer may significantly delay the process or leave you without a visa. Many of them will require two or three passport-sized pictures, often with a requirement that they be signed and dated on the back and sometimes certified by a notary. Getting your signature, the notary's signature and statement crammed into the space on the back of the picture is sometimes a fascinating experience. We are still somewhat in the dark as to why it must be certified. It is bad enough to admit that the picture on the other side is really you (they are always at least as unflattering as your driver's license picture) but to have to have a third party confirm that you look that bad seems somewhat cruel. Ah well, this is the first of many indignities you will have to suffer!

Countries with which the U.S. has warm political relationships usually do not give you more than the usual amount of bureaucratic delay. Some others may make it more difficult and hints for a bribe to facilitate it are not unknown. For some of those countries, the price of an expediting service may be worth it to you to avoid the headache.

TICKETS, TRAVEL ARRANGEMENTS, AND LODGING ON THE WAY

Many of the groups you go with may take care of all of this for you. If you have to take care of the particulars yourself, still ask the group if they have a travel agency with which they are happy. Since many mission trips are not on the usual tourist circuit, most travel agents know very little about how to get you there. It is therefore best to use an agency with experience in booking mission trips and especially those familiar with the country you are visiting. There are often "missionary rates" on various airlines that can make a real difference in cost, but given the multi-level booking schedules for all airlines, many agents are not familiar with those fares that may be advantageous to you. Someone with experience on the small airlines found in developing countries will also know which ones to avoid, how much potential delay time to build in, and the like.

If you are traveling with children or with lots of luggage, it is particularly helpful to schedule your flight to avoid the busiest times of day at airports (8 to 10 AM, 4 to 7 PM). Be sure that your agent knows you are bringing extra luggage. Increasingly, airlines will refuse extra bags if they have not pre-approved them. Also, the fees for extra baggage can be considerable and you have to seriously consider whether what you plan to carry is worth the expense.

You can download a list from www.S3Ministries.com that gives you the names of some agencies that have been known to handle a large number of such trips. There are undoubtedly others who may do every bit as well.

Some miscellaneous considerations:

▶ It may be considerably cheaper on the shorter trips if you can stay at least fourteen days.

▶ If your travel agent has recommended a national or regional airline, it may be cheaper, but the quality of service can be poorer. This may be evident in the quality of the plane, of the food, of the personal service and in reliability. The chance of schedule disruption is sometimes much higher on these small airlines and it is not unheard of for some flights to be cancelled for days or even permanently, leaving you to scramble for alternative modes of transportation. Another drawback of small airlines is that there are often no reciprocal agreements that will allow you to get frequent flyer miles. Transfer of luggage is also a problem. If they do not have reciprocal agreements for baggage handling, you may have to get a visa to come into the country, get your luggage, check your luggage once again with the second airline (which usually does not honor the two-suitcase, 23 kg rule that covers you when coming and going from the U.S.), pay any extra charges for what is now "overweight" or "extra" luggage and then go back through immigrations to catch your plane.

▶ Speaking of frequent flier miles, many airlines around the world have reciprocal agreements with U.S. airlines. Be sure to sign up for the appropriate frequent flier membership well in advance of your trip in order to minimize the chances of confusion and failure of proper posting of the credit to your account. Take the card with you to make sure it gets credited at each leg of the trip. Some airlines will not honor your request if you do not have the original card from your airline. You can still submit the ticket stubs for frequent flier credits when you get back, but you have to keep track of the stubs and submit them within the appropriate time constraints. If you have a credit card that gives you frequent flier miles for purchases, be sure to use it to pay for your tickets. One long trip to Asia or Africa can give almost enough miles for a free domestic trip.

▶ Your schedule: do not allow your agent to schedule you too tightly between flights. You will have enough stress without worrying about making a 45-minute connection. This is especially true when traveling with children. Schedule at least 2 or 3 hours between flights in order to give you a chance to walk around and to make sure your luggage and your family all make it on the next flight.

▶ Most short-term missionaries heading somewhere have strained their weight and luggage restrictions to the breaking point because they are carrying things for the project or for the missionaries. If you need to take extra baggage, notify your agent and/or the airline several days in advance and see if the airline has any program that will allow you to take extra luggage at a reduced charge (a diminishing number of companies will do it for free if you ask nicely and tell them you are on a missionary trip). Do NOT expect the same courtesy if you show up at the airport without having notified them ahead of time. Even so, the final decision is up to the ticket agent at the airport, and they do not have to honor any previous commitment made over the phone nor the commitment made by another airline with whom you are connecting. This can be frustrating and is one reason to arrive at the airport in plenty of time so these details can be worked out.

▶ Some U.S. airlines are now requiring that you confirm your baggage (and pay for it) via the Internet before you come to the airline. There is usually a benefit financially by doing so. Be sure to bring your receipt to your check-in at the airport to avoid confusion.

▶ A reminder for the trip home: Confirm your ticket at least 72 hours before you leave. In many countries, you cannot do this at the airport and have to do it by phone during regular business hours. One possible help: on occasion, we could not do it in country because of the failure of phone lines, strange business hours and the like. We were able to e-mail back to our family and travel agent and they confirmed our flight from the U.S. (where 24 hour service is more likely to exist for your airline).

▶ If you need special meals (either for yourself or for your children), please notify your agent at the time you book the trip. Some fliers routinely ask for diabetic meals for themselves because they tend to be lighter and more digestible—and carry the added benefit of being served first!

SEAT ASSIGNMENTS

If at all possible, have your travel agent book your seats at the time you make the reservation. If that is not possible, ask them to book them at the earliest possible date (make a note in your calendar to call them to ensure they have not forgotten to do this for you). In selecting your seats, ask your agent for the configuration of the plane's seating. How many aisles does the plane have? How many sections are thereby created? How many seats in each section? Where are the bulkheads, kitchens and bathrooms? Where are the engines? This information may help you choose your seats wisely. There are some general advantages and disadvantages of various seating locations that are worth reviewing:

▶ Front of the plane: these are best if your connection times are tight because you can get off the plane quicker but are usually the most crowded since the seats tend to be assigned from the front to the back. These seats tend to have less air and engine noise, especially in aircraft with wing-mounted engines. If you have problems with air-sickness, these are not as good as the ones over the wing but better than the ones behind the wing.

▶ Over the wing: just in front of or over the wing are the best for those with motion sickness but obviously the wing obstructs the view. Sometimes the airflow over the wing or the engine location can make these seats noisy.

▶ Back of the plane: These tend to have the highest probability of the adjacent seat being empty but people sitting here are usually the last ones to leave the plane. The last row in any section may not recline properly because of the bulkhead behind it and it has a higher chance of having less knee room. The ride in the very back of the plane tends to be bumpier and if you are prone to motion-sickness, do not select these seats. Any seats near the toilets or bulkheads can be noisy and the traffic may interfere with your rest. Because of the trailing noise from wing-mounted engines or because of proximity to tail mounted engines, these seats tend to be noisy.

▶ Window seats: these let you sleep without being disturbed by those wishing to move about. It gives you the ability to lean against the wall and window while sleeping. Obviously, the view is better. This seat (along with the center of the center section) is best if you have a child needing a restraint system because placing the child restraint system here does not interfere with evacuation in case of emergency.

▶ Aisle seats: it is easier to get up and to move around or to use the rest room. Long-legged passengers have the advantage of a little extra leg-room but at the risk of having your knee or foot traumatized by the carts and people in the aisles.

▶ Seats near exits in planes with multiple doors: the increased speed of exiting the plane may be helpful if any connection is tight.

▶ Emergency row (exit row): these usually have more legroom. Emergency row seating is usually not assigned in advance and increasingly, airlines are charging extra for these seats. If you are flexible in your seating plans, arrive early at the airport and ask if such seating is available. Children under the age of 15 and those with diminished hearing, problems with language fluency or physical disabilities that prevent them from opening the emergency exits are not allowed to sit there.

▶ Bulkhead seats: these have more legroom but usually have sub-optimal views of the movie screens and have no under-seat storage. All carry-ons must be stored in an overhead bin which may be behind you. Armrests usually do not lift up and therefore if there is space next to you, it is more difficult to stretch out on the seats. Bulkhead seats are especially valuable if you have children (see below).

Seating Considerations for Children

Taking your children can be a blessing but it requires special planning. Remember that children should be properly restrained both in the plane and during transit to and from the airport. A restraint system must be both FAA and airline approved. It should also be of such a size that it can fit in the limited width of an economy class seat (not all child restraint systems are that narrow). See Chapter 9 for a further discussion. In addition to the things mentioned above, consider the following:

▶ Be sure your travel agent knows your children's ages. Otherwise, you may be required to make a last minute move and you may not all be able to sit together as you would prefer.

▶ Bulkhead seats are especially valuable if you have children because of increased floor space for playing and sleeping. You are usually close to the flight attendants. Bulkhead seats are the best ones for infants who do not pay for a seat. Upon prior request, some airlines will provide a small "skycot" (portable bassinet) for infants under 10 kg to occupy during the flight. The child must be held during take-off and landing. Since the arm rests do not lift up, it is hard for the child to stretch out to sleep. Also, if the plane is stuck on the ground, putting your carry-on in the overhead which may be behind you, can make a child's demand for a drink, food or toy _now_ impossible to meet.

▶ One of the parents who are traveling with children should probably sit in an aisle seat to accommodate frequent trips to the bathroom to avoid repeatedly inconveniencing some poor stranger.

▶ If only one parent and one child are traveling together (or for that matter, if two adults are traveling together), and the seat configuration is three across, consider booking aisle and window seats in the same row. If the plane is not full, you will have the entire row. Lift up the armrests and you will be able to stretch out. If it is full, one of you can then take the center seat. If there are two adults and a nonpaying infant is traveling with you, this strategy sometimes works to your advantage as well. If the seats remain empty, you can avoid holding the child the entire trip and put your baby in the center seat. Make sure that your car seat is approved by the National Highway Traffic Safety Administration and that your airline approves its use in their plane (see Chapter 9).

▶ Not a seating issue, but worth a reminder: several airlines offer fast-food type meals for kids that you must order in advance (sometimes the day before). If you forget to reserve them, bring some kid-friendly snacks in case the standard meals do not appeal to your children.

▶ Some airlines are now allowing you to book a second seat at the same price as your first seat. This gives you room to stretch out but at less cost than a business class ticket. The legroom is still not the same however. This may be worth considering for a long overseas trip (such as to South Africa or Asia). Usually, you have to call the airline directly to get this type of reservation.

DRIVER'S LICENSE

Road vehicle accidents, not malaria, disease or rebel activity, are the leading cause of death for missionaries. That statement is not to scare you but to warn you that driving in the rest of the world is not like it is in North America. That said, you will need a license if you plan to drive there. Some countries let you use the U.S. driver's license, but it is probably wisest to obtain an International Driving License. This form is merely a certification that you have a valid driver's license and that statement is translated into ten other languages. It is available through the AAA Club. There is a $15 fee and two passport photos are required (which can be taken on site in most AAA offices). It is accepted in approximately 180 countries worldwide. Sometimes you must present both your U.S. driver's license and the International Driving license to the local police upon arrival and pay yet another special fee in order to drive in those countries. Failure to be properly licensed can be expensive and the consequences inconvenient, so please check before you drive.

INSURANCE FOR YOUR BELONGINGS

▶ Make sure that your homeowner's insurance will cover the items you are taking on the trip if they are stolen or lost.
▶ Make sure your homeowner's insurance will cover your home in your prolonged absence. Some policies will cover the house and its contents only if it is being regularly looked after. Make sure you know what your policy says and that you comply with all stipulations.

INTERNATIONAL CERTIFICATE OF VACCINATION

This document is available from your health department. Which immunizations are required and which are recommended vary from country to country. Please see Chapter 6 for a more detailed discussion of immunizations.

PROFESSIONAL LICENSURE

If you are going to work as a professional, please read this carefully. Some countries are very strict about licensure and others do not require anything at all for a short-term trip. Some allow you to work under the supervision of someone who is already licensed in that country. Check with your missionaries or with your agency to see what is needed. Usually someone in the country will need to go to the licensing board of that country to confirm what you need and to get you copies of the forms you need to fill out. If you need to get a license in the country, most licensing boards usually require a certified copy of your license, specialty certification and letter of good standing from the your state licensing board. They often request certified copies of your diploma, certified translations of the diploma into English, certified certificates of residency, and occasionally other documentation such as a police report from your home country. If you are one of those many people who have graduated from schools that feel that the bigger the diploma, the smarter their graduates appear, it is sometimes hard to get a good photocopy. Companies and stores that specialize in reproduction of blueprints are often your best bet at getting a large enough photocopy made. Keep the original copy (is that an oxymoron?) in a safe place for you to use to make future photocopies. Translations of your diploma may be hard to get if you don't know someone who speaks Latin or whatever language your diploma is printed in. Often, the best place to obtain that translation is from the Dean's office of your medical school or other professional school and it usually has to be a notarized copy.

Interestingly enough, it is often harder for nurses to get professional permission or licensure than it is physicians or dentists. Allow enough time to work through the barriers that are raised. Even if you are told that a license is not needed, taking photocopies of your credentials with you may prevent unpleasantness if some local official wishes to cause problems. Also, in some cultures, it is wise for you to pay a call of greeting to the local officials just as a matter of courtesy. Check with your missionaries about the necessity of such a call.

Many missionaries, both career and short-term, try to work in a country without getting formal licensure. This can create much unpleasantness and even lead the government officials to close your short-term project or to the permanent closure of the long-term work. Whether or not you feel their system requires respect and compliance, they certainly do and are often very sensitive about it. Put yourself in their shoes—would you accept it if someone from another country came to your country and started practicing your profession without confirmation of their skills and without going through the legal process? Failure to comply can ruin your Christian testimony in that country.

OTHER HELPFUL PIECES OF PAPER TO TAKE

Health Insurance Cards

Although most hospitals overseas will not take direct payment from the insurance company, having a photocopy of your card with you is wise. Some N. American health insurance policies do NOT cover you while overseas. It may be wise to seek supplementary health insurance. If you opt to get an additional health insurance policy that covers you and your family while overseas or that covers evacuation to a medical facility, take that information with you as well. On our website (www.S3Ministries), there is a list of helpful websites. It has a list of many companies who can provide health insurance, travel insurance, expatriation insurance and even terrorism insurance.

Insurance for Medical Evacuation and Expatriation of Remains

It may be wise to consider insurance which pays for you to be evacuated if you are seriously ill. Make sure it covers you worldwide (or at least the country where you will be visiting), that you can go to the hospital of your choice (as opposed to one selected by the company) and that there is not a limit on the expenditures (it can be frightfully expensive). Also, if you should die overseas, you will find that it can cost as much as $100,000 to return your body to your home. Insurance to cover this potential disaster is a wise choice and is often required by sending agencies.

Insurance for Terrorism

Some companies are also providing insurance for acts of terrorism. Most insurance policies exclude acts of terrorism. It is difficult to get terrorism insurance as an individual but a few insurance companies offer the option (Adams and Associates International, www.aaintl.com, is one of them). The insurance may also be available through your sending agency.

Cash

Currency and currency equivalents are also very nice (and necessary to have) on such trips. The issue is always one of security versus exchange rates. There are several options: personal checks, U.S. cash, traveler's checks and plastic. Each has some advantages and drawbacks, so look into what is best for your trip *before* you go.

Personal checks are increasingly having a place. Many agencies and mission groups overseas will accept them (usually at a good rate of exchange), so stick in a few to cover the possibility. Banks and stores, especially in the developing countries, usually do NOT take them. They are secure even if they are not always liquid. Do not plan on them being your only source of cash. There are stories of dishonest people trying to use your account information and your signature to forge checks, so be careful.

United States currency and Euros are rapidly becoming universal currencies and can be used for tips at airports when you have not yet been able to cash money or when your new currency notes are too large to be used for tips. Take small denominations—$1, $5 and $10—for purchases in airports and for tips. Twenty-dollar bills are often required to pay for visas and for airport departure taxes. Check on that as you enter the country and if they are required, tuck them away so you will have them when you leave. You may need American currency to pay for visas upon entering a country. Whether $50 or $100 bills are best to use for routine exchange is debatable and that should be checked with the missionary on the field or someone who has recently traveled there. Often $100 bills will give you a better exchange rate than smaller bills and depending on the country, increasingly are giving better exchange rates than traveler's checks. What is important is to make sure the bills you have are new[1], intact, and without spot or blemish, and that they are of the latest anti-counterfeit "big picture" type. Go to the bank before you leave North America to get them but you may have to call before you go to ensure that they have enough of the latest type. Money exchangers and merchants, even in small out of the way places, seem to know all about the types of currency and will often reject any bill that is less than perfect or that is of an old series. They will often give you a less favorable exchange if it is more than a few years old. It can leave you stranded without cash if you ignore this warning. Currency has the real advantage of being very liquid and the disadvantage of being an attractive target for thieves. Take it in a money belt or body wallet if you have a significant amount and/or divide it up between your wallet, briefcase, purse, or something that you will keep close to you or on you at all times. It is better to divide it and lose part of it than to gamble and lose all of it.

WARNING! If you are carrying more than $10,000 in cash or liquid financial instruments into or *out* of the U.S., be certain to declare it to the U.S. Customs at your port of departure. It is illegal to leave

---

[1] For example—at the time of publication (2010), many exchange bureaus will not take money printed before 2006 or if they do, at a significant discount.

without declaring it. Failure to comply with this regulation can have serious consequences. Likewise, know the regulations about how much cash you can carry INTO the country you are visiting. Some countries will "tax" you on extra cash over their limit and failure to comply and declare such funds can have serious consequences, including forfeiture of all the money and/or time in jail. This information can be hard to find out. Check with your travel agent, guidebooks for the country, on the Internet and if necessary with the country's embassy before you leave.

Traveler's Checks

These have the advantage of perhaps being the most safe of all forms of money, but are so only if you follow the simple precautions. Keep track of your numbers (and where you spend each one) in a separate place from your traveler's checks. That will allow them to be replaced if they are stolen. Get the checks in a variety of denominations so you don't have to exchange too much money. If you are traveling with your spouse, if possible, get the checks that will allow either one of the two individuals who signed the checks initially to sign it as the only person the second time. That keeps you from having separate checks and allows a little more individual freedom on your shopping trips (whether that is good or not will have to be worked out with your spouse and is beyond the scope of the advice of this book!). Some places will not take them at all (in which case you had better have enough cash). In some countries, traveler's checks give the best exchange rate but it is increasingly *not* true in most other countries. Check before you go. Sometimes the difference can be as much as 10 percent in the exchange rate.

Credit and Debit Cards

They are increasingly accepted in many third world countries. Check with someone in country as to the best ones to use: VISA and MasterCard are the most commonly accepted worldwide. American Express has the advantage of not having a limit if you need to arrange some high cost transportation in an emergency but is less widely accepted. If you are using a debit or credit card and can find an automated teller machine (ATM) that accepts it, the exchange rate is usually better than cash or traveler's checks. However, the presence of machines that are compatible with your card's system is spotty. Do NOT assume that they are available unless you confirm their presence ahead of time. If you can use the credit card for your purchases, lodging, meals and so on, you will often get the best rate of exchange possible. This is because these big companies are exchanging huge amounts of currencies every day and thereby demand (and pass on) the best rates. There is often a separate fee from your bank for foreign currency exchange (usually about 1%) but it still works out to be one of the better exchange rates even including that fee.

One danger inherent in the use of credit cards is the issue of identity theft. There is a new TravelMoney card which is a debit card, charged with cash before you go. It is accepted at any place which accepts a Visa credit card and diminishes the risk of misuse of your credit card or identity theft. If you use your credit card, as a matter of common sense, take the carbons from the stores where your credit cards are used. If someone begins to illegally use your credit or debit card while you are on a mission trip, you will not know about it until much later. It is wise to notify your credit card company (or your bank if you are using a debit card) that you are traveling in such-and-such country so that they don't stop what they would ordinarily consider to be a suspicious charge from an unusual place but will be on heightened alert for fraud. Calling back to the States to get your card working again can be difficult and expensive.

Taking a credit card in case you have to arrange airline flights, lodging or other types of emergencies is still a good idea. However, only take one or at most two in case one is not working. Empty your wallet or purse of all extra cards as a security measure. If you don't bring it, it can't be lost or stolen. Make sure that you photocopy the entire contents of your wallet and leave one copy at home and take one with you, carried in another place. You may need this information if it is lost.

Foreign Currency

Having some foreign currency before you leave the airport, especially in the amounts necessary to pay for taxis, tips, food and incidental expenses for a day or two, is a great idea. It is possible to exchange money before you go by using services like AAA (http://www.aaa.com/AAA_Travel/TravelMoney/foreign_currency.htm). Some people will exchange money at a U.S. airport bank or one of the big airports in transit instead of waiting until you get overseas where you are tired and the lines may be long. Usually the commission charged and the exchange rates are not as favorable as they will be within the country. Also less common currencies will not be available. If you are going to do this, exchange only the amount you will need for the first day. Each time you exchange one currency for another, it will cost you money. Avoid changing from one currency to another, e.g., don't go from dollars to schillings to Kwacha to dollars.

One option is to look for an ATM in the airport when you land in-country. The airport may be your best chance of finding an ATM in some of these countries and will usually give you an excellent exchange rate.

A CHECKLIST

- ❑ Passport photos
- ❑ Passport
- ❑ Visa(s)
- ❑ Photocopies of passport, visa, extra photos
- ❑ Ticket
- ❑ Frequent-flier card
- ❑ Traveler's checks
- ❑ Cash
- ❑ Credit card
- ❑ International certificate of vaccination
- ❑ U.S. driver's license
- ❑ International Driver's License
- ❑ Photocopies of professional licenses, etc.
- ❑ Letter of invitation
- ❑ Letter of charitable intent
- ❑ Certified copy of birth certificates
- ❑ Certified copy of marriage license
- ❑ Power of attorney
- ❑ Health power of attorney for dependents
- ❑ Photocopy of your health insurance card including traveler's insurance
- ❑ Children's health record
- ❑ Itinerary and contact information
- ❑ List of preferred workmen for your home
- ❑ Permission to pick up mail

Money exchangers are in the business to make money. They will do it either as a transaction fee, by giving a less than fantastic exchange rate or most commonly a little of both. Some advertise that they have no transaction fee but then they make it up on the exchange rate. There will be a charge to you to exchange money in both directions (although some money exchangers have no commission on changing back to home currency if exchanged by them originally) so do not exchange more than you need at any given time. Ask your hosts how much you need to exchange. The amount will depend on what you will need to buy, how good the shopping is, how many souvenirs you want, how easy it will be to get more exchanged, and so on. Ask your hosts where they get the best exchange rate. They will know. If that is not possible, comparison-shop the rates if it you are able to do so. There can be big differences in commissions, exchange rates, and the ultimate answer to the question "how much of this new funny money do I get for my cash when everything is said and done and paid?" is what is important.

WARNING! Unless you like meeting new people in smelly jails, avoid "Black Market" exchanges. Even if you can somehow square this with your conscience as a Christian, there can be severe penalties if caught. Some countries do tolerate a so-called "gray market" in which there is a recognized and accepted difference between the official exchange rate and the everyday exchange rate, but this should be approached with caution. Your testimony as a Christian is at stake as well as your money and perhaps your freedom.

Telephone Cards

Prepaid telephone cards, especially those accepted by companies with worldwide distribution, can be very helpful and make phone calls home much less expensive. Even if you cannot use it from the country where you are, it may be helpful during your travels to and from the country.

Letters of Charitable Purpose and Invitation

If you are carrying more than a few items of obvious value (medical supplies, drugs, diagnostic equipment, electronics, etc.), a letter from your mission group explaining who you are and that what you are carrying is a gift to the missionary work may help get you through customs without penalty. Gold seals, embossing and several signatures always make such a letter look more impressive. A letter from someone in country, especially local or federal politicians or someone in the bureaucracy welcoming you to the country and asking the customs department to facilitate your passage, often helps, especially if it is in the national language or language of the customs agent.

Approval for Importation of Bulk Medications and Controlled Substances

Generally, importation of these drugs may not be worth the bother. If you *need* to bring large amounts of bulk medications or controlled substances into the country, the proper paperwork must accompany you. For bulk medications, it is best to get approval before you arrive by sending the list ahead containing brand and generic name, strengths, numbers and expiration dates. This may take a while; therefore allow plenty of time. For controlled substances, have the hospital you are visiting tell you how best to get the necessary approval and ask them for their assistance. They can usually do it more effectively by working within the country. Be sure to check with Drug Enforcement Agency in the U.S. before exporting them. Jail time on either end is not worth it.

Also, the World Health Organization has pushed a program to prevent the importation of expired drugs. Most countries will not permit the importation of expired drugs.

Birth Certificates and Marriage Licenses

If you are going to stay for a longer period of time, some countries will require that the missionaries register as aliens, special workers and similar designations. This may require a certified copy of your marriage license and birth certificates for you and each of your dependents.

The Back-up Option

In addition to the photocopies that you carry with you, we have more than once found it helpful to have scanned every paper we might need. We then sent them as attachments to an e-mail account that we knew we could access anywhere in the world via the web in case we needed to have another copy (our own webmail, Google e-mail, Yahoo e-mail, etc.). Also, you may wish to leave a photocopy of all of these in a folder that a friend or relative would have access to in order to get them to you in case of a problem.

OTHER PIECES OF PAPER TO LEAVE AT HOME

If you have children that you are leaving with others, make sure they have your health insurance information (including a copy of your insurance card). Make sure those guardians have a health power of attorney for the children and a complete medical history (including significant health conditions, immunizations, medications, allergies and names and contact information for their physicians and dentists).

If you are traveling alone, make sure you have left with your spouse or family member an unlimited power of attorney. This is necessary in case they have to do banking, deal with the IRS, open or close business accounts, and a thousand other details that could crop up. Make sure they know where your will is, your health power of attorney, the key to your safety deposit box and any other important pieces of information.

Leave a list of people who you like to have work on your house if something happens (plumber, electrician, heating repairman, etc.), and the contact information for your house, car, health and any other kind of insurance including the agents' numbers (with your account or policy numbers). Make it clear whether they can or cannot drive your car. If your car is being driven at home while you are driving a rental car, your policy usually will not cover the rental car. You must have a separate car rental insurance policy in effect in that case.

Your home security system: make sure there is someone to

respond to any real or false alarms. Notify the monitoring service of your absence and alternative numbers for them to contact. Review the system with your family or friends who will cover problems. Show them how to turn it on and off, bypass portions if necessary and give them the account number, password and security codes.

Mail: if you have your mail held, or if a package cannot be delivered, the post office is sometimes reluctant to release it to a stranger. You have two options. The first is to have your mail forwarded to someone who has your checkbook (to pay unexpected bills) and your power of attorney. There is a limit on the amount of time that the post office will forward mail, but this is a good option for a relatively short trip. Alternatively, have the mail delivered to your house but make sure it is collected regularly to avoid giving notice to any thieves that you are not home. Have a notarized statement or limited power of attorney written up giving someone you trust the permission to collect your mail in your absence. Likewise, if you are expecting something significant, make sure a person has permission to open that mail and notify you of its contents. Unexpected mail from certain sources might also need to be opened (e.g., IRS, your law firm, your accountant, your bank, etc. depending on your circumstances), so the person with your power of attorney should know about anything important that you are expecting. You should make arrangements with them about the best way to pay unexpected bills.

Leave a full itinerary and contact information for all times during your trip. You should record all flight numbers, flight times, a phone number for contact on the field, a fax number on the field, the mailing and email address and also the contact information of the parent group with which you are serving.

LIVING WITH DOCUMENTS OVERSEAS

Always carry some sort of official looking document with your picture on it wherever you go off the mission compound or out of your lodging if you are not staying in a compound. Some people carry their U.S. driver's license or international driver's license because they are easier to replace than a passport if they are stolen from you. Some U.S. embassies are now providing a passport card that functions as a national ID card so you don't have to carry your passport.Sometimes carrying a photocopy of the passport suffices. Your passport itself may be necessary for certain official transactions including the exchange of currency, renting vehicles, signing into hotels, etc. If at all possible, do not allow the passport out of your sight. Try to substitute a photocopy and if they insist on taking it, be sure to ask for a receipt.

Always keep your visa and residency papers up to date if you are in the country for longer periods of service.

Lastly, always assume any official who asks to see your papers means business. Do NOT joke or protest. In virtually all countries others than ours, people can be required, for no apparent reason, to prove who they are and why they are in a certain place. "Innocent until proven guilty" is a uniquely American right that you leave behind; "guilty until proven innocent" is more universally applied. There is no universal Bill of Rights, no worldwide Miranda rights, "no nothing" once you leave the borders of your own country.

CHAPTER 5

SPIRITUAL PREPARATION

*"There is nothing special that happens to you on a
757 crossing the ocean."*
—Harry Gebert, MD, medical missionary

These words by a veteran missionary are a humorous reminder of
a serious truth—your heart must be right *before* you go. If you are not
a soul-winner on this side of the ocean, you will probably not be one
there. If you do not spend time in the Word or in prayer here, you will
probably not do so there. You would not dream of entering a marathon
without running endless miles before the event to build up your sta-
mina, endurance and strength, yet many short-term missionaries will
make the mistake of going on their mission without proper spiritual
preparation. It may not be in vogue here in North America to talk seriously about spiritual warfare. Sometimes the concept is hard to take
seriously in the comfort of your home. However, it is real. The presence of the Holy Spirit, the peace of God, and the knowledge based on
experience that you can trust him will make a difference in your trip.
This does not mean that before you go you have to be transformed into
a reincarnation of Dwight L. Moody, Charles Spurgeon or be the next
Mother Theresa, but it does mean that you have to have a solid relationship with God before you go.

Proper preparation must be a top priority, but unless you make it
happen, it will not happen. To carry our running analogy a little further,
there are mornings you must drag yourself out of bed to run when you
do not really feel like it. You do it because you realize that you must discipline yourself and work hard in order to achieve your goal. Spiritual
preparation takes the same dedication. Start early and train hard.

Proper preparation requires clarification of your call to go. Some
people get very uncomfortable with the idea of talking about a "call to
missions" in the context of short-term missions. Although it usually is

not the audible voice of God, you must have a sense and a conviction that God's will for your life includes your proposed trip. You must "know" that you will have a defined purpose in God's economy and plan, even if you have no idea what it is. If you are going on short-term mission just for the "experience," you should probably just take a good vacation. There is an increasing tendency to emphasize the effect of the short-term missions on the participant and trips are being promoted with this as the main benefit of the trip. This is reflective of our culture's "Me Generation." While it can not be argued that a short-term mission trip will have an salutary effect on you that will be far beyond your expectations, it is perhaps an error to make that the *primary* justification for the trip. Your overriding motivation for the trip must be that you have realized that God has called you and your family to provide service to the Lord, the missionaries on the field, and the hurting people surrounding them. You are going to try to communicate in whatever way you can that Jesus Christ is Lord and He has saved you personally. You are going because of a realization that an understanding of the Great Commission has made it imperative for you and your family to help bring the good news of His salvation to every man, woman and child. You have a personal responsibility to fulfill the Commission. You are obeying.

In order to discharge this privilege, duty and sacred responsibility fully, we must strive to be filled with the Holy Spirit. We must ask for His help to empty ourselves of "Self"—all our visions of self-glory, our improper motivations, our problems, our worries, our ego and whatever else that may get in the way. We need to learn how to be as transparent as possible so that when the people to whom we minister see us and our actions, they see Jesus Christ. We must rely as completely as possible on the Holy Spirit in order to face uncertainty and live our lives in a way honoring to Christ. With language and cultural barriers being what they are, we may truly be the only Bible that they ever read.

Whoa! This is getting much more spiritual that you counted on! After all, you are only a layman (or maybe a medical professional or some other category. . . .) But before you try to get a refund on your tickets and unpack your suitcase, it may help to get a grasp on a few important concepts that might make this process easier for you. There will be times on this trip where you will be stretched so far that you can no longer recognize yourself. You may be holding a child who is starved; she is so lethargic that she cannot even cry. You may see people dying of diseases that would be easily treated back home. You may be with people living in cardboard, plastic or mud hovels. You may find yourself totally bewildered by the culture or customs. You may find

> *"If I knew I was not 'prayed up' or that no one was praying for me while I was on the trip, I would not go"*
>
> —A veteran of several trips

yourself so sick that you can't figure out which end to present to the toilet, let alone do anything "spiritual". You may see thousands dying without Christ—and seemingly unwilling to listen. You *must* have a practical understanding of your underlying theology in order to survive. If you do not, you will become a victim of your own good intentions. The devil is more than willing to tell you how inadequate you are and how far you are in over your head.

The first thing you must understand is that God knows exactly what and who you are, and you will not surprise Him. The second is that you can do all things beyond your own abilities because you can do them through Christ's power (Philippians 4:13, *"I can do everything through him who gives me strength"*). Third, you are not responsible for the results, only the attempt. Ephesians 2:10 reads, "For we are God's workmanship, created in Christ Jesus to do good works, *which God prepared in advance for us to do."* (italics added). If He prepared the works in advance, He knows what will come of it.

You must understand exactly *why* you are where you are. *You* are God's mission. Let me explain. The Lord's prayer is well-known. Some people say it daily. Some churches use it regularly in their liturgy. Did you realize that this prayer of Jesus encapsulates the basis of for all mission efforts of the church? Are you on that trip because you believe in the importance of the concepts that Christ himself taught?

"Our Father, which art in heaven"—He is a caring God who is truly and fully God, higher, wiser and more powerful than we are.

"Hallowed be thy name"—His name is holy, honored and wonderful. Do we believe it and treat it as such?

"Thy Kingdom come, thy will be done on Earth as it is in Heaven"—that's it! That is missions. The rest of the prayer and the rest of the Gospel are just details. In order for God's kingdom to come and for His will to be pre-eminent over a fallen creation, Jesus Christ himself came down from heaven and became God-man. Why? Not only to redeem us (for we could not do it ourselves) but because it was the only way to effect a cure of the sin present in the universe. Jesus was Emmanuel—God with us. God the Son was the first misisonary and defined the mission. The only valid mission of the church today is to continue to represent God to a fallen world. To be, in our own individual flawed ways, God with man, so that someday we can truly say with all the redeemed around the throne "for Thine is the Kingdom and the power and the glory forever, Amen." All the other good things that we do in the name of missions often gets so confused in our mind so that we cannot separate the true purpose behind the misison and the methods we use to reach it. All the good we may do in our stumbling mission attempts is *not* the mission. God's relationship with man (and by extension, with you) is the mission. Sometimes, God willing, it is focused outwardly and people become saved and we help God to relieve suffering. That is what we often think about when we think about missions. However, sometimes and perhaps more often than not, God's work is inward, within our own hearts and souls. Our personal relationship with God is what is worked upon. The great martyred missionary, Jim Elliott, wrote, "So many missionaries, intent on doing something, forget that His main work is to make something of them. . . ." That is true for short-termers too! You are on this trip because God has a work to do in your own heart and life.

To be effectively used or in order to be effectively altered, we must maintain a growing, personal relationship with Jesus Christ. Practicing the disciplines of prayer, Bible study, church attendance, meditation and time alone to listen to God are vital and critical to the process of becoming more Christ-like. Prayer is not just asking God to move in our lives. It is the process of God's moving us into conformity to *His* will. He will not do this unless we pray.

It is often difficult to have a meaningful prayer life, especially if you are not used to doing it. Do not set arbitrary time limits or feel you have to use formal terms of address in order to pray properly. Prayer is just spending time with a God who loves you and there is no "right" way. Be thankful that as children of God, we have the Spirit that allows us to call God Almighty "Abba," "Daddy." He is thrilled to hear from His children. Talk—and listen.

The important thing is for you to begin praying right now. It is never too early nor too late to seek the Lord and His guidance in this proposed trip. Make sure that someone is praying with and for you as well. It is sometimes helpful to pray together regularly with a family member, member of your church or an accountability group, friend or fellow traveler for a dedicated time of prayer for specific and more intimate concerns. If you are traveling with your family, you should definitely have times of group family prayer. The prayer should begin now, continue throughout the trip and after you return.

Pray about every aspect of your missions experience. Listed below are some ideas that you may find helpful in preparing your heart and that will affect the outcome of your service to Him. The list is by no means exhaustive and the Holy Spirit will bring many more Scripture passages to your mind. He will lead you to pray about other concerns. This list, or one that you have modified to list the specifics for your trip, may be duplicated and given to each member of your support team.

Suggestions for Prayer[1]

▶ Explore your own salvation and the blessings from it. Read 2 Corinthians 4:1–11. Spend time thanking God for your salvation and praise Him for specific blessings which come from knowing Christ.

---

[1] This and the subsequent list have been modified from lists in uncopyrighted material by the Volunteer Missions International division of the International Mission Board.

These include (but are not limited to) forgiveness for our sins, certainty about our eternal destiny, the privilege of praying and knowing that God hears, power for living now, and the opportunity to give ourselves away in behalf of His Kingdom.

► Ask God to fill your life with His power for this venture. Jesus said, *"If anyone wishes to come after Me, let him deny himself, and take up his cross, and follow Me"* (Mark 8:34). Only the Holy Spirit can deliver us from the demands of our selfish natures. Envision every area of your life: your relationships, your vocation, your personal resources, your physical health, everything—and surrender each area afresh to the Lord Jesus. Confess and repent of sins the Holy Spirit reveals to you. Make restitution where it is needed.

► Pray for a "me last" attitude which claims no rights or privileges for yourself. Our attitudes, both at home and overseas, should be the same as Christ's. In Philippians 2:5–8 we read that even though He was God, He took on Himself the role of a servant and displayed an attitude of humility and helpfulness, of willingness to identify with people and to accept the cost of obedience to God. In the end, it cost Him His life.

► Pray for an awareness that what God wants from you may not be what you feel is your strongest suit, but that *"obedience is better than sacrifice"* (1 Samuel 15:22).

► Pray for the missionaries, their families and for your interaction with them. Pray that you would have a spirit of encouragement and not of criticism. It is crucial that you put aside now any tendencies toward criticism. Negative comments from short-term volunteers are rarely upbuilding to career missionaries who are paying a great price to make Christ known.

► Pray for those to whom you go to minister. Pray that they will be strengthened and encouraged by your presence. Pray also for the patients you will treat, that God will sensitize you to their needs, and that they will see Jesus Christ in you.

► Keep your eyes, ears, and heart open to what God may be showing you.

► Claim Christ's victory over the adversary. Pray that Satan might be prevented from disrupting plans in any way. Pray for the Lord and His angels to intervene where evil forces are at work.

▶ Pray for the witness of believers in the area, for boldness and encouragement.

▶ Pray for churches in the area to reach out to people and their needs.

▶ Pray that lost people will become open to hearing about Jesus and then accept Him as their Lord and Savior.

▶ Pray for those in positions of leadership within the country, for their salvation and witness.

▶ Pray for national and missionary families to be united through the Holy Spirit.

▶ Give honor and glory to the Lord for your participation in this trip.

▶ Pray for the other team members: for their health, ministries, and spiritual growth.

▶ Pray for opportunities to serve, witness, and speak.

▶ Pray that you will remain open to any type of missions work, including here at home.

Prayer and Bible study are the main foundations of spiritual preparation but the following are additional things that can help to put you in the right state of mind and spiritual readiness:

▶ Learn a simple way to lead someone to Christ. Remember that you are not the one doing it. It is the power of God's word and the Holy Spirit that will draw them to Himself. You do not need to have extensive knowledge of various arguments against tenets held by other cults and world religions. Most of those to whom you will witness have little sophistication in those matters, and those who do can be referred to the missionaries or someone else more qualified. Your responsibility is to tell what God did in your life and what He is willing to do in theirs. See Chapter 14 for advice on how to develop a testimony suitable for sharing in a new culture.

▶ Read stories of faith and missionary biographies and reflect on the unchanging nature of God. If He did it before, He can do it again.

▶ Read books emphasizing the church's call to missions. Several suggestions are listed in the bibliography in Appendix A.

▶ Read books about missionaries that have served or are serving in the country where you are going.

▶ Study Scripture passages before you go and/or do a mission related Bible study on the trip (two are suggested later in this chapter).

▶ Collect reminders of His faithfulness, e.g. Lamentations 3:21–25: *"Yet this I call to mind and therefore I have hope: Because of the LORD's great love we are not consumed, for his compassions never fail. They are new every morning; great is your faithfulness. I say to myself, 'The LORD is my portion; therefore I will wait for him.' The LORD is good to those whose hope is in him, to the one who seeks him."*

▶ Start a journal to chronicle your experiences with what God is doing and continue it throughout the trip to record both the physical and spiritual journey.

▶ Ask missionaries, agencies and nationals for stories about the history of spiritual outreach by the work or agency in that country.

▶ Look up the country (and surrounding countries) you will be visiting in Patrick Johnstone's *Operation World—The Day-to-Day Guide to Praying for the World*, other reference materials, or on the Internet (e.g., http://prayercast.com/ or www.operationworld.org). Pray for a better understanding of the needs of the people and the works that are ongoing in the country.

Preparation of your heart and soul is more important than what you pack. Along with your passport, visa, money, and Bible, make sure you take a properly prepared heart and mind, bolstered by ongoing prayer.

SUGGESTED READING

(See the Appendix A for a more exhaustive list.)

Blackaby, Henry T. and Claude V. King. *Experience God: Knowing and Doing the Will of God*. Nashville: Lifeway Press, 1990, ISBN 0-8054-9954-7

Bonhoeffer, Dietrich. *The Cost of Discipleship*. New York City: Touchstone, 1959, ISBN 0-684-81500-1

Borthwick, Paul. "Missions—God's Heart for the World." Downers Grove, IL: Intervarsity Press, 2000, ISBN 0-8308-3090-1. Nine studies for individuals or groups.

Gaukroger, Stephen. *Your Mission, Should You Accept It...An Introduction for World Christians*. Downers Grove, IL: InterVarsity Press, 1996, ISBN 0-8308-1366-7

Hale, Thomas. *On Being a Missionary*. Pasadena: William Carey Library, 1995, ISBN 0-87808-255-7

Hoke, Steve and Bill Taylor. *Send Me! Your Journey to the Nations*. World Evangelical Fellowship, 1999, ISBN 0-87808-294-8

Hunt, T.W. *The Mind of Christ*. Broadman/Holman, 1997, ISBN 0805463496

Ives, Jane. *Transforming Ventures: A Spiritual Guide for Volunteers in Mission*. Nashville: Upper Room Books, 2000, ISBN 0-8358-0910-2

Johnstone, Patrick. *Operation World, 21st Century Edition: When We Pray, God Works*.Paternoster Publishing, 2001, ISBN 1850783578

Lisech, Howard and Bonnie Lisech. *Abide in the Vine (14 day Devotional Bible Studies)*. Orlando: Deeper Roots Publications, 1995, ISBN 1-930547-16-1— Also available in 21 and 50 day editions

Lisech, Howard and Bonnie Lisech. *Ripe for Harvest (14 day Devotional Bible Studies)*. Orlando: Deeper Roots Publications, 2000, ISBN 1-930547-07-2— Also available in 21 day

Lisech, Howard and Bonnie Lisech. *Walk as He Walked (14 day Devotional Bible Studies)*. Orlando: Deeper Roots Publications, 1997, ISBN 1-930547-00-5— Also available in 21, 30 and 50 day editions

Miller, Darrow. *Discipling Nations: The Power of Truth to Transform Cultures*. Seattle: YWAM Publishing, ISBN 1-57658-015-6

Pippert, Rebecca. *Out of the Salt Shaker and into the World*. Downers Grove, IL: InterVarsity Press, ISBN 0-8308-2220-8

Piper, John. *Let the Nations be Glad! The Supremacy of God in Missions*. Grand Rapids: Baker, 1993, ISBN 0-8010-7124-0

Tucker, Ruth. *From Jerusalem to Irian Jaya*, Grand Rapids: Academie Books (Zondervan), 1983, ISBN 0-310-4593-1

30-DAY SPIRITUAL PREPARATION[12]		
DAY	POINT OF FOCUS	SCRIPTURE READING
1	Spiritual Renewal for Service	Psalm 51
2	Taking Time to Pray	Mark 1:35–45
3	The Word and the Way	Psalm 119:2, 19, 105, 165
4	The Power to Serve	Acts 1:1–12
5	Christian Depression	1 Kings 19:1–18
6	Here I Am, Let Me Go!	Isaiah 6:1–12
7	Fit to Serve	Ephesians 5:1–17
8	Availability Plus Christ	John 6:1–14
9	Commissioned to Serve	Matthew 28:19–20
10	Empowered to Serve	Matthew 28:16–18
11	The Unlikely Witness	John 4:1–42
12	The Expected Result	John 4:1–42
13	Making the Ordinary Extraordinary	Acts 4:1–19
14	Revive Us Again	Psalm 85
15	Overcoming Difficulties	Numbers 13:25–33
16	Removing the Stones	John 11:39–40
17	The True Measure of Greatness	Matthew 20:20–28
18	Differences Between Good Missionaries	Acts 15:36–41
19	When You Cannot Finish the Task	Luke 10:25–35
20	Acting Like What You Are	Mt 21:18–19; Gal 5:22–23
21	Overcoming Prejudices	Jonah 1:1–3; 3:1–20; 4:1–3
22	Serving with Gladness	Psalm 100
23	Serving with Gratitude	Psalm 103
24	Serving with Compassion	Jonah 4
25	Serving with Urgency	John 9:1–7
26	Serving with Inner Strength	John 15:1–16
27	Serving with Love	John 21:15–23
28	Serving with a Team Spirit	Romans 12
29	Serve for Common Purposes	1 Corinthians 1:23–31; 2:1
30	Proclaiming Liberty to the Poor	Isaiah 61:1–6

[2] Prepared by Volunteer Mission International division of International Mission Board

ALTERNATIVE STUDY

Study the following verses to see what the New Testament teaches about missions and our approach to them:

Matthew	5:14–16	John	4:34–38
	6:19–21, 25–33		13:34–35
	9:36–38		21:15–17
	10:32–33, 39, 42	Romans	10:14–15
	16:24–27		Chapter 12
	18:5		13:11–12
	21:28–32		15:26–27, 30
	22:36–40	II Corinthians	1:3–5
	25:31–46		5:14
	28:18–20		8:1–5, 12–15, 20–21
Mark	1:17–18		9:6–15
	3:35	Galatians	2:10
	8:34–38		3:28
	9:41		6:9–10
	10:26–31	Philippians	2:4
	12:28–34, 41–44	I Timothy	6:17–19
Luke	6:38, 46–49	James	1:27
	8:21	I Peter	4:10–11
	9:23–26		5:8–9
	10:1–7, 25–37	1 John	3:16–24
	12:22–34, 48		
	14:12–14		
	16:13		
	18:16–17, 27–30		

CHAPTER 6

HEALTH TIPS FOR THE TRAVELER[1]

Health issues are always a concern when you consider travel to a distant destination. Most people can travel almost anywhere with a little foreplanning and common sense.

GENERAL HEALTH CONSIDERATIONS

If you have any health problems, you should confirm with your doctor that your chronic conditions will not preclude safe travel. If you have problems with getting around, that is not a hard and fast reason not to go, but any disability or need for help must be carefully planned for. Most countries, especially the developing countries, do not provide for the disabled in any fashion. Make sure your teeth are in good repair before you go. Modern dentistry can be a rare commodity on the mission field.

It is probably wise to have your physician check you before you go. At that time, it is wise to take along the following checklist since many physicians are not travel experts. Discuss these with your physician and obtain his advice and if appropriate, the necessary prescriptions:

▶ From your optometrist or ophthalmologist, a copy of your eyeglass or contact lens prescription.

▶ Prescription for malaria prophylaxis and prescription for self-treatment (see section below).

▶ Any needed vaccinations (see section below).

▶ A letter on official stationery may help you with customs or security inspection points if you need to bring along syringes, needles, narcotics, implanted metal devices or anything else that looks suspicious.

---

[1] Nothing in this chapter is intended to take the place of personal medical attention and advice from your medical care provider. Please be aware that recommendations change frequently.

A translation of the letter in the local language(s) might come in handy.

► If you have heart disease, a copy of your EKG (scanned or miniaturized if possible) would be handy to have.

► If you have diabetes, discuss how the abnormal eating pattern and sleeping pattern of your long airplane flight will affect your glucose levels. Together with your healthcare provider, plan an approach to your disease.

► Prescriptions for your routine medications, remembering to include oral contraceptives. Having enough medication to carry one full set in one place of your luggage and one full set in your carry-on is sometimes advisable, especially for the most critical medications that cannot be replaced on the mission field. If you have a prescription benefit on your health insurance plan, they may not pay for the duplicate set and you will have to pay for them yourself in order to have that security and peace of mind.

► Prescription for ciprofloxacin (or other fluroquinolone), azithromycin or rifaximin for traveler's diarrhea (fluroquinolones are also effective for marine organisms if you will be near or in the ocean reefs as part of your trip).

► Prescription for metronidazole (Flagyl®) is recommended by some for treatment of giardia, amoeba, some diarrheas, and some cases of vaginitis. This drug is usually easily available throughout the developing world.

► Prescription for a broad-spectrum antibiotic (e.g. cephalosporin or amoxicillin type of drug) in case of pneumonia, sinusitis, urinary tract infection or skin infections.

► Prescription for short acting sleeping pill, helpful for the plane trip and for the first few days of altered sleep secondary to jet lag.

► Prescription for acetazolamide and perhaps dexamethasone if you are going to high altitudes (see section below).

► Prescription for gastric upset (H-2 blocker or ion pump inhibitor) if you are going to a country with spicy food or if you have a history of gastritis or ulcer. Many of the older ones are available over the counter.

▶ Prescription for a mild narcotic in case of need. Codeine (usually with acetaminophen) has the advantage of potential use in suppressing a cough and slowing diarrhea as well as in helping pain.
▶ Prescription for treatment of conjunctivitis.
▶ Prescription for anti-nausea medications: metaclopromide, promethazine, chlorpromazine or others.

Always get advice from the professionals before an international trip, even if you are returning to a place you know well. Check with your travel agent or the State Department to see if there are any outstanding travel alerts in force. Check with the Center for Disease Control or with your health department for the latest guidelines for your country of destination. They can change rapidly.

Short-term missionaries and other travelers often assume that their health insurance covers them anywhere in the world. *Many times this is not so*, and failure to check can leave you responsible for some large bills if you are hospitalized and have not obtained insurance to cover you on your trip. If they do not, check with your carrier to see if they offer a supplemental policy. Sometimes your agent or your mission agency can recommend another company that offers such a policy.

The International Association for Medical Assistance to Travelers (IAMAT, www.iamat.org) has a worldwide referral network available to members. The membership card is free and ensures that you will have the care at the published treatment rates. These doctors in the network speak English, have had their qualifications reviewed and agree to accept the published fee schedule (Office visit: $100, House/hotel call: $150, Nights/Weekends: $150). The address is IAMAT, 1623 Military Rd #279, Niagara Falls, NY, U.S. phone (716) 754-4883; Canada phone (519) 836-0102.

Plan what you would do if a catastrophe strikes and pray that it does not. Most mission hospitals are not in places where you will be comfortable receiving care for a serious medical or surgical condition. Evacuation is often the best option but can be difficult and expensive to arrange if you have not given some thought to it before the need arises. There are many companies that provide these services to various parts of the world and most have some sort of pre-paid insurance plan that may be worth your money. Check with your parent organization, travel agency, local missionaries and/or the Internet to identify the best companies serving the area where you are going to be. Insurance that will cover expatriation of your mortal remains (return your dead body) may also be wise given the high costs of returning a corpse to your home (as much as $100,000).

Although the suggestion may strike some as unnecessary and unnerving, knowing the blood types of your traveling companions will allow you to know who might serve as a presumably lower risk blood donor. If you are going to be traveling in countries where accessibility to medical supplies is uncertain, you may want to carry along your own syringes, needles, intravenous fluids and tubing sets. If you opt to do this, make sure you have a letter from your physician explaining why you have these items. This may avoid problems with the customs officers.

If you get into any sort of trouble with the police, regulations or need any help, contact the U.S. embassy immediately.

HELPFUL PHONE NUMBERS

Center for Disease Control in Atlanta, Georgia
1. International Traveler's Hotline: (404)-332-4559 (24 hours a day, prerecorded)
2. CDC Information: 800-232-4636
3. Malaria treatment hotline (for professionals) (770) 488-7788; (770) 488-7100 after hours.
4. Traveler's health hotline: (877) 394-8747

U.S. Department of State
Overseas Citizens' Emergency Center: 800-407-4747; from overseas, (202) 551-4444; http://travel.state.gov/travel/tips/emergencies/emergencies_1212.html.

ALTITUDE SICKNESS

Several acute, sub-acute and chronic disturbances can occur at heights above 2000 meters (6560 feet). The risk factors include a lack of sufficient time to adjust to the lower oxygen levels in the atmosphere, individual susceptibilities, sickle cell disease and the amount of physical activity. The faster you get to that altitude and the more active you are, the more likely you are to have symptoms. Susceptability to the condition has no correlation with the person's physical condition.

The onset of the disease is initially manifested by headache (usually severe and persistent), malaise, drowsiness, nausea and vomiting, pallor and even cyanosis. In the next stage, altered neurological function can include irritability, difficulty in concentrating, dizziness, ringing ears, changes in vision and insomnia. There can also be shortness of breath, altered breathing patterns, palpitations, fast heart rate and even weight loss. As the disease progresses, it can progress to cerebral edema, pulmonary edema, and even death.

Prevention consists of a slow ascent if at all possible. A maximum of 300 meters a day is recommended. Adequate rest and sleep, reduced food intake and avoidance of tobacco and alcohol are commended. Avoid any overexertion in the first few days until you have acclimated. Since on a short airplane ride to a high locale (e.g. La Paz, Bolivia) does not allow time to get used to the elevation slowly, you can start taking acetazolamide (Diamox) 250 mg 24–48 hours before the trip and continue to take it twice a day for 72 hours. The same drug can be used for treatment of the condition. The side-effects of acetazolamide include parathesias (odd tingling and "pins and needles"), a large urine output (it is a diuretic), and it can alter the taste of carbonated beverages. Dexamethasone is sometimes used as a prophylactic drug (4mg every 12 hours beginning the day of the ascent, continuing for 3 days at the higher altitude and then tapering over 5 days), and may be part of the therapy if you become symptomatic.

The mainstay of therapy is descent to a lower altitude as quickly as possible; even a drop of 500 feet can make a difference in symptoms. Oxygen therapy helps and more severe cases can be treated with hyperbaric therapy if that modality is available. Acetazolamide, dexamethasone (especially for brain symptoms), prochlorperazine (antiemetic and respiratory stimulant) and vasodilators (e.g. nifedipine) may all have a role in the initial care of such patients.

AUTOMOBILE AND VEHICULAR TRAVEL

It is sobering to realize that motor vehicular accidents are the leading cause of death for missionaries. Statistically, the most dangerous thing you will do on your trip is get in a vehicle. Since such travel is not entirely avoidable, there are some things you can do to diminish your risk.

▶ Ride only in mission owned vehicles. Presumably they are better maintained than the average vehicle on the road.

▶ If possible, choose the back seat.

▶ Always, wear seatbelts if available. Don't be surprised when there are none.

▶ Avoid riding motorcycles but if necessary, always wear helmets.

▶ Driving and drinking don't mix.

▶ Avoid traveling in overcrowded public vehicles. Although they may be big, maintenance and safety are not their strong point. Another drawback is the aroma. It may not kill you, but can be stifling.

▶ If you must rent a car and drive yourself, request the larger models of rental cars with seatbelts when available. This gives you more protection in case of an accident.

▶ If you are driving in a country that drives on the "wrong" side of the road, be very, very careful. You may be an excellent driver but your reflexes in emergencies can take you in exactly the wrong direction.

▶ If you are driving, make sure you understand the traffic rules and patterns. Traffic circles, odd stoplight patterns and the like can be overwhelming and lead to errors in driving.

▶ If you are driving, find out what you are to do in case of an accident. Some embassies recommend that you do not leave your car and exchange licenses and the usual amenities of home. If there is not a policeman in sight, drive directly to either the embassy or the police station. Staying with your car can be dangerous to you and in some third-world cities, deliberate accidents are used as a way to extort money from you. ▶ If you have a hired driver, caution him not to take chances and reinforce that he is being paid by the hour and not the trip.

AVOIDANCE OF EXPOSURE TO POTENTIALLY CONTAMINATED BODY FLUIDS

Diabetics and other individuals at high risk should carry a personal supply of needles and syringes. Do not undergo elective or cosmetic procedures such as tattoos, ear piercing, and acupuncture while out of your home country. Since this book is written with misisonaries as a target audience, warnings against illicit intravenous drug use (which has considerable health risks and legal consequences at home as well as abroad), and illicit sex will hopefully be unnecessary. Devise a contingency plan for emergency medical care during travel in the event of accidental injury or serious illness. Explore the use of the agencies described in the beginning pages of this chapter. Evacuation insurance can be a godsend. Medical personnel treating patients should, of course, use universal precautions. Transfusion should be avoided unless reliably effective screening for Hepatitis B and HIV is routinely carried out on the donated blood.

HIV PROPHYLAXIS FOR MEDICAL PERSONNEL[2,3]

Given the wide-spread and increasing incidence of HIV infection in many of the developing countries, there is an understandable concern about the risk of contracting the disease, especially among those

[2] Some of this material, including the recommendations, is adapted from Current Medical Diagnosis & Treatment, 2010, page 1220 and the CDC's http://www.cdc.gov/ mmwr/preview/mmwrhtml/rr5409a1.htm (as accessed on March 6, 2009). Given the rapid flux of information in these areas, the reader is advised to check with his physician, the latest CDC recommendations (www.hivatis.org), and recent medical literature for any changes to these recommendations.

physicians who routinely do invasive procedures and among relatively inexperienced students and residents. Avoidance is always the best option and prevents the acquisition of other serious diseases as well, particularly Hepatitis C and B. Routinely use gloves (double-gloving for OR personnel), masks and protective eyewear (where reasonable and appropriate) to avoid contact with bodily secretions. Do not recap needles and dispose of "sharps" appropriately. Do not pass "sharps" from one person to another to avoid accidental injury. Although the risk of contracting the virus varies according to many factors (type of injury, type of sharp, amount of blood or secretion, and viral load of the patient), the average risk of HIV transmission from a needle stick with blood from an HIV-infected patient is about 1:300. The risk from contamination of mucous membranes (eyes, mouth, nose) is too low to quantitate accurately and estimated to be less than one in a thousand.

Since, if there is a positive ELISA screening test, most hospitals in the third world do not have the capability of doing confirmatory tests (e.g, Western Blot) and also since it is usually impossible to get CD4 lymphocyte counts or any sort of viral-load testing done, it is probably safest to assume the highest risk scenario. Low risk contacts include contact of secretion on unprotected, unbroken skin; contamination of mucous membranes (splash), and with such exposures, there is probably no indication for HIV prophylaxis. Prompt hand-washing, preferably with dilute (1%) sodium hypochlorite (bleach), or copious irrigation of the mucous membrane with water is sufficient. Medium risk contacts include superficial skin scratches with the contaminated object and superficial punctures with solid core needles. Encourage bleeding from the puncture site with the use of pressure and promptly wash your hands, preferably with dilute (1%) sodium hypochlorite.

---

[3] Note: This section is not important to the majority of people going on short-term mission trips—at least those who will promise to avoid blood, promiscuous sex and intravenous drug use. Those on dental and medical ministries should probably read it. A more comprehensive chapter on health including more information on HIV can be downloaded at www.S3Ministries.com.

Immediately test the patient for HIV and if the diagnostic testing will take more than four hours to get a result, begin two-drug PEP (Post-Exposure Prophylaxis) antiviral therapy as recommended by the CDC. High risk contacts include deep punctures with hollow core needles, deep lacerations with contaminated instruments and other forms of significant contamination from patients who have advanced clinical disease. Encourage bleeding and promptly wash your hands, preferably with dilute (1%) sodium hypochlorite. Immediately test the patient for HIV and if the diagnostic testing will take more than four hours to get a result, begin antiviral therapy as recommended at www.hivatis.org or the CDC (www.cdc.gov).

If you are stuck with a needle or sharp from a patient with unknown HIV status, have the patient tested if possible for HIV, Hepatitis B and C. If positive for HIV, start prophylaxis as soon as possible (preferably within 4 hours). If the patient cannot be tested within that time frame, perhaps it is wisest to start the medication with a two-drug regimen while awaiting the test results. It can be safely stopped if the test returns negative. If it is not possible to test the patient, strongly consider full prophylaxis if the patient has any disease condition that fulfills the criteria for the diagnosis of AIDS.

Also, if you are exposed, do a baseline HIV screening test on yourself if possible and follow-up with tests at 6 weeks, 3 months, and 6 months (some also advise another test at a year, especially if you contact Hepatitis C from the stick). Since both Hepatitis B and C are statistically more common and more dangerous to your health, you should be monitored for those as well.

Let us reiterate: most missionaries and visitors do not need to worry about this. There is no hard and fast rule about whether a short-term medical missionary should carry medications for HIV prophylaxis on a short-term mission trip. The risk of transmission of the disease in most cases is realistically very low despite the associated exaggerated fear that goes along with it. The price for these three drugs for a month's therapy in the United States is high, approximating $1,000–$1,200. Insurance drug plans will not usually cover their cost under these circumstances. Sometimes they can be purchased by physicians through their hospital, pharmaceutical companies or buying groups at cheaper wholesale prices. Increasingly, the drugs are available in most developing countries at much lower cost. The author used to routinely take three drugs for prophylaxis with him on his travels but now buys them in the country of destination if the hospital does not have them because of the high risk nature of exposure associated with his surgical speciality. Realistically, the risk of infection is actually greater wherever hollow-core needles are used, e.g., the outpatient clinic and wards. If the drugs are not used (as is usually the case), they are donated to the mission hospital for use by the missionary staff and hospital staff in the event of an inadvertent exposure to one of them. The donation would ordinarily be tax-deductible and helps to offset the cost of the drugs. *The fear of AIDS should not be a reason not to go—the safest place for any of us to be is in the center of God's will for our life.*

MALARIA

Perhaps there is no disease in which there is more confusion and concern than there is about malaria. Since it is a disease which is largely unknown in North America, the reaction to it tends to be polarized. There are those who under-react, pooh-poohing the significance of the disease, and there are those who over-react, afraid to go because of fear of contracting the disease. Neither response is a wise one.

For the under-reactors, please consider the following quote. Philip Briggs, writing in typical understated British style in the Bradt travel guide on Uganda, says in his description of the need for malaria prophylaxis, "Some travelers prefer to acquire resistance to malaria rather than to take preventative tablets, or they twitter on about homeopathic cures for this killer disease. That's their prerogative, but they have no place expounding this ill-informed drivel to others. Travelers to Africa cannot acquire any effective resistance to malaria, and those who don't make use of prophylactic drugs risk their life in a manner that is both foolish and unnecessary." [4] The *Consumer's Report* says, "Given how dangerous malaria can be, no one recommends doing without an anti-malarial drug in regions where the disease is prevalent. Which one you take…depends on where, when and how long you travel, as well as your medical history, your preference, and your finances." [5] Amen! A word to the wise should be sufficient.

To the rest, the risk is manageable and requires good common sense and a willingness to follow your doctor's orders. Fact #1: What is somewhat scary to contemplate but absolutely necessary to understand is that virtually none of the present malarial prophylaxis regimens *prevent* the contraction of malaria. Prophylaxis merely prevents the majority of patients taking it from becoming ill until the parasite has gone through its cycle and is eliminated from the body. There are important corollaries to that fact. First, an ounce of prevention is worth a pound of cure. Avoidance of being bitten by mosquitos is an important goal. Secondly, you must understand how your particular prophylactic regimen must be taken. This is in order to have adequate blood levels of the drug before you are exposed and to maintain those levels long enough afterward to treat the possiblility of ongoing parasite infestation. Thirdly, some malarial types can hang around in your body within the liver and spleen and be effectively protected from the effect of the drugs, only to emerge after your prophylactic regimen is up. They then cause clinical malaria at a time and place remote from your trip. Fact #2: It only takes one bite from the wrong mosquito, therefore, *all* travelers to an endemic area should take prophylaxis. Since the female *Anopheles* has no buzz, it is truly the one you don't hear that gets you.

Before proceeding further, it is important to emphasize that none of this discussion is meant to stand in place of any other qualified and expert advice. Pay attention to your physician's recommendation. Either he or you should contact the CDC Travelers' Health Section

---

[4] Briggs, Philip. Uganda—The Bradt Travel Guide" 3rd edition. Bradt Publication (UK) The Globe Pequot Press (USA), 1998.
[5] "Lariam's Legacy," Consumer Reports, March 2002, pp 60–61.

(770) 488-7788 or by Internet http://www.cdc.gov (choose the Travelers Health category). Emergency consultation can be obtained after hours (770) 488-7100. Questions on malaria prophylaxis and care should be directed to CDC Malaria Hotline for the latest information (404) 332-4555. There is now facsimile capability to the malaria hotline. By following the instructions, callers can receive on their fax machines information on the risk for malaria and on malaria prevention measures in Africa, Southeast Asia, South America, Central America and the Caribbean, Mexico, the Indian Subcontinent, and Oceania; special information for children and pregnant women; and a world map indicating areas with malaria transmission. This service is available 24 hours a day.

In order to understand the rationale behind the prophylaxis protocols, you must understand a little about the disease. Malaria actually refers to the disease caused by five different species of the parasite (genus plasmodium): *P. vivax, P. malariae, P. ovale, P. falciparum* and the new one on the block, *P. knowlesi.* This disease has been eradicated from most temperate zone countries but continues to be a major health problem in the tropics and sub-tropics. Worldwide, each year it causes 300–500 million cases of clinical disease and results in at least million deaths per year. It is endemic in parts of Mexico, Haiti, Dominican Republic, Central and South America, Africa, the Middle East, the Indian subcontinent, Southeast Asia, China and Oceania.

Once thought to be spread by bad air (*mal* + *aria*), it is spread by a single type of mosquito, the female *Anopheles* mosquito. Both the male and female *Anopheles* mosquito subsist on fruit and nectar, but the female requires a blood meal every three days or so in order to get enough protein to reproduce, hence the spread from one person to another as she seeks a blood meal. There are no animal reservoirs for any variety except the rare and newly recognized *P. knowlesi.* It is occasionally spread by the transfusion of infected blood or by mother-infant transmission at birth. The incubation period for the disease varies by species. *P. falciparum* is approximately 12 days (range 9–60 days), *P. vivax* and *P. ovale* 14 days (range 8–27 days with rare cases up to 8 months) and *P. malariae,* 30 days (range 16–60 days). The prevalence of these diseases vary by locale with *P. vivax* being responsible for the majority of the cases. *P. falciparum* is the predominant species in Africa and the only one in Hispaniola. It also tends to cause the most severe disease. *P. malariae* is widely spread but less common. *P. vivax* is uncommon in Blacks because they lack a blood antigen that the malaria prefers (Duffy factor). *P. ovale* is generally rare but replaces *P. vivax* in West Africa. *P. knowlesi* is a primate malaria from Indonesia which is now being diagnosed rarely in humans and it tends to cause severe illness. It tends to be sensitive to all malaria drugs. Normally, your missionaries will know which species causes the most problem in the area where you are working.

The mosquito becomes infected by ingesting blood from a person who has active malaria. The sexual forms of the parasite (micro- and macrogametocytes) develop within the mosquito and the sporozites in the salivary glands of the mosquito are injected into the next human during the mosquito's next meal. There are two developmental stages in the human. The sporozites first travel to the liver and take up residence within the cells of the liver. This is the exoerythrocytic ("out of the red cells") stage. All four types of malaria mature within the liver cells becoming tissue "schizonts." Only in *P. vivax* and *P. ovale* infections do some stay in a dormant form within the liver cells ("hypnozoites"). These two forms of malaria are the least common forms of malaria but reactivation of these dormant hypnozoites account for the patients who have recurrent disease 6 to 8 months later.

The tissue schizonts escape from the liver and invade red cells in the blood stream, multiplying therein. Forty-eight hours later (24 hrs for *P. Knowlesi;* 72 hours for *P. malariae*), the red cells rupture, releasing a new crop of parasites (merozoites). This cycle can occur time and time again, giving the classic fever every forty-eight hours (a tertian fever for the medical purists among us), or with *P. malariae* every seventy-two hours (a quartan fever). The continued cycle of rupture of red cells leads to the anemia, often becoming chronic anemia. Without treatment, *P. falciparum* usually terminates this cycle within 6 to 8 months but can last for 18 months, *P. vivax* and *P. ovale* as long as 5 years and some *P. malariae* as long as 50 years.

In the early stages, typical malarial attacks feel very much like a bad case of influenza. Shaking chills (the "cold" stage) are followed by high fever (as high as 41°C or 105°F) and marked sweating. This is usually over a 4–6 hour period and can be accompanied by fatigue, headache, dizziness, muscle and bone aches, gastrointestinal symptoms (nausea, vomiting, diarrhea, cramps), and dry cough. After four or more days, enlargement of the spleen and liver are common. Because of the cyclic nature of the infection, these attacks will occur every 2–3 days and the patient may feel well, though fatigued, between the episodes. Serious complications including cerebral malaria, severe anemias, pulmonary edema, renal failure, liver failure, hypoglycemia (compounded by quinine therapy), adrenal insufficiency syndromes, abnormalities in cardiac rhythm, and other system disturbances can occur. Please refer to a standard medical text on the topic for a more in depth understanding and for diagnostic and therapeutic approaches.

From the study of malaria alone, it is now obvious that it is wise to avoid being bitten. That advice is even more logical if you consider dengue fever, yellow fever, filariasis, viral encephalitis and the 30 or more other mosquito-carried rarely-diagnosed viral illnesses, all of which can make your trip memorable in the worst way. Mosquitoes can be divided generally into two types: daytime and nighttime biters. Those mosquitoes that transmit malaria and Japanese encephalitis (*anopheles* and *culex* mosquitoes) bite most intensively after sunset, whereas *aedes* mosquitoes, which transmit dengue and yellow fever, are predominately daytime bitters. Most people receive most of their bites at night.

The common sense precautions to avoid being bitten include:

▶ Long sleeves, long skirts or trousers and socks, all of a tightly woven material, should be worn after dark.

▶ Mosquito DEET repellent on all exposed skin. DEET provides effective protection when applied to skin.[6] It is effective in relatively small amounts if it is spread evenly and completely over all exposed areas. Be aware that DEET has little "spatial activity," meaning that

[6] http://medicalletter.org/freedocs/repellents.pdf , accessed January 3, 2009

nearby, untreated skin is vulnerable. Most insect repellents work for about 3–4 hours but may need to be reapplied more frequently if you sweat heavily or get wet from rain. Adults, to achieve the necessary protection, should use a repellent that contains at least 15% DEET and some experts recommend a minimum of 25% DEET. Repellents with DEET concentrations of 55%–100% are available, but the higher concentrations are probably unnecessary and there are concerns about the possibility of toxicity, especially in children. The higher concentrations do retain efficacy longer (e.g, 30% DEET lasts 4–6 hours, 95% DEET lasts 20 hours) The low concentration products (those with a concentration less than 15%) may be acceptable for the prevention of nuisance bites in your back yard, but low-concentration DEET repellents may not provide enough margin of protection against the various species of mosquitoes that can be the carriers of killer diseases. There is an Ultrathon preparation that provides extended activity (12 hours) with relatively low concentration (33%). According to the EPA, which has done extensive testing, "DEET is the safest and most effective repellent available" when properly used. Despite the common hype, Avon's Skin-So-Soft® (the type without the added proven-effective repellents) has been scientifically shown to be ineffective in preventing mosquito bites and given the severity of the potential risks if you are wrong, its use cannot be advised in these situations. The chapter on traveling with children has more on the alternative proven-effective agents.

▶ For those deeply concerned about the possible risks of DEET: Picardin was approved by the CDC in 2005. It is available in solutions of 5–10%. Oil of lemon eucalyptus is also registered by the Environmental Protection Agency and is comparable in its effectiveness to lower levels of DEET. Long-term studies are not available on these two agents and given the risk of malaria and other serious diseases if your or your child are bitten, the decision is yours.[7]

---

[7] James R. Roberts, WB Well and MW Shannon "DEET Alternatives Considered to be Effective Mosquito Repellents, accessed http://www.aap.org/family/wnv-jun05.htm January 3, 2009

▶ Don't attract the mosquitos. Don't wear after-shave, cologne, perfume or any skin lotion that is perfumed.

▶ Open windows at night only if screened and if the windows are the screens have been inspected for a tight fit and a lack of holes or tears. Always keep your screens and doors shut in your hotel rooms.

▶ Before retiring, check room for mosquitoes around ceilings, in curtains and closets and kill them. Spray your bedroom with permethrum-based insecticide an hour before you retire. It knocks down, or kills, insects that come in contact with it. Permethrin is a related insecticide that is applied only to fabric. Permethrin adheres tightly to fabric and will last through multiple washings. It will not harm or stain fabric, even silk. Unlike DEET, permethrin will not soften or melt plastic or synthetic material. It is effective against mosquitoes, ticks, flies, and other insects. It is biodegradable and non-toxic to humans. Another insecticide similar to permethrin but available only overseas is deltamethrin. The best way to avoid insect bites is to apply DEET or Picardin to your skin and permethrin or deltamethrin to your clothing. Several brands are effective and widely available in the U.S. Similar insecticides are usually available in the country where you are serving. Another alternative for the control of insects inside the house are pyrethroid mosquito coils that can be burned with flame or pyrethrum impregnated wafers that can used in a little device plugged into the electrical outlet. These slowly release the permethroid insecticide. There are now similar plug-in devices that vaporize a liquid.

▶ A mosquito net is a good idea for your health as well as for pandering to your sense of the romantic adventure. The best are those that are impregnated with permethrin (0.2 g/m^2) They are often cheaper overseas than in North America. Contact your missionary host to see if the beds already have them and if not, offer to pay for them if they can purchase them and hang them prior to your arrival. The most portable of mosquito nets are collapsible ones that cover just head and arms and tuck under the sheet or cover of the bed. They are handy if you are moving from place to place but some people find them claustrophobia inducing.

▶ The mosquitoes carrying malaria do not fly well in turbulent air. If your room has a fan, use it and direct the air flow over your bed.

PROPHYLAXIS FOR MALARIA

For many reasons, despite intensive past and ongoing efforts, a reliable vaccination for malaria has never been developed and people who are exposed can develop only partial immunity. That is why even those nationals who have had repetitive attacks can have recurrences when something lowers their immunity or when they face a new strain. Chemical (pharmaceutical) prophylaxis remains the best option for those who are not partially immune (the majority of us) but the shifting patterns of resistance and the drug side-effects make the recommendations sometimes less than straight forward. The best option for Americans to check with the latest recommendations given by the Center for Disease Control in Atlanta at the numbers and/or URL given earlier. To emphasize it again, the following discussion is not to be substituted for the advice of your physician and the CDC.

The general principles of malaria prophylaxis stem from the understanding of the life cycle of the parasite. The drug must develop adequate blood levels by the time the parasite begins its reproductive cycle within you and must continue long enough to have a reasonable chance stopping the reproductive cycle. Ideally, it would act within the liver cells and in the blood stream, but no presently available drug does that well and safely. The recommendations that are made are different depending on whether there is chloroquine resistance present in the country you are visiting or not. The sensitivity of *P. falciparum* is the determining factor for drug choice for prophylaxis.

It is often helpful, especially for those taking once a week prophylaxis, to make a point of taking it on the same day of the week. Sunday is a special day for most Christians and is often suggested as a day to start. With the exception of Malarone, all the prophylactic drugs are recommended to be taken for four weeks after your return. Mark your calendar or figure out some way to remember to continue it for four weeks after you return home. It is easy to forget when you are back in the U.S. and the excitement of the trip has died down. Most of the regimens below are very well tolerated, but any drug can have a side effect. By starting the drugs at the recommended times, most side-effects will be evident before you go. That allows you the luxury of switching to another regimen before you are someplace where there are no good alternatives. See the CDC website if it becomes necessary to switch prophylactic regimens.

The wrong prophylaxis is often used by those who do not seek expert opinion. Make sure you have good, high-quality information as to whether the malaria in the area you are going to visit is susceptible to the drugs you plan to use. This informaiton is available on the CDC web site (www.cdc.gov). "The resistance of *P. falciparum* to chloroquine has been confirmed in all areas with *P. falciparum* malaria except the Caribbean, Central America west of the Panama Canal, and some countries in the Middle East. In addition, resistance to sulfadoxine–pyrimethamine (e.g., Fansidar) is widespread in the Amazon River Basin area of South America, much of Southeast Asia, other parts of Asia, and in large parts of Africa. Resistance to mefloquine has been confirmed on the borders of Thailand with Burma (Myanmar) and Cambodia, in the western provinces of Cambodia, in the eastern states of Burma (Myanmar), on the border between Burma and China, along the borders of Laos and Burma, and the adjacent parts of the Thailand –Cambodia border, as well as in southern Vietnam."[8] It goes on to say, "Travelers should be strongly discouraged from obtaining chemoprophylactic medications while abroad. The quality of these products is not known, and they may not be protective and may be dangerous. These medications may have been produced by substandard manufacturing practices, may be counterfeit, or may contain contaminants."[4]

One last word of warning from the CDC: "Overdose of antimalarial drugs, particularly chloroquine, can be fatal. Medication should be stored in childproof containers out of the reach of infants and children."[4]

---

[8] From http://wwwnc.cdc.gov/travel/yellowbook/2010/chapter-2/malaria.aspx accessed on January 3, 2010

WARNING! Some of the regimens below are NOT recommended by the FDA/CDC, but are mentioned for the sake of completeness. This is therapy which should be decided in consultation from an medical professional who is conversant with malaria and in the regional variations of the disease.

Chloroquine Phosphate

Dose: 500 mg salt (300 mg of base) given once weekly. Pediatric dosage: 5 mg base/kg given once weekly

Starting date: 1 week before entering the endemic area (some recommend 2 weeks).

In country: Weekly while there.

Stopping date: Take for 4 weeks after leaving the endemic area (some recommend 6 weeks)

Advantages: Safe in pregnancy (see the paragraph on malaria in pregnancy) and children; weekly administration. Well tolerated. Inexpensive (approximately $5 per month).

Disadvantages: Variable resistance; Common side-effects include gastrointestinal symptoms, mild headache, pruritus (especially in blacks), dizziness, blurred vision, anorexia, malaise and hives (all of these may be diminished in frequency and severity or prevented by taking after meals or in divided twice-weekly doses). Not effective against the liver schizonts of P. vivax and P. ovale.

WARNING! Take with food and water, but taking it within four hours of the ingestion of preparations that contain kaolin, magnesium trisilicate or calcium carbonate can cause erratic and diminished absorption. There is a theoretical limit of 100 grams of chloroquine base to prevent ocular damage (that is roughly equivalent to six years of prophylactic use). Patients who are on chloroquine at the time of rabies vaccination may have a suppressed immunse response.

If the malaria is *resistant* to chloroquine (every place else other than the Caribbean, some areas of Central America and some ares of the Middle East), there are several regimens, each with advantages and disadvantages:

Malarone® (atovaquone/proguanil)

Dose: one tablet daily. Contains 250 milligrams of atovaquone and 100 mg of proguanil.

Starting date: One tablet (with food or milk) before entering the endemic area.

In Country: Daily (with food or milk).

Stopping date: Daily for 1 week after leaving.

Advantages: Well tolerated. Effective against liver stages of P. vivax and P. ovale because of the proguanil contained within the pill.

Disadvantages: Although it is effective against P. falciparum it has undetermined suppressive activity against other forms. Can cause vivid dreams, insomnia and dizziness, similar to mefloquine but at a lower rate of incidence. It has recently been approved for use in the United States. It can be used in children over 11 kg (24 pounds). Do not use in pregnant or breast-feeding women. Do not use in patients with severe impairment of renal function. Costly (approximately $130 a month). Requires daily dosage.

Mefloquine (Larium®; others)

Dose: 250-mg tablet salt (228 mg of base) for adults once weekly with food and water.

For children: 10–19 kg, 1/4 tablet once weekly with food and water
20–30 kg, 1/2 tablet once weekly with food and water
31–45 kg, 3/4 tablet once weekly with food and water
Greater than 45 kg, 1 tablet once weekly with food and water

Starting date: 1 week before exposure (some recommend 3 weeks before).[9]

In country: Weekly.

Stopping date: 4 weeks after exposure ceases.

Advantages: Weekly administration. It is the preferred method of

---

[9] The long half-life of this drug results in a steady-state level being achieved in 7 weeks. Side-effects may not become evident for 3–7 weeks. Steady-state interval can be reduced to four days, revealing adverse reactions within a week, by taking 250 mg daily for three days in a row, then resuming weekly doses. This is NOT standard practice and can result in a higher incidence of side-effects.

malaria prophylaxis by the CDC (although this may change in the near future).

Disadvantages: The common side effects are no greater in incidence than with chloroquine: nausea, vomiting, epigastric pain, diarrhea, headache, dizziness, fainting and extra heartbeats. Severe neuropsychiatric symptoms are rare (estimated to be 0.01% to 0.066%); insomnia and vivid dreams are reported more often. Symptoms seem to be higher in older people and in women. Taking a half tablet twice weekly and taking the pill at night may reduce some of the symptoms. A *Consumer's Report* article[10] relates that in the first placebo-controlled study of travellers aged 4–80 and both sexes, 29% reported one psychiatric side effect and 19% of the total group rated those effects moderate or severe. Both of these groups were double the rate reported in the Melarone group (see above). Five percent of the study patients dropped out because of the severity of the symptoms (four times the rate of patients who dropped out in the Malarone group. These symptoms usually disappear with a few days after the drug is stopped but can last weeks or months due to the long half-life of the drug. If prophylaxis is continued for more than a year, periodic testing of liver function and ophthalmological testing should be done. Mefloquine is relatively expensive: retail prices $34 to $40 per month in the U.S.

WARNING! Mefloquine is contraindicated in the presence of cardiac conduction abnormalities, liver impairment or a history of psychiatric or neurologic disorder including epilepsy. Do not administer concurrently (or within three weeks) with quinine, quinidine or halofantrine. Concomitant use with tetracyclines or ampicillin can increase blood levels.

Mefloquine has been recommended in the past to be taken in a every other week regimen after three months of weekly prophylaxis. This is no longer recommended because of an increased rate of malaria. Also, it was thought to be contraindicated when beta blockers and calcium channel blockers are being concomitantly taken. This recommendation is no longer considered valid although you will still find it

---

10 "Lariam's Legacy," Consumer Reports, March 2002, pp. 60–61.

written in many places. Pregnancy was also considered a contraindication but the CDC has recently advised that it can be used throughout pregnancy. Certainly it would seem wise to base use in the first
trimester on a risk-benefit assessment. Conception should preferably
be avoided for the duration of mefloquine usage and for two months
after the last dosage.

Doxycycline
> *Dose:* 100 mg daily.
> *Starting date:* Two daily doses before exposure.
> *In Country:* Daily.
> *Stopping date:* 4 weeks after leaving the area of exposure.

Advantages: Can be started with short notice of the trip.
Relatively inexpensive (retail approximately $12–15 per month).
Effective in areas of mefloquine resistance (e.g. Thailand, Cambodia,
Myanmar, Papua New Guinea and some areas of Africa). Effective for
those unable to tolerate mefloquine.

Disadvantages: Requires the traveler to remember to take a daily
dose. Infrequent gastrointestinal side effects. Take with lots of water to
avoid esophageal irritation but do not take with milk. May cause fun-
gal vaginitis (women may be wise to carry a self-treatment antifungal
regimen).

WARNING! May cause hypersensitivity to the sun. Always use a
high sun protection factor (SPF) sun screen and avoid the sun as much
as possible. Not for use in pregnancy, nursing mothers, children less
than 8 years of age or persons with hepatic dysfunction. Safety for
long-term prophylaxis is unknown.

Primaquine (Can be used as terminal treatment under a physicians
care. Should be used as prophylaxis only in those areas where *P.
vivax* is the principle type of malaria. Patients should *always* know
their G6PD status before taking this drug to avoid the risk of life-
threatening hemolytic anemia).
> *Dose:* 30 mg base (52.6 mg of the salt) orally daily.
> *Starting date:* Start 1–2 days before travel to malarious areas.

In Country: Daily.

Stopping date: Take for seven days after leaving such areas.

Disadvantages: Contraindicated in patients with G6PD deficiency and also during pregnancy and lactation unless infant has a documented normal G6PD level.

Chloroquine Combined with Proguanil (Proguanil is not available in the U.S.)

Dose: Chloroquine weekly as above; Proguanil, 200 mg daily while in the endemic area and daily for 4 weeks after leaving.

Advantages: Well tolerated with rare side effects of nausea, vomiting, hair loss and mouth ulcers reported with proguanil. Safe for pregnant women.

Disadvantages: Less effective regimen, recommended only for use in countries with a low frequency of chloroquine resistant faciparum malaria, such as southern Asia (excluding Bangladesh), the Philippines and parts of the Middle East. Proguanil not available in the U.S., but can be purchased in other countries.

WARNING! See chloroquine. Proguanil should not be used in persons with hepatic or renal dysfunction.

Drugs that are used to treat the disease but are NOT recommended for chemoprophylaxis by most experts include halfantrine, Fansidar (combination drug containing pyrimethamine and sulfadoxine), amodiaquine, pyrimethamine alone, artemisinin and related drugs, proguanil and quinine. One drug combination used for prophylaxis in some countries, but not available in the U.S., is the combination of pyimethamine and dapsone (Maloprim). Resistance is increasing to this drug. It is tasteless and therefore often used for children, but has a risk of wiping out the bone marrow's production of certain white cells (granulocytes) and is less effective against *P. vivax.*

Malaria and Pregnancy

Pregnant woman should be protected from malaria because malaria during pregnancy can be particularly severe. The very safest alternative is to, if at all possible, avoid both the disease and the prophylaxis by not going. If that is not reasonable, then attempt to travel in the second trimester. In chloroquine sensitive areas, chloroquine and proguanil are recommended for chemoprophylaxis. Both are safe and the combination has a higher efficacy of protection than chloroquine alone. In chloroquine resistant areas, mefloquine is the drug of choice, preferably not used in the first trimester but still safer in that three months to mother and fetus than the consequences of coming down with malaria. Doxycycline and primaquine should NOT be used. Malarone (atovoquone/proguanil) is currently not recommended for use by pregnant women.

Treatment of Malaria While Traveling

A definite diagnosis is certainly desirable and you should obtain medical consultation as soon as possible in order to obtain repetitive smears in an attempt to make a diagnosis if possible. However, *if you cannot obtain medical consultation within 24 hours,* it is safer to empirically institute malaria treatment early in the course of the disease if malaria is suspected but cannot be proven. Those for whom this book is written should probably have medication for self-treatment along with them in case they develop fever or flu-like symptoms but it must be emphasized that follow-up by a qualified medical practitioner is advised. Realizing that most readers will have been on some prophylaxis medications and that sensitivities of malaria in different parts of the world vary, the following general recommendations are in force at the time of the writing of this book. *NB: Do not treat the disease with the drug you are using for prophylaxis.* In chloroquine-sensitive areas, use chloroquine as a three-day course (1 gram of the salt as an initial dose followed by 500 milligrams at six, twenty-four and forty-eight hours). In choroquine-resistant areas where the malaria is sensitive to Fansidar (pyrimethamine 25 mg and sulfadoxine 500 mg), use three tables of Fansidar as a one-time dose. In chloroquine-resistant areas where the malaria is resistant to Fansidar, use Malarone (atovaquone plus proguanil) 4 tablets daily for three days or if available in the country where you are, artemisin derivatives (or artesunate) are alternatives. These artemisin type drugs are not available in the United States.

The artemisin/artesunate drugs should not be taken alone because of the high risk of recurrent disease. It is usually in in combination with another drug (artmisin combination therapy), e.g. Artemisinin—lumefantrine; Artemether—lumefantrine (Co-Artemeter); Artesunate—mefloquine; Artesunate—amodiaquine; Artesunate—sulfadoxine/pryimethamine; Artesunate—doxycycline are all examples.

Mefloquine, halfantrine and quinine for treatment of uncomplicated disease in this situation are not recommended because of their toxicity in the face of acceptable alternatives. The recommended treatment regimens may not be considered the sole or complete treatment for disease in your local area and it is again emphasized that follow-up is advised with someone with expertise in the disease in the area where you are.

Summary

The complete medical treatment of malaria is beyond the scope of this book but it is important to re-emphasize three principles for the short-term missionary who contracts the disease. The first is a repeat of an earlier statement: No prophylactic regimen can prevent all cases of malaria. Second, it is safer to treat the flu like malaria than it is to treat malaria like the flu. If you come down with the disease on a given drug regiment, do *not* use that drug to treat the disease. Third, after you return home, any severe viral-like syndrome in the next year after your return should be assumed to be malaria and treated promptly. Any unexplained fever that lasts more than 24 hours, a prolonged severe headache, severe muscle and joint pains or persistent diarrhea or vomiting unresponsive to treatment may be malaria. Seek immediate treatment even if you have to treat yourself. Don't let your doctor brush you off, even if you have to go to a university center or a clinic specializing in travel medicine to be seen. Delay in seeking care or in being treated can be deadly. Malaria antigen tests (blood tests) do exist but are not fool-proof and the CDC recommends confirmatory blood smears. Because of the rarity of the disease in North America, many laboratories do not have the experience of having seen hundreds of such cases, therefore the technician may miss the parasite on thick blood smear even when they look for it properly. Insist on at least three malaria thin and thick smears *read by an expert experienced technician.* If that is not possible, have your doctor consult with the CDC Malaria Hotline.

As you have read, those who have been infected with *P. ovale* and *P. vivax* may have persistant parasites within their liver cells. Those patients with *known P. ovale* and *P. vivax* infections or with a high exposure in an area where those are common forms of malaria *and* who have not taken primaquine for prophylaxis, should consider treatment with primaquine upon return to their home. It should be taken after returning home during the last 2 weeks of chemoprophylaxis. The dose is 26.3 mg of the salt (15 mg base) daily for 14 days. It is generally well tolerated, but can have significant toxicity. The most important is the possibility of a hemolytic crisis in patients with glucose-6-phosphate-dehydrogenase (G6PD) deficiency. All patients should be tested before the drug is given, especially those from Mediterranean, African, or certain East Asian extraction. Pregnancy is a contraindication as well as autoimmune disorders and concomitant administration of quinine. Patients with a low risk of exposure should not routinely take the drug but should have all malaria-like symptoms within a four year period evaluated by your physician.

MEDICAL KIT

Assemble a traveler's medical kit appropriate for your destination, length of trip, and general health. Pack it in your carry-on luggage. In general, the best way is to use medications packed in blister packs, use plastic bottles (rather than glass) for liquids and take only small quantities in the amount you think you will need in order to save room. Make sure you have spare eyeglasses or contact lens with you as well. A small eyeglass repair kit with screwdriver, magnifying lens and

extra hinge screws can be very helpful. Bring a tweezers to remove splinters and stingers. The medical kit should contain:
▶ Prescription medications as described in the beginning of this chapter. Keep them in their original container (preferred) or in a small pill case or bottles labeled with name, strength, expiration date and instructions.
▶ Over-the-counter medications to include the following. The amount to take depends on your usage and length of time you will be gone.
• Cough drops/throat lozenges
• Decongestant
• Pills for motion sickness
• Antihistamine: diphenhydramine can be used for sleep, allergic reactions and cough and cold symptoms.
• Acetaminophen
• Ibuprofen or other non-steroidal anti-inflammatory
• Loperamide (antidiarrheal)
• Laxative (travel, change in diet, and dehydration can interfere with your regularity)
• Bismuth subsalicylate tablets if that is what you are going to use for diarrhea prophylaxis or treatment (it is not as effective as appropriate antibiotics)
• Small tube of antiseptic or antibiotic cream
• Small tube of 1% hydrocortisone cream
• Itch relief cream or solution
• Lip balm (preferably with sun screen activity)
• Antacids, H-2 blockers (e.g., cimetidine, ranitidine), or ion-pump inhibitors (e.g. omeprazole)
• Antifungal powder, lotion or cream
• Women: a course of anti-fungal vaginitis treatment
• Oil of clove for toothache
▶ General first aid: gauze bandages, adhesive bandages of assorted sizes, tape, scissors, hemostat, small tube of petroleum jelly, and if appropriate for your circumstances, a small suture kit with a selection of skin sutures, lidocaine and needles and syringes.

PREGNANCY AND TRAVEL

Travel can be planned most safely between the 18th and 32nd weeks of pregancy. Commerical flying in pressurized cabins is safe. Do get up and move more often, taking frequent walks. Adequate fluids should be taken during the flight.

Ideally, all immunizations should be taken before pregnancy. Live virus products (measles, rubella, yellow fever) should not be given. Oral typhoid vaccine should probably not be given. Vaccines against pneumococcus, meningococcus and hepatitis A are safe. Hepatitis A immune globulin is safe. Influenza vaccine is encouraged for all pregnant women who will be in their last six months of pregnancy during flu season. The appropriateness of other vaccinations during pregnancy can be checked by consulting with the CDC.

Water should be purified by boiling rather than by iodine purification, since the latter may provide an excess of iodine to the fetus.

Do not use bismuth subsalicylate or prophylactic antibiotics to prevent traveler's diarrhea. Use oral rehydration fluids and treat bacterial diarrhea with azithromycin or erythromycin if treatment is necessary (consult a medical professional before starting it).

See the on-line version of the CDC Yellow Book (www.cdc.gov) for the most up-to-date CDC recommendations.

REST

It seems odd to mention this, but do not overwork or overextend yourself. The missionaries want you to enjoy your experience and come back. The work will wait; the opportunity to understand the culture and the people may never come again.

RETURNING HOME

If you become ill after your return, the first two things to think about are malaria and parasites. If you have a febrile or viral illness that seems out of proportion to the usual cold, see your physician immediately, and let him know you have been in areas where malaria is endemic. At the risk of offending my colleagues, it is unfortunate that many physicians do not know much about malaria and have been taught that they must prove the disease before treating it. That delay can have serious consequences, especially in people who have not acquired partial immunity from previous attacks. Since the disease is rare in North America, many labs do not have the experience in making the diagnosis and therefore their ability to pick up the parasite may be less than optimal. If you do not feel that you are being treated optimally, insist on referal to someone with experience in travel medicine.

Some people advise self treatment with worm medicine (mebendazole or albendazole) just before or after arriving home. There is little risk in doing so and it is a personal decision. However, remember that these drugs do not affect protozoa such as giardia, amoeba and Cryptosporidium. If you have chronic gastrointestinal symptoms (nausea, constipation, flatulence, food intolerance) or weight loss after returning, remind your physician of your travel history and these possibilities. The diagnosis can sometimes be hard to make.

SAFETY, PERSONAL AND FOR YOUR POSSESSIONS

Some short-term missionaries act as if they are visiting some huge theme park put on for their own personal benefit and are oblivious to the dangers that are present. Most places should be treated with the same degree of caution and common sense you would have if visiting a big city in your home state or province. Enjoy it but stay aware of your surroundings. Don't go into a stairwell (such as those leading into a subway, hallway or an underground tunnel) if there aren't at least two other people in sight. If it looks like an area of town that you should not be in, then get out. If you need directions, go into a shop to inquire—don't ask a stranger. Don't be out at night if you can avoid it; never go out after dark unless the street is well lit and busy with pedestrians. If you take a taxi, note the number and look at the picture ID of the driver as you step in. Be situationally aware at all times. Follow your instincts, if you sense danger, leave. Ask your hosts for advice and then follow it.

You should always carry your passport or government-issued ID with you, preferably in a body wallet— do NOT leave it in the hotel or in your room unless you are certain that the room is secure. You will likely need it to cash traveler's checks as well. Guard your valuables by keeping them with you, or putting them in the hotel safe. Do not leave them in your room.

Pickpockets and purse-snatchers are ubiquitous but they look for easy pickings. Men should carry their wallet (or preferably a slim money clip) in their front pocket with their hand over it. Some experienced travelers carry a dummy (empty) wallet in their back pocket so the pickpockets go for the wrong thing. Women should carry purses over their shoulder and keep their hand on the clasp when walking in the city. Keep small change and small bills in a change purse and use that when your paying for purchases. If you can, reverse your back pack so the zippered compartments are against your back and not ready to be unzipped. The best solution is a body wallet. Worn around the waist, suspended from a strap around the neck or (best of all) worn around the leg, they are invisible under the clothing. You really don't need to carry very much money, so carry only what you can easily replace. Wear a whistle around your neck. Whether to carry something for your defence like Mace or pepper spray is debatable, but do know you must pack it in your checked suitcase in order to be able to take it on the airplane. You cannot carry it in your purse or in your carry-on, because it is considered a weapon by the airport security department. They will confiscate it from you. If you take pictures, carry your camera around your neck to minimize the risk of snatching it.

Walk with purpose and don't dawdle even during the day. Stay together in groups or at least in pairs. Don't wear expensive jewelry (including diamond rings) or expensive watches. Keep even inexpensive watches out of sight under your sleeve or in your pocket if you are wearing something sleeveless. Do not dress to look like a "rich tourist." Dress in such a manner that you are not an offense to the local mores (especially in Moslem countries).

Don't pet street animals; bites (and even rabies) are possible. Use your own judgment whether to give beggars your spare change. Don't give children money. (If you must give something, give pens or pins and kids like gum or crafts.) Such largesse can quickly degenerate into a true mob scene that can be dangerous to you.

Pay attention when someone on a bike is approaching and don't walk close to the curb. Both of these can be an invitation to a purse-snatching. Don't make eye contact with gangs. They'll try to intimidate you.

If you are accosted, give them what they want. You can replace it all (being well prepared by this book, you have the photocopies of everything and have written down the numbers of your traveler's checks). Your life is harder to replace. As soon as your assailants turn and begin to leave you, yell "thief" at the top of your lungs and begin to blow your whistle. Most of us would not expect much response from the average citizen in our own countries, but you may be amazed at the help you receive from bystanders. Sometimes their response is vigorous and if caught, the assailant can be in mortal danger. Report the theft to the police, but do not be terribly surprised if it does no good! If you have to give up your passport to the thief, the loss needs to be reported to the embassy as soon as possible.

Personal safety in your hotel room is also a matter of common sense. Always keep the door locked with all extra chains and locks in place. Do not open the door for anyone you do not know or you do not expect. Never keep your valuables out in a place visible from a window. Keep valuables in the hotel safe. Make sure you are familiar with the recommended exit route in case of fire or other emergency.

SNAKES, BUGS, SCORPIONS AND OTHER NASTY THINGS

They are more afraid of you than you are of them—although with some of you, it may be mighty close to a draw. Consult the nationals or missionaries about your concerns. After they quit teasing you, they will tell you what you need to know.[11] Ask if there any bugs, caterpil-

---

[11] By the way, no matter what the missionaries say, there is no such snake as a "step-and-a-halfer," i.e. a snake so venomous that if bitten, the victim only makes it a step and a half. Almost anyone can make it two steps...

lars, worms or plants that are around that you and your children should not handle, climb in or touch. Use common sense. Don't put on your shoes without checking them out for unwanted visitors. Don't pick up a towel or piece of clothing without shaking it out. Don't pick up crawly things no matter how pretty or fascinating they are. Don't approach wild or even domestic animals unless you know it is safe. Never walk at night without a flashlight. Always wear footwear— wearing appropriate foot gear can prevent infection from parasites, fungi, insect bites (chiggers, ticks, sandfleas), and other injuries (snakebites, cuts, puncture wounds). Consider wearing flip-flops in the shower to prevent acquiring athlete's foot (tinea pedis).

SUN AND SUNBURN

The sun in the tropics and at the higher altitudes can be vicious, burning you before you are aware of the discomfort. This is especially true if you are on doxycycline as a malaria prophylaxis or any tetracycline or phenothiazine for other medical reasons. These drugs can make you sensitized to the sun. Do as your mother said: wear a good sunscreen or sunblock (at least 15 SPF), wear long-sleeves, wear a hat, and avoid dehydration. Drink plenty of fluids.

Sunglasses are great for your personal comfort but be sensitive to the cultural considerations. In a country where communication may already be a problem, covering the eyes may make it worse. Your eyes are the "windows to your soul" and taking your sunglasses off so whoever you are talking to can see your eyes may prevent unintended miscommunication.

SWIMMING AND WADING

In areas endemic for schistosomiasis (bilharziasis), do not swim, bathe or wade. In some areas (e.g. Lake Victoria in Africa), even the spray from the lake water can be of concern. If accidental immersion occurs or wading is necessary to cross a steam, rapidly and briskly towel wet skin to decrease the chances of infection. The infective larvae tunnel directly through the skin in a few hours and toweling briskly can knock them off. They are not visible. Rubbing with alcohol may help as well.

If you return home and develop either an acute febrile illness or a chronic syndrome of vague gastrointestinal or genitourinary symptoms associated with fatigue or general systemic symptoms, be sure to remind your doctor that you have been in an area with endemic schistosomiasis.

TRAVELER'S DIARRHEA

Montezuma's Revenge, Traveler's Two-Step, Delhi Belly, Bali Belly—Known by dozens of different names, traveler's diarrhea is a common problem for travelers. Whenever change involves a marked difference in climate, social conditions, or sanitation standards and facilities, diarrhea becomes likely. Although a luxury hotel would seem to offer a lower risk, it is not foolproof. And one sure way to get it is to believe the missionary when he or she says, "It's okay—we eat this all the time."

The typical symptoms of travelers' diarrhea (TD) are diarrhea, nausea, bloating, urgency, and malaise. TD usually lasts from 3 to 7 days. It is rarely life threatening. Areas of high risk include the developing countries of Africa (Central, East, North, Southern, and West), the Middle East, Asia, and Central America.

Traveler's diarrhea is caused 4 out of 5 times by new strains of bacteria that your intestine has not seen before and therefore not built up an immunity to them. Strains of *E coli* that produce toxins that target your gut, Shigella species and *Campylobacter jejuni* are the most common bacteria causing these problems. Other possible bacterial agents are aeromonas, salmonella, and noncholera vibrios. Parasites such as amoeba and giardia and viruses such as adenoviruses and retroviruses are also causes. There may be up to ten loose stools a day, often accompanied by cramps, nausea, occasionally vomiting and rarely fever. The stools do not usually contain mucous or blood.

Systemic signs of illness are infrequent. For 90% of those stricken, the illness usually subsides spontaneously with 1–5 days. Signs of more serious disease are bloody stools, persistent vomiting, a temperature greater than 102° F or diarrhea lasting more than a week. Prevention is better than treatment. Besides washing your hands frequently and never eating from street vendors, the best advice is "Boil it, cook it, peel it, or forget it." The principles for what to eat and drink are outlined in Chapter 11. You can live without salads and raw vegetables and fruits for the duration of your trip. Please do unless you know the food has been properly prepared by yourself or others. This seems to be a major problem for some folks but consider it this way: you have paid too much money and traveled too far to spend several days of it deciding which end to present to the ceramic throne (or floor level squat toilet, or long-drop latrine, or . . .). Washing hands well before eating and drying helps. Impregnated hand wipes and waterless antibacterial washes are helpful and are a good way to ensure clean hands. Carry your own toilet paper (often it is not available in public toilets). Since the disease can be water-borne, shower with your mouth shut and do not brush your teeth with the tap water. Have a liter or container of "safe" water in your bathroom to help you remember.

Unfortunately, there are no vaccines effective against traveler's diarrhea. Antibiotic prophylaxis is effective against some of the causes of traveler's diarrhea but only prevents about 60% of the cases of diarrhea. It is recommended for a limited number of travelers. Those travelers with serious underlying disease (inflammatory bowel disease, cardiac disease in the elderly, diabetes, immunosuppression) are candidates. Those in whom any interruption of their work is unacceptable make up another group who may consider prophylaxis. The drugs are started upon entry into the country, continued through the stay and for 1 to 2 days after leaving. Prophylaxis for stays of greater than 3 weeks is not recommended because of the costs and possible drug toxicity. Prolonged or high dose prophylaxis using antibiotics can lead to vaginitis and antibiotic-induced diarrhea. Bismuth subsalicylate (Pepto-Bismol®, others) is effective (less so than the antibiotic regi-

mens) but turns the tongue and stools black, interferes with doxycycline absorption (especially a problem if that is the malaria prophylaxis you are using) and should not be used with other salicylates
because of the aspirin that is part of the formulation. The most effective regimens are two tablets carefully chewed or two ounces taken
four times a day. Numerous once-a-day regimens for antibiotics are
efficacious but can be expensive. Norfloxacin (400 mg), levofloxacin
(400 mg) ciprofloxacin (500 mg), or ofloxacin (300 mg) are acceptable
choices if taken once a day and for two days after return.
Cotrimoxazole and doxycycline may work but are no longer suggested because of high levels of microbial resistance. An approved nonab-
sorbable antibiotic, rifaximin, is effective as well (200 mg one to three
times a day). To repeat, prophylactic antibiotics for diarrhea are not be
recommended for most travelers.

Treatment consists of rehydration and symptomatic treatment
with anti-diarrheals. Replacement of lost fluids with oral rehydration
salts will frequently prevent nausea and vomiting and hasten the cure.
Patients who are systemically ill with high fevers or dysentery (bloody
stools) should not be treated with agents that slow the motility of the
gut (e.g. loperamide and opioids). Oral rehydration salts are widely
available in other countries and in the U.S. are known as Ceralyte,
ORS, Infalyte, Pedialyte, Gastrolyte and others. Other drinks (juices,
soft drinks, Gatorade and water) are helpful but milk should be avoided both because of a possible lactose intolerance induced by the infection and because it may aggravate the situation by causing an osmotic
diarrhea. In an emergency, make up a solution with 8 teaspoons of
sugar and half a teaspoon of salt to a liter of water. Loperamide
(Imodium AD, Maalox Anti-Diarrheal, Pepto Diarrhea Control) is
given as 4 mgm as a first dose and then 2 mgm after each loose stool
to a maximum of 16 mg a day. There is some evidence that loperamide
may actually prolong the duration of the diarrhea but will make it less
severe. Many experts recommend no antibiotics unless 48–72 hours of
oral rehydration solution has proved ineffective. If there is a need for
a more rapid recovery, a single dose of ciprofloxacin (750 mg), lev-

ofloxacin (500 mg), norfloxacin (400 mg) or ofloxacin (300 mg) cures most cases (those antibiotics may be taken up to three days if necessary). If the diarrhea is severe, associated with fever or bloody stools, or persists despite the one-dose antibiotic treatment, do not use loperamide or opioids. Instead, begin 3–5 days of ciprofloxacin 500 mg twice daily, levofloxacin 500 mg once daily, norfloxacin 400 mg twice daily or ofloxacin 300 mg twice daily are all options. Azithromycin (10 mg/kg/d for three days) is the drug of choice for pregnant women, children and those who travel to areas of high prevalence of fluroquinolone-resistant *Campylobacter* (e.g. Thailand and India). Rifaximin is approved for treatment of E.coli in travelers >12 years old but should not be used in cases where there is a fever or blood in the stool. It is contraindicated if the organism is *Campylobacter jejuni* and in pregnancy. Cotrimoxazole (TMP/SMP, Bactrim®, Septra®), doxycycline and ampicillin probably should not be used any more because of the high resistance levels in many areas.

Most pediatricians also advise against the use of loperamide and other antimotility agents in children less than two and use other medications and antibiotics in children with great caution. Azithromycin is considered first line antibiotic treatment in children (rather than fluroquinolones).

The most common parasitic cause of traveler's diarrhea is *Giardia intestinalis*, and treatment options include metronidazole, tinidazole, and nitazoxanide. Although cryptosporidiosis is usually a self-limited illness in immunocompetent persons, nitazoxanide can be considered as a treatment option. Cyclosporiasis is treated with TMP-SMX. Treatment of amebiasis is with metronidazole or tinidazole, followed by treatment with a luminal agent such as iodoquinol or paromomycin.

Food poisoning can be avoided by the same precautions. Dine in reputable restaurants or in homes where you know proper precautions have been taken, select only freshly cooked food that is still very hot and avoid shellfish, salads and creamy desserts.

Sometimes, you feel you have no choice. You find yourself in a situation where not eating would be too great an insult and hinder your testimony and friendship. If that is truly the case, remember the prayer, "Lord, thank you for this food and protect me from it" and consider taking 500 mg of ciprofloxacin when you return back to your lodging! For more extensive information on food and water precautions and on travelers' diarrhea, please read http://wwwnc.cdc.gov/travel/content/safe-food-water.aspx and wwwnc.cdc.gov/travel/yellowbook/2010/chapter-2/travelers-diarrhea.aspx

TUBERCULOSIS

Tuberculosis is increasingly a problem in the world. For all travelers, skin-testing for previous exposure to TB before you go is wise. Testing after your return is also probably wise, especially if you provided health care to patients with a high likelihood of having the disease. If you convert, proper prophylactic treatment (usually with isoniazid) has excellent results.

There is no prophylactic antibiotic regimen approved for tuberculosis. BCG is a term that refers to a series of available vaccines named after the original modified bacterium (bacillus Calmette-Guérin). Although widely used in developing countries, it does not protect well against contracting the disease and seems to be most effective against certain manifestations of systemic tuberculosis. It also will turn the skin test positive losing a potentially valuable form of patient monitoring. "Vaccination of health care workers should be considered on an individual basis in settings in which a high percentage of tuberculosis patients are infected with strains resistant to both isoniazid and rifampin, in which trasnmision of such drug-resistant [organisms] are likely, and in which comprehensive tuberculous infeciton-control precautions have been implementsed but have been successful"[12] It is contraindicated in those with immunosuppression.

___

[12] Stephen J. McPhee, M.A. Papadakis (eds). 2010 Current Medical Diagnosis & Treatment. New York: Lange, 2009, page 258.

USING THE TOILET

Yes, it is certain that your mother has trained you well in such things but you may still face a situation she was not familiar with. The fastidious person may have a real problem with some of the pissoirs, long-drop latrines, squat toilets, and less than hygeinic toilets that you might find. Women in particular seem to have more of a problem with this, but "holding it" and not drinking water are definitely NOT the best solutions and can lead to some wicked urinary tract infections.

One hard and fast rule is to always carry your own toilet paper. If possible, carry a small bottle of waterless hand cleaner, a small package of pre-moistened wipes or a small bar of soap. If packing and carrying them is easily done, you might be thankful for some dispoable toilet seat covers.

In many countries, you do NOT flush the toilet paper, tampons or sanitary napkins. The plumbing cannot handle the challenge and the people waiting in line behind you will not be happy with you if you block the pipes. Ask your local missionary before you use the facilities or look around for a small wastebasket that has been left for such an eventuality. This method of disposal is distasteful to many North Americans. Is the wastebasket for toilet paper? A few minutes reflection will reveal the truth—they often have no other amenities (such as soap, towel or water) so they would not have a wastebasket either unless it was for a real purpose. It is not just an accoutrement of their decorating scheme. If you find yourself going out to the village, taking a small zip lock bag to put your used toilet paper, tampons or sanitary napkins in may be the best solution.

Many people with latrines sprinkle things in them intermittently to keep down the odor. Ashes, lime, moth balls, and other things are used. You may see those chemicals, ashes and materials within the latrine. If you are using the latrine as a visitor, it is probably not necessary for you to do anything with them. If you are sharing the latrine on a regular basis, check with the hosts to find out what they would like you to do in that matter.

For most North Americans, the squat toilet represents the greatest challenge. Those citizens of the world who have used squat toilets all their lives look at our high ceramic devices and wonder how anyone could eliminate body wastes in the sitting position or wonder upon which part they should perch. North Americans look at the floor-level holes (sometimes with little blocks on either side upon which you place your feet) and wonder how anyone can eliminate in that position. It is not always easy to keep long skirts tucked up and concentrate on your aim. As we grow older and less limber, the position becomes less dignified and certainly less obtainable. Since necessity is the mother of invention, you can handle it, but a little practice at home may make it a more facile maneuver. Pre-moistened wipes can be a life-saver the first few times.

VACCINATIONS [13, 14]

Your itinerary and your previous immunization record determine the need for vaccinations. There are those that are recommended for general health purposes (and travel has little or nothing to do with whether you need them) and those that are recommended depending on your itinerary.

Travelers considered at low risk are those traveling for less than one month, staying on tourist routes and having little exposure to ill patients. Those who are high risk are those who will be there for longer periods of time, travel frequently, have significant medical exposure and are off the usual tourist routes. If you are a short-term medical missionary, this is probably the category in which you fall. All travelers should get the immunizations required by the countries you are visiting (e.g., yellow fever) and make sure that all the routine immuniza-

[13] These recommendations are taken from the CDC website and the 2010 *Current Medical Diagnosis & Treatment.* New York: Lange, 2009 edited by Stephen J. McPhee and M.A. Papadakis. Since such information may change often, please consult your physician or the CDC website for the latest information.
[14] A more comprehensive version of this chapter with more material on vaccinations can be downloaded from www.S3Ministries.com.

tions—tetanus, diphtheria, measles, mumps, rubella, polio, varicella and perhaps hepatitis A (vaccine or immune globulin)—are up to date. Influenza and pneumococcus are other serious considerations depending on your health factors. High risk travelers should definitely have the hepatitis B vaccine series completed and consider typhoid, meningococcus, rabies, and cholera Japanese B encephalitis(in roughly the order of importance depending on where you are traveling). Plague and cholera vaccines are no longer commercially available in North America. Consult the Health Information of International Travel (The Yellow Book), published each year by the CDC or consult the web site (http//www.cdc.gov) for the latest recommendations. Your physician can discuss with you whether there is a proven and acceptible regimen that will still give you acceptable protection if you have waited longer than you should.

Ideally, these vaccinations would begin at least six months before you leave, but two months is about the bare minimum to hope to get good antibody response. Since dosages, regimens and recommendations vary from time to time, please consult your physician. The vaccinations are listed below for the purpose of ensuring that you have thought about them and then discussed any deficiencies in your immunization record with your doctor. Some general principles apply:

▶ Prevention by careful attention to water, food and hygiene is important even if you are vaccinated against the disease—none of the vaccines provide complete protection.

▶ Live attenuated vaccines (measles, mumps, rubella, yellow fever, BCG and oral typhoid vaccine) should not be given to pregnant women, immunosuppressed people or household members of immunosuppressed people.

▶ If you are receiving two or more live virus vaccines, both should either be given on the same day or at least a month apart for maximum antibody response.

▶ Also, immunoglobulin should not be given for three months before or at least two weeks after a live virus vaccine because it may prevent the vaccine from provoking the desired antibody response. Immune globulin does not effect polio, yellow fever, tetanus or typhoid vaccines.

► Most vaccines can be given on the same day in scattered sites, but some (intramuscular typhoid comes to mind) can cause significant discomfort and are best done on different days.

► For the vaccinations not usually given to children and especially for those under the age of 2 and for pregnant women, check with the CDC for their recommendations.

► Make sure that you get your last shots in a series at least 10 days before your departure date in order to let any fever and pain to subside and to make sure you are not having any adverse reactions. Hepatitis A immune globulin can be given at any time before departure but it is wise to give yourself at least a three day hiatus between the shot and your departure to allow resolution of any subsequent pain and fever.

SUGGESTED READING

Aroney-Sine, Dr. Christine. *Survival of the Fittest: Keeping Yourself Healthy in Travel and Service Overseas.* Monrovia, CA: MARC, 1999, ISBN 0-912552-88-3

Dawood, Dr. Richard. *Traveller's Health: How to Stay Healthy Abroad.* Oxford University Press, 2002, ISBN 0192629476

Rose, Stuart R. *International Travel Health Guide (13th edition).* St. Louis: Mosby , 2005, ISBN 0323040500

Schroeder, Dick. *Staying Healthy in Asia, Africa, & Latin America, 5th ed.* Avalon Travel Publishing, 2000, ISBN: 1566911338

Wilson-Howarth, Jane. *Essential Guide to Travel Health: Don't Let Bugs, Bites and Bowels Spoil Your Trip.* London: Cadogan Guides, 2009, ISBN 1860114245

CHAPTER 7

PACKING

How do you remember all you have to take and avoid taking too much?
How do I get it there? What do I leave?

All of us have stood at the last minute before the mountain of things we "just have to have with us," culled through the pile packing every suitcase to its fullest and then gotten there and realized we have forgotten something. It will happen to you again, but here are some general rules of packing:

▶ Take fewer clothes and more money than you expect to need.

▶ Don't pack any suitcase you can't physically carry. If your trip has severe weight restrictions (e.g., a private small plane is part of your itinerary) or if you must make multiple, rapid connections from one

"He who would travel happily must travel light."

—Antoine deSaint-Exupery

form of transportation to another, pack and repack until you have pared your luggage down to the required weight or to the size that you can carry ALL of your luggage at least a few hundred yards.

▶ Remember that just because you are taking it with you, that doesn't mean that you have to bring it back.

▶ If you are taking something for the missionaries or their work, remember that what they specifically asked for takes higher priority than what you thought they "might" like.

▶ Decide which camera you are most likely to use (or at very most, two) and then take extra batteries and twice as much film or memory as you think you will use.

▶ Keep the most critical things (e.g., passports, visas, international certificates of vaccination, airplane tickets, money and credit card) on your body.

▶ Have a change of clothes and your necessary cosmetics, medications, one change of underclothes, and personal hygiene items in your carry-on in case your luggage doesn't make it.

▶ Because of the occasional mishap with lost luggage, don't pack anything you can't afford (financially or emotionally) to lose. Also consider cross-packing—some of your spouses' clothing in your suitcase and vice-versa in case one of them is temporarily lost.

▶ Start making your list early and jot down ideas about what you might like to take with you as they come to you.

▶ Ask somebody who has recently visited the field or the missionaries themselves for their ideas and help to judge whether something is appropriate for you to take.

Appendix D is a packing list which can also be downloaded on our website (www.S3Ministries.com). **WARNING!** It is neither complete nor do you ever have to take all of those things. They are listed just to help you *consider* whether you want to take them. Obviously, the climate and conditions of your trip will affect the clothing you take, but they will also affect what you might want to have in the way of medications, emergency supplies and the like. A trip to the polar conditions of Siberia would obviously be different than the rain jungles of the Amazon region. A trip to the high altitudes of Bolivia is different than the low altitudes of Togo. Even the climate at the time of the year you are going can affect your list. And then there are rainy seasons—the rainy season consists of daily 4 p.m. rains in some areas of the world that last an hour and is certainly different than the monsoons of some areas of the Indian subcontinent that are true frog-stranglers.

SIZE AND WEIGHT RESTRICTIONS

This is an area that changes frequently and it is ultimately YOUR responsibility to make sure that your luggage complies with the rules. Just because Mrs. So-and-so was able to take her grand piano in her luggage last time doesn't guarantee that you can do so this time. And just because we write about it below, doesn't mean it still is necessarily so. Please check with your airline and your travel agent just before you go as to what regulations apply for your trip.

Usually, the North American airlines will allow two pieces of checked luggage and one piece of carry-on luggage on international flights (but this is no longer true on domestic flights). Some frequent flier programs will allow more if you are in the higher levels of those programs. The dimensions of the checked luggage must add to a total no more than 62 inches. Measure the greatest length of your suitcase, the greatest width and the greatest depth and add them together. The weight limit is now usually 50 pounds (23 kg) on outgoing flights. Some airlines will stretch that limit to 70 pounds. Some airlines will charge you for the excess weight between 50 and 70 pounds and refuse to carry anything over 70 pounds. Although *sometimes* they will take the average weight of your pieces (allowing you to scrape by with a heavier piece of luggage) or the ticket agent at check-in *may* allow a bigger piece, you run the risk of one of two penalties.

> *"If you wish to travel far and fast, travel light. Take off all your envies, jealousies, unforgiveness, selfishness and fears."*
>
> —Cesare Pavese

The first hurts your wallet. The distance you are traveling and the amount of excess weight affect the extra fee you are charged for your baggage. Fees in the range of $100–$200 per extra bag are not unusual. For the best up-to-date advice and the least number of fees, check with the airline and your agent before you pack to make sure. Should you pay it? Depends. Some airlines, *if you call ahead*, will allow you as a missionary to take extra pieces of luggage at no charge. Call yourself or ask your travel agent to check on this for you. Airlines are not obligated to do so and increasingly, in response to financial and other pressures, many airlines do not. Also, not all airlines will honor an agreement you have with another airline to carry an extra bag, even if they are "partners" for frequent flyer miles and no matter what their advertising would seem to imply. Therefore, check with each airline and make sure all airlines that you are using will honor the agreements.

The second penalty that is sometimes imposed is the refusal to allow you to take the bag. Depending on the conditions of your flight (how full it is, how much weight the plane is carrying), the airline agents have the option of not honoring any agreements for extra luggage. That happens rarely but can be a real problem if it does.

Anyway, back to the question, "Should you pay the extra luggage fee?" Same answer: it depends. How badly do you want the stuff to go on the trip with you? And the answer to that question is often answered indirectly by how well you packed. Let's look at some factors that affect the answer and then look at the math. First, your bag is more likely (albeit not guaranteed) to arrive where you are going than if you ship it internationally by some alternative method. Second, it is cheaper to take things by commercial airline than it is to send it by commercial carrier and much, much faster.

Let's now do the math as a storybook problem. Dr. Smith, short-term missionary, is at the airport ticket agent and has planned to take an extra suitcase along with her. The agent states that the suitcase is 70 pounds but the extra luggage fee is $140. Dr. Smith knows that the airline is giving a special reward to the agent who collects the most money this month in extra baggage fees. Quickly doing the "gozintas" (70 gozinta $140 twice), she comes up with a price of $2 per pound. Since she knows the price for the post-office airmail and other express carriers can be from $5 per pound to $50 a pound and may still take weeks or even months for packages to arrive at her mission trip destination, should she: a) announce loudly that she is a missionary and argue, in general making a nuisance of herself and impressing all around with her Christ-like demeanor; or b) know that she has packed wisely, planned ahead to take only what she needs, and allowed for the possibility of having to pay the fee knowing that she and the missionaries on the field need what she has?

Admittedly, most people will get that question right but going through the thought processes involved does help you decide what to take and how much of it to take. If you can take just enough for what you need, take powders instead of liquids, distribute your weight carefully between suitcases, and choose your things to take with you wisely, you will do okay.

Many airlines have a 7–10 kilogram (15–22 pound) weight limit on your carry-on piece of luggage and may have unique size limitations. As we have all heard, "they must be able to fit in the overhead bin or under the seat in front of you." It has been our experience that they don't usually enforce those weight restrictions on the North American airlines (although they can), but it is increasingly more likely to be enforced on some of the overseas airlines.

Speaking of overseas airlines, some of the smaller carriers have a weight limit of only *one bag weighing 20 kilograms* (instead of 23 kilograms) unless you are flying first class or business class where a higher weight limit may pertain. This can be a very expensive lesson to learn since they often charge very high rates for extra luggage, sometimes demanding it be paid only in American currency, sometimes only in the local currency (which you are unlikely to have in that amount), and sometimes refusing both traveler's checks and credit cards. Your first flight to a destination, no matter how many small airlines you fly, is covered by your first check-in. It is the subsequent check-ins for flights between countries or back to the U.S. where you might get burned. Check this carefully before you leave and be very careful about accepting any layover which may suddenly drop your allowable weight from two bags and hundred pounds to one bag weighing only 44 pounds. It can get expensive and annoying.

When making several airline trips from one overseas airport to another, any errors in weight can get expensive. We have found that carrying a portable digital luggage scale (made of plastic) has been very helpful.

One other thing. The federal aviation authority has *strict* rules about what can be carried aboard a plane and these change from time to time and do so suddenly. Remember, this is like your childhood days: "my ball, my rules." Well, these are their planes, their airspaces and their rules. They take it seriously. You are not a special exception, no matter what your mother told you. The ultimate decision is theirs and no logic will sway them. Check their website at www.cas.faa.gov for the latest information before you go.

You must declare hazardous materials to airlines. Violations carry a civil penalty of up to $27,500 for each occurrence and, in appropriate cases, a criminal penalty of up to $500,000 and/or up to five years imprisonment.

▶ At the time of writing, all of the following are banned from ALL luggage (http://www.tsa.gov/travelers/airtravel/prohibited/permitted-prohibited-items.shtm#1):

- fireworks, sparklers and explosives
- butane lighter refills
- paints, solvents or drain cleaners
- bleaches

▶ Your carry-on cannot contain:

- Larger containers that are half-full or toothpaste tubes rolled up are not allowed. All liquids, gels and aerosols must be in three-ounce or smaller containers. All liquids, gels and aerosols must be placed in a single, quart-size, zip-top, clear plastic bag.
- knives (even pocket knives), scissors or shears with pointed tips or blades longer than four inches
- toy guns, any gun replica or real guns or ammunition
- straight-edged and certain other razors
- box and carpet cutters,
- ice picks
- "cutting instruments" of any kind
- baseball bats, golf clubs, hockey sticks, ski poles, spear guns, darts, bows and arrows, pool cues, etc.
- Mace, pepper spray or any weapon of self-defense
- hammers, tools longer than seven inches in length, saws, crow-bars and drill bits.

▶ Some overseas airlines may also preclude

- knitting needles
- duct tape and similar strong tapes
- nail clippers

To sum it up, here's a good rule of thumb: if you have the slightest doubt that an item you're carrying might be construed as a sharp, potentially dangerous item or a weapon of any kind, then pack it in your checked luggage. Even better: minimize what you carry on board as much as possible but never put essential medications, valuables such as jewelry and expensive or fragile equipment such as cameras in checked luggage.

SUITCASES, TRUNKS, BOXES OR DUFFEL BAGS?

One additional rule to the ten listed in the beginning of this chapter: "Your luggage will not return unscathed." Or unpummeled, or uncut, or unbroken, or unthrown, or undropped, or. . . . So, put away your beautiful Corinthian leather luggage and drag out some other bag. It should be:

▶ Sturdy. Soft-sided luggage (including duffel bags) may be easier to handle and has more give if you pack something of odd shape, but may not protect the contents as well and may not resist the thief's sharp knife. Your call.

▶ Size: The biggest sizes (26") were designed to carry 70 pounds of luggage. The next smallest size (~21–24") tends to be nicely and fully packed with 50 pounds.

▶ Wheeled (if you accept the fact that many places the wheels just won't work): The little wheeled carts with straps to hold your luggage may be useful on smooth surfaces but they are just more thing to keep track of and besides, there are no smooth surfaces where you are going.

▶ Disposable and/or foldable: If you are carrying a lot of things over that you don't plan to carry back with you, being able to roll or fold a bag up allows you to take it home. An alternative is to spend some time at yard sales, garage sales and thrift stores where you can often pick up old luggage that is sturdy enough (perhaps with the addition of

"It was all very well for an Englishman like Mr. Fogg to make the tour of the world with a carpet-bag; a lady could not be expected to travel comfortably under such conditions."

—Jules Verne

some duct tape or strapping) to make it one way to wherever you are going. You can leave it there. Even if you bring it back, you don't mind if it gets beaten up a bit more in some airport somewhere.

Hint: We often use the plastic trunks that fit within the 62" size limit. These have the advantage of being very rugged, cheap (even with a needed long-shanked padlock, they can often be obtained for $20–$25 for the entire package), having good hinges and reasonably good clasps (although they should be strapped shut with strapping or duct tape). Tape your name and address securely to the outside. They also are welcomed as storage containers in most places. The only drawback in using them is that they sometimes will attract the attention of customs agents upon landing. There are strategies for minimizing unwanted attention discussed in Chapter 8. Warning: Larger sizes than the 19.5 gallon models may be okay if you are leaving from North America and IF the airlines permit the outsized luggage, but you are warned again that many foreign airlines will refuse to carry them or charge outrageous fees for overweight or oversized luggage.

One variation on that idea is packing part of your goods in a large cooler (greater than 50 quart capacity) that can then be left on the field. Please check with the missionaries as to whether this would be a desirable thing for them. Often missionaries can buy meat or other frozen foods in the main city and this allows a way to transport them to the mission compound. These coolers do not have secure clasps, so it must be reinforced well with strapping and/or tape (a problem if the TSA inspects it and doesn't secure it well afterward) and usually best if it is packed with something relatively light.

▶ Don't take cardboard boxes. They get beat-up in transit, don't necessarily protect the contents well and tend to attract the attention of custom agents on the other end.

Label your luggage well. You never realized how many people have a suitcase of your model and color until you are looking for it on a busy baggage carousel. Make sure that you have put your name, address and phone number on outside, using sturdy tags. Also place one address label inside the suitcase. This precaution may prevent your suitcase from being lost forever if the outer tags come off. Be certain to write BOTH your home address and your destination address. The latter is to help them find you when they lose your luggage. *[Oh, we beg your pardon for that Freudian slip; we of course meant "if" they lose your luggage.]* If we are using trunks as described above, print or use your computer to print up a large label with your U.S. address, the local address and with the name of the sponsoring organization prominently displayed. Tape it securely to the lid. Seeing the local address and name of a recognized mission seems to help at times with customs when the agents glance at it.

Make sure your luggage is easy to identify. It helps you find it and it helps you make sure across a crowded room that your luggage is not leaving accompanied by someone else. A large "x" in colored tape on the side, colored yarn on the handle, distinctly colored or shaped luggage tags are some ideas that can make your luggage identifiable from across the room. You are limited only by your imagination and your sense of embarrassment. If a whole group is traveling together, have everyone mark the luggage the same way. That way when a few members of the group get assigned the job of picking up all the luggage, they know to look for the identifying mark or item.

Keep a detailed list of the contents of suitcases. You may need to report the loss! Also, a list of contents sometimes will satisfy the custom agents' curiosity about what you brought, demonstrate that you are not trying to hide anything and prevent long searches of your baggage.

WHAT CLOTHES DO I TAKE?

There are some general principles that apply here and we will cover the details in subsequent paragraphs:

▶ If you look and dress like a tourist, you will be perceived as one. On the parts of your trip where you are just a tourist, this is fine, but the rest of the time you should dress in a fashion comparable to the local professionals or laymen. That is what you are.

▶ Take modest clothing. Modest is defined by the culture where you will be, not by what is considered modest in your culture. See Chapter 10 for a discussion on adapting to cultural mores.

▶ Dress appropriately. Do not over- or under-dress. Many cultures dress up for any event and know the kind of clothes you have in your closet. Failure to dress appropriately may be considered as insulting by the nationals. North Americans by and large dress to reflect their opinion of their selves. In many cultures, how one dresses reflects the person's opinion of others. Although casual clothing may be acceptable in your home congregation, many cultures take dressing up very seriously. If there are questions, check with the agency or missionaries before you go. You are on the King's business and to dress in a way that detracts from that message is counter-productive.

"When preparing to travel, lay out all your clothes and all your money. Then take half the clothes and twice the money."

—Susan Heller

▶ Take wrinkle-free non-iron clothes that are easily cared for. Take color coordinated clothes that can be mixed and matched for different looks. There are only so many times you can wear the same outfit without getting tired of it.

▶ Do *not* wear whites. Depending on how dirty the water supply is, they may well return a nice shade of tan.

▶ Consider buying your clothing at a thrift store and plan on leaving them overseas. The clothes may make appreciated gifts to the nationals and this may solve some of the problems with weight restrictions on the return visit—especially if you bought a lot of souvenirs!

▶ If you need special clothing or uniforms (white jackets, scrub suits, surgical hats and masks), take them with you. Don't expect them to be there at your ultimate destination in sizes guaranteed to fit you, especially if you are a more generously sized individual. Plan to leave them for the staff. Extra scrub suits in the smaller "non-American" sizes are great gifts for the staff.

▶ Take sturdy and comfortable shoes that are well broken in. In temperate climes, take one pair of good walking or sports shoes and one pair of sturdy casual shoes that can double for your Sunday-go-to-meeting shoes. In hotter climes, a pair of sandals is often appreciated. Rubber flip-flops may be desirable to wear while relaxing and in the shower. Since in many cultures, you are expected to remove your shoes, it may be desirable to take a pair of house slippers with you. Those that can fold or be rolled to fit into your pocket or purse may be appreciated once you are there.

▶ Despite your long-suppressed and burning desire to wear safari clothing and look dashing—they quickly look terrible. Crepes, jerseys and cotton/polyester types of material that drip-dry quickly without much wrinkle are often best for many climates. Obviously, it depends on the climate, altitude, and local weather. On one trip, we sweltered in near-100 degree heat in the high latitudes of Moscow and shivered in the high-40 degree coolness in the high altitudes of Equatorial Kenya.

▶ Leave your expensive watches and jewelry at home. It makes you a target for thieves, marks you as a "rich American" among the people you are working with and makes you feel bad if you lose it.

WOMEN'S CLOTHING

▶ Six sets of underclothes packed (one of those six are packed in your carry-on) and the ones you will be wearing.

▶ Six tops and the one you are wearing. In many cultures, bared shoulders are not acceptable, so a top with sleeves is preferred. Avoid tank, tube or sleeveless tops.

▶ Three skirts or slacks. In some Third World countries, pants may be considered inappropriate for women to wear because they are indicative that the wearer is a "loose woman." If that is the case where you will serve, it is suggested that one or two of the skirts be loose culottes or dresses. Hemlines should be long, usually to mid-calf. One woman working in Equatorial Africa strongly recommends that the dresses be made with pockets. She had no desire to carry her purse on daily errands but found that keeping track of the necessary keys, pens and so on very difficult to do without pockets.

▶ If culturally appropriate or to wear on the trip to and from, a pair of slacks or jeans. Shorts are much less commonly culturally appropriate except for times you are spending in resort areas.

▶ One Sunday dress.

▶ If you will have any chance to use it, bring a (modest one-piece) swimsuit and cover-up.

▶ A hat is optional, but it can protect from the sun, rain or cold.

MEN'S CLOTHING

▶ Six sets of underclothes packed (one of those six are packed in your carry-on) and the ones you will be wearing.

▶ Six shirts (one of those six are packed in your carry-on) and the one you wear (include one that will be used with your sport coat). Tee shirts may be appropriate but no tank tops. Avoid wearing pseudo-military or camouflage clothing.

▶ Necktie (or two)

▶ Two pairs of pants plus the one pair you are wearing. One should complement your sport coat. There are travel slacks made that have many hidden pockets and zippers that double for a body wallet and give you places to hide your money, papers and important items. They are usually dressy enough to function as your "good" pair of slacks.

▶ One pair of jeans

▶ One pair of shorts if culturally appropriate. Here it is not a question of modesty but merely that men in those cultures may not wear them and consider you odd for doing so.

▶ A sports coat. Wear this on the plane since it gives you a place for tickets and documents (as well as warmth on the chilly plane). It will be needed for church overseas, especially if you are asked to speak or represent your group. Again, some companies make special travel sport jackets that are wrinkle resistant and have a number of hidden pockets.

▶ Light jacket, sweater or sweatshirt. A windbreaker can often double as rain gear. If rain will be a frequent event, a poncho that folds flat may be appreciated.

▶ Light foldable rubber boots or galoshes to put over shoes, especially helpful in rainy areas.

▶ Swim trunks.

▶ Sturdy belt, suitable for all of your clothing.

▶ A hat is optional, but it can protect from the sun, rain or cold.

TIPS ON PACKING

▶ Rolled clothes pack tighter, taking up less room. Breakable items can be placed in a plastic bag, sealed and rolled within the item of clothing. Rolling works best for socks, T-shirts, blue jeans and clothes made of rayon, polyester or any other thin, durable fabric. Do *not* roll blouses, neckties, suits or articles of silk or linen. Fold dress shirts, blouses or anything that is 100% cotton (have your cleaner fold them for you). Fold bulky items such as sweaters.

▶ Clothes with a shiny, smooth lining (e.g. suits, dresses, blazers and pants) will wrinkle less if they are turned inside out before packing and turned right side out after unpacking.

▶ Be sure to pack any potential unused spaces (e.g., the insides of shoes, the center of a roll of duct tape) with socks, underwear or similar things.

▶ If you are color-blind or taking children, put each day's outfit in a plastic re-closable bag and seal it. It keeps it clean and makes it easy both to find your things and re-pack if necessary. It also eliminates arguments about what to wear.

▶ Use plastic containers with lids (Rubbermaid®, TupperWare®, small pocket tackle boxes, etc.) to organize your items. Pack each one to the fullest by itself. This makes it easier to pack and repack (especially if the customs agent has emptied your suitcase!). These containers are also a wonderful gift to leave with someone on the field.

Slide into an outside pocket of your luggage enough extra large trash bags, like those used for yard pickup, that are big enough to put your suitcase in it. On occasion, you may not be able to get your luggage out of the rain and these will keep it dry.

▶ Pack your clothes in the order they will be worn so that you won't have to dig through layers.

▶ If room in your suitcase is at a premium, wear your heavier or bulkier clothes while traveling instead of packing them.

▶ To keep neckties from wrinkling, place them over the center page of a magazine you are taking for a missionary. Close the magazine and pack it flat.

▶ Do not pack food items and soap or scented toiletries in the same suitcase. The food can pick up the flavor of the scent.

TOILETRIES, BED AND BATH

Carrying a towel and washcloth is a good idea. Many hotels in developing countries do not furnish washcloths. Alternatively, the special swim towels available at sporting stores or dive shops are very handy. They are only about a foot square but dry with wringing and can be used as a washcloth or a towel if needed. They take up very little space. Similar towels that are larger can be found in the car-wash area of your local discount store. Carry the washcloth or swim towel in a small re-closable plastic bag in your carry-on. Baby wipes, and/or anti-bacterial hand cleanser may be desirable.

Depending on your sleeping arrangements, having your own sheets and pillowcase may be desirable. An alternative is a "sleep bag" made of silk that you can use to line your bed when you are sleeping in questionable surroundings. They may give you some peace of mind and being made of silk, can be folded very small and easily hand-washed. Check whether it is wise to bring your own mosquito net, and whether it is available on the field (if so, find out if you have to make arrangements to have one purchased ahead of time for your use that first night). There are small one-person folding mosquito nets available from camping, sports, and military surplus stores as well as from mail-order companies. They fold down into a small package. Try it out at home before you go to see if you need any additional string or other supplies. Some people find them rather claustrophobic.

Besides the usual things listed in the packing list (See Appendix D—

Packing   119

it can be downloaded from www.S3Ministries.com), there are some general principles to consider. Men should bring a shaving kit (razor and soap) that does not require electricity. Woman should never count on being able to buy their favorite toiletries in another country and should never require a blow dryer or curling iron to be presentable. Tampons, menstrual pads, and other items for feminine hygiene are often not available and sufficient amounts should be taken with you. Both sexes need:

▶ Toilet paper: take out the cardboard roll and squash it flat or buy the specially rolled paper from a camping store. Alternatively, use the small travel packs of Kleenex®. Toilet paper can be a rare commodity in the Third World, especially when you need it *now*!

▶ You might desire to take some saline nose drops in your pocket or purse. The air on the plane can be very dry.

▶ A small mirror, unbreakable if possible. Lightweight plastic mirrors are available in camping sections of discount stores and in camping stores.

▶ Toothbrush, toothpaste, soap, and deodorant are necessary. Shaving gel or foam is optional. Some camping stores have a liquid soap that is multipurpose for cleaning, dishes, and clothes.

▶ No perfume or cologne. It attracts mosquitoes.

▶ Any supplies you need for contact lenses, including a spare set of lenses.

▶ A minimum of cosmetics. For women, base, a little blush and neutral lipstick is enough in most mission situations. Take only the ones you will use. Body lotion may be desired.

▶ Take enough of what you need but no more than enough. Most are toiletries are liquid and are heavy. Tape the lids of bottles that hold liquids securely and put powders in doubled zip-lock bags.

PERSONAL MEDICATIONS

The list of appropriate medications obviously may vary on location and according to personal health considerations. Many of these are discussed in more detail in Chapter 6 on health. However, for the sake of completeness, they are mentioned again here:

▶ Prescriptions for routine use: carry in your carry-on at least enough to make sure you are okay if your main suitcases are lost. Some people recommend carrying enough mediation for the entire time in both your carry-on and your suitcase. Make sure you carry them in an original prescription bottle to avoid problems with customs and their concerns about drug smuggling. Don't forget your contraceptives or you may have an unexpected souvenir.

▶ Carry extra syringes and needles for your personal use should you be asked to take an immunization at a foreign airport for entry into the country or should you find it necessary to take personal medication while you are away from home. If you are diabetic and have cleared this trip with your doctor, do not forget your insulin, syringes, glucose testing devices and so on.

▶ After discussion with your doctor, you may wish to carry prescriptions for the following things (see Chapter 6). Make sure you fully understand when and how to take them and what conflicts there may be with other drugs.

• Traveler's diarrhea
• Altitude sickness
• Antimalarials
• Broad-spectrum antibiotic
• Medications for gastric upset, especially if you are going to a country where the food is spicy.

▶ Take a small first-aid kit (adhesive bandages, tape, etc.) and the following over-the-counter drugs with you:

• Motion sickness pills
• Antidiarrheal (e.g., loperamide)
• Anti-inflammatory drugs/analgesics
• Antihistamines/decongestant
• Cough drops, throat lozenges, and/or cough syrup
• Tube of antibiotic ointment
• Tube of hydrocortisone crème
• Antifungal powder or crème
• For woman, a course of anti-fungal treatment for vaginitis

- Lip balm (with sun-screen capabilities)
- Thermometer (the contact strip type)[1]
- Tweezers for splinters or stingers
▶ Sun block (SPF greater than 20)
▶ Insect repellent (DEET in the 20–30% range is the best). Use a liquid preparation rather than a repellent in a can (for weight considerations and FAA concerns). Avon's Skin-So-Soft®[2] is a great moisturizer but has been proven not to be an effective mosquito repellent. Remember, these mosquitoes can kill you.
▶ Nail-clippers or a manicure set.

OTHER THINGS

The list of things you might also need can be endless. Things are listed below (sometimes with comments) in order to stimulate your thought process. Download the packing list (www.S3Ministries.com) and fill in the blank lines to make up your list:

▶ Your professional equipment (stethoscope, instruments, medications, etc.)

▶ A credit card sized calculator, preferably solar powered. These help with many things including local currency transactions and bartering in the market when you don't speak the language. Just key in your offer. They will take it and key in their counter-offer.

▶ Your reading glasses, your sunglasses, extra contact lenses and a spare pair of prescription glasses. Make sure that you have your ophthalmologist fill in the prescription information on your yellow International Certificate of Vaccination in case you have to have some made overseas. Take a small eyeglass repair kit with extra screws of the right size for your hinges and nose pads (and include a few extra nose pads of the right size and type).

---

[1] Mercury-containing thermometers are banned by some airlines.
[2] We are referring to just the Skin-so-Soft® product. There are other forms of Skin-so-Soft that have effective repellents as part of the formulation. See the discussion on repellents in Chapter 9.

▶ If you wear dentures, don't forget your denture adhesive and a tube of contact cement that can repair the dentures in case of a crack or lost tooth.

▶ Laundry supplies including a net bag for use in washing delicates, for use as a dirty clothes bag and also to function as a shopping bag. Carry a clothesline, some clothespins and a doubly sealed bag of laundry soap. Sewing kit for repairs including some safety pins. Some people like to throw in a few lightweight plastic clothes hangers. Buy a flat, flexible sink stopper in case you have to do handwashing and there is no sink stopper.

▶ An inflatable travel pillow, eyeshades and earplugs. Many airlines now furnish them on transoceanic flights. They are useful once you land and are having trouble sleeping due to jet lag and strange noises.

▶ Your camera is essential (see Appendix F). A point and shoot type of camera is okay for the average photographer. A disposable waterproof camera gives you added flexibility in some situations. Most serious photographers will want a 35 mm or digital single lens reflex with interchangeable lens that will give you much more versatility. A telephoto lens will help if you are taking wild animal shots at a distance but also allow you to get close-ups of people without getting into their personal space. The pictures will be much more candid and vibrant for that. A wide-angle lens is sometimes helpful, especially if you are in an urban setting. A suitable macro lens is also good. Some of the little creatures and flowers you will see are amazing. Digital cameras give you the benefit of being able to see right away if you got the picture. They are also great ice-breakers when you show the pictures to your subject and his or her family and friends.

Don't forget: If you have a film camera, take plenty of film (10 to 20 rolls of 36 exposures). It is usually expensive overseas and increasingly hard to find. Airport X-rays usually aren't a problem unless you use very high-speed film. A lead foil bag can protect film. They are sold at camera stores.

• Extra batteries for camera and flash. Batteries in special sizes are difficult to find overseas. If using digital, make sure the memory device is adequate. You will not reliably find more overseas. Make sure your recharger is compatible with the voltages where you will be.

• Take the camera in a well-padded bag.

• Lens brush for dusty conditions.

Your video camera may be optional if you are taking something else, but they are a great way to get the sound and movement of your experience. Too bad there is nothing that can quite capture the aroma of the developing country! The new, smaller digital cameras with a good zoom lens can be ideal and serve as both a still and a video camera. Don't forget:

• Take extra batteries and charger that can use 220 volts and 50 Hz.

• Take appropriate adapter plugs so you can plug in your charger.

• Take enough recording cassettes. They are very expensive and hard to find overseas.

• Take a well-padded case.

• Make sure that you have a large enough memory card or many memory cards. Consider taking a card-reader with you if you are taking your computer or have access to one. Frequently downloading of the pictures gives you an automatic back-up in case you lose the card or the camera.

▶ Disposable toilet seat covers.

▶ Spare shoelaces for all pairs of shoes.

▶ Swiss army knife or pocket tool kit.

▶ Travel dictionary or electronic translator.

▶ Water purifier or filter. See Chapter 11 for a more complete discussion. There are companies who make a sports-bottle type of water purifier that uses ultrafiltration, iodine resin cores, and activate charcoal to remove infectious organisms and bad tastes from the water. This will allow you to use water from almost any source safely. Alternatively, an ultraviolet system or a filter plus chemical decontamination of the water to prevent viruses are options. If you don't want to use those, take at least one bottle of bottled water for the airplane trip but you have to buy it once you have gone through security for your gate or you will lose it.

▶ Duct tape or fiber-enforced strapping tape. A million uses. Leave for the missionaries if you don't need it on the way home. Some security checkpoints will object to your carrying it in your carry-on luggage.

► A fanny pack or folding backpack. Some people have advised lining these with a fine wire mesh to prevent pickpockets from slitting the pack with the razor and removing the contents without having to remove it. There are commercially made versions that have slit-proof straps and pockets. Some people advise against fanny packs since only North Americans wear them and to do so is to advertise your vulnerability.

► Emergency snacks (peanut butter, crackers, nuts, granola, trail mix, candy, etc.). Remember, gum (and spitting) is not socially acceptable by some Asians. It is illegal in Singapore and can get you arrested!

► Bible.

► Notebook or journal. Stationery, envelopes, ballpoint pens and stamps (especially "forever" stamps) may be desirable. Carry one pen in your pocket when you travel for filling out entry and custom forms, writing postcards and the like.

► Other reading material.

► Photos of your home and family. Consider laminating them to preserve them from the dirt of many hands. Avoid photos that show your possessions or the obvious wealth of the American life style.

► Postcards, magazines or booklets about your city and State.

► Brochures and pictures of your church.

► A watch. Waterproof (a dive watch) and an alarm are nice features to have. Make sure you have put in a fresh battery before you leave.

► An umbrella.

► Outdoor thermometer. A small one will fit into the cracks of your packing.

► A permanent marker (we prefer a fine point marker).

► A whistle. It's great for signaling and in case of personal attack (God forbid).

► Binoculars.

► Disposable cigarette lighters. Great for starting fires and lighting candles. Must be packed in your checked luggage.

► Cable ties of various sizes. They can be used as an ersatz padlock, hold things together and have many uses. Some airlines refuse to allow them to be carried in your carry-on luggage.

▶ Envelopes (often hard to find overseas) and U.S. postage stamps so that anyone on the field returning to the U.S. can mail your letters here for faster delivery. Also, take enough stamps to give or sell to the missionaries for their personal use to do the same thing. The "forever" stamps work especially well for this given the regular raises in postage costs. If you don't buy special envelopes that have a strip over the adhesive (Peel and Seal®), put waxed paper between the envelope flap and the envelope if you are going to a tropical climate. Otherwise, your envelope may seal before you use it.

▶ If you have room, small 2-way radios can come in handy to communicate between the hospital and home, in bazaars, etc.

▶ There are available specially modified "can safes" that look like common products (shaving cream, drinks, etc.) but are hollow with a screw-in bottom. These allow you to "hide" valuables in plain sight but probably should not be used to hide things of great value. Use more secure safes for those items.

Pack these things in either zip-lock bags or in see-through small plastic compartmentalized trays such as the ones that are used for pocket fishing tackle boxes. Those boxes are available in the sporting areas of discount stores. They have the advantage of being waterproof as well. It is a great way to store all the extra little things.

ELECTRONICS

Americans have become dependent on many electronic devices, but traveling overseas with them is not always straightforward. Please see Appendix G for more detail. Most of the countries of North, Central, and South America as well as the Caribbean use 110 volt, 60-Hertz currency and you have only to use an adapter. However, much of the rest of the world uses 220 volts, 50-Hertz electricity and the difference can be problematic.

For those whose eyes are already beginning to glaze, let's make it very practical. If you put plug something designed for 110 volts into a 220–volt outlet, it will fry the circuitry rapidly and become worthless.

Ideally, you will have appliances (irons, curling irons, blow dryers and most computers) that can handle either 110 volt or 220 volt. Most of them require that you flip a switch. Failure to do so will burn out the 110 portion if you plug it into 220 volts or make it non-functional if it is set on 220 volts and you have it plugged into a 110 volt outlet.

If your device doesn't have that two-way switch, you will need to get a transformer and a set of plug adapters. As with their money, every country seems to want to set the shape and size of their electricity outlets, and, of course, none seem to match. At your local travel, electrical supply store, or discount store, you can buy a set of plug adapters. Make sure you have both the adapters and a transformer. The strength (rated in watts) of the transformer is variable but in general, the more money you pay, the bigger, heavier and more robust it is and the more likely it can handle high wattage items. The little transformers available in your local discount store often cannot handle the wattage of a large hair-dryer, so make sure it is rated for as many watts as your devices require. If not, they will burn out rapidly and you cannot use your device.

The potential problem with transformers is that they are designed only to cut the voltage by a certain percentage. For example, a 230-volt incoming current would be cut to 115 volts and this would be ideal. There are still a problem for certain motorized devices and those devices with internal "clocks." The voltage may be changed to the appropriate level but the frequency has not changed from 50 Hz to 60 Hz. There is no easy fix to this dilemma and as a result, many motorized items will run slower and hotter on the lower frequency. Some may not function.

Even without that problem of frequency, most of the world's electrical companies do not deliver highly uniform voltage and a purported 220 volts may be anything from 110 to 330 volts. It may vary from minute to minute. Most of us are familiar with surge protectors and it may be wise to include one in your luggage if you are going to be using 110 volts. If not, a surge protector for 220 volts is harder to find in North America and you may want to make that one of your first purchases in the country. Surges are familiar, but serious problems with lower voltage are not as familiar to us. Many electrical devices dislike this "brown-out" as much as they dislike electrical surges and many pieces of equipment may eventually die because of it. The fix is not as easy. An uninterrupted power supply (essentially a battery and inverter hooked to a voltage monitor) is the only option, but they are too big to carry and too expensive to buy overseas unless you have a major project going on or will be there long enough to take one with you or buy one in the country.

Battery-operated equipment avoids this problem, but it may take a large number of batteries if the device has high power consumption. Batteries may or not be available in the developing countries but are usually either of poor quality or very expensive for quality, brand name batteries.

So what should you consider taking?

▶ A flashlight with extra batteries. A small magnesium light or LED flashlight running on 2 AA batteries may be sufficient depending on your use. Be sure to take an extra bulb as well if you are not using an LED flashlight.

▶ A battery-operated travel alarm or a watch with an alarm. Make sure your batteries are fresh before you go.

▶ Hair-dryer with a 220/110 switch. Small and light are the operative terms. Consider sharing one with another person on the trip so you both don't have to pack one. Check the wattage for it and compare it to the transformer you plan to use.

▶ Curling iron with a 220/110 switch. Again small and light. Share. Check the wattage and the transformer capabilities.

▶ Travel iron or steamer with a 220/110 switch. Share with a fellow traveler to minimize luggage weight.

▶ Digital sound recorder to record sounds, peoples or your own thoughts. Don't forget extra memory, connecting cords and batteries.

▶ Small, short-wave radio if you want to keep up with the news. Sony and Radio Shack make small ones half the size of a paperback book. The price range for such radios is in the $50 to $300 range. Digital circuitry is more expensive but a search/scan function saves hours of slow scanning through all of the channels.

▶ If you insist on using an electric razor, make sure it has a 220/110 volt switch or batteries with sufficient half-life to work throughout the trip.

▶ A coffee pot or heating coil. These are high-wattage, so again make sure the transformer can handle it.

▶ Mobile cellular telephone that has tri-band or a quad-band capacity (confirm which you may need in your country of service) so you can buy a SIM card in the country where you are going. Alternatively, check with your N. American provider to see if they offer international service on your present phone, but make sure that your desired country is covered and that you have a 220v/50Hz phone charger (many sold in the U.S. do not tolerate 220v). Several companies will also rent you a telephone for international use. If you don't have a suitable phone, it is very easy to buy a cheap functional phone for about $30 in the country where you are going. If you choose not to take a phone, but do take your laptop, don't forget your headphone/microphone combination so you can call via Skype (www.skype.com).

A final bit of advice on this topic: Surges and brownouts are a problem only if the devices are plugged in. Get in a habit of unplugging your appliances as soon as you are finished with them or they are finished recharging. You may be glad you did.

GIFTS FOR MISSIONARIES AND NATIONALS

Carrying items to the mission field is a very important part of your ministry. In most developing countries, the mail is very unreliable, and items are often stolen before they arrive. Additionally, the cost of sending items from the United States is very expensive. One short-term missionary spouse put it this way, "It is a crime if you arrive on a station with any unused weight allowances carrying only your personal stuff." You will have only limited room in your baggage, so you must prioritize the items you take so that the most critical items reach the hospital. There are three different categories of items that you may be asked to take:

▶ Items that the ministry, clinic or missionary directly requests that you bring. These items should have the highest priority, and you should make every effort to take them. Getting out of the missionaries something they really want or need is sometimes very difficult and requires patience and repeated contact. Of course, it seems that they usually don't think of it until the day before you are scheduled to leave and they want something esoteric like a left-handed monkey wrench with an attached modem made by a now-defunct company, but the treasure hunt is part of the fun.

▶ Items that you know will most likely be needed. You know because the agency has told you, the work or missionary has published a general list or because of you're past experience. Critical medications and supplies that are not easily available in country would fall in this category.

▶ Items that the friends and family have asked you to carry with you. These items are usually of a personal nature and can be everything from Christmas gifts to videos to family photos. Although these things are very meaningful, they are often not essential and should therefore have a low priority (but ahead of the non-requested gifts you had thought to take). You have to be willing to say "no." Those who request that you carry items for them may have no idea how much you already must pack. Certainly use every ounce of your allowed weight. You are not obligated to take extra baggage unless you wish to do so. If you must take excess baggage, please contact your travel agent or airline with the dimensions and weight. As mentioned earlier, sometimes it will be allowed free of charge. If you have to pay for the excess baggage, please feel free to bring that to the attention of the hospital or missionaries. You should contact the missionary in charge or the visiting staff coordinator to let them know about the expected cost. Try to supply a percentage of the cost to be assessed toward each person who had things included in the baggage. Another option is to charge the cost to the project you are funding through your parent organization. Check with them before doing so to see if this is allowable. The third option would be to pay these expenses out of your pocket as a gift to those you are visiting on the field. **WARNING!** Pack items you are taking for others in your luggage among your own stuff. Take any new items out of the packaging and separate the instruction booklets from the item. Do not carry them in boxes. Always carry the receipts with you for the item in case they are needed in a discussion with the customs agent. You may need receipts even for your own things that look new, just to prove that they are yours. Electronics are perhaps the thing that will set off the most red flags. If you are hit for customs and want to pay the duties for the missionaries that is fine, but if you are bringing something at their request and if the duty fee seems too high, it is appropriate to ask for a receipt for the item (making sure the serial number, model number and a good description are noted) and leave it with the customs agent. The missionary can come back and pay the duties for the item and have the advantage of arguing in the same tongue.

If you have extra room and your luggage is still light after all of the above, here are some ideas for things for the missionaries. It is not by any means an exhaustive list:

► Clothing for the missionary children.

► Entertainment items:

• Up to date magazines and newspapers

• Recorded videos of recent sporting events or television specials

• DVD movies (being sensitive to the language and violence issue)

• New novels or non-fictional works that may be of interest to them

► New items to help the missionaries worship

► Christian videos/DVDs for the children

► New Christian music (keeping in mind their interests in music). This can be a recording or new sheet music and songbooks of worship music.

► New Christian books, Christian novels, Bible study handbooks, personal devotional books, etc.

► CDs, DVDs or videos of your pastor or other famous pastors or singing groups

▶ Special food items. These made a great hostess gift. If you brought a lot, ask your host missionary to divvy it up amongst their compatriots.

• Marshmallows, powdered drinks, gelatin deserts, popcorn, pepperoni are perennial favorites.

• M&M's, Hershey Kisses, Chocolate and butterscotch chips, coconut, nuts (walnuts and pecans),

• Salad dressing mixes, Dream Whip, Chili or Taco seasoning, mixes of all kinds for baking and cooking

• American peanut butter (ask first if it is available in country)

▶ Paper products and stamps. High quality paper is difficult to get in many places and is expensive. Stationary, greeting cards, thank-you notes are appreciated. Stamps for their home country are often appreciated since they can send letters back with you or some other visitor to be mailed in America. The recently introduced "forever" stamps make great gifts because their value is always equal to the latest change in first-class postage.

▶ Soaps, lotions and cosmetics. One missionary waxed rhapsodically about a bottle of American dishwashing soap!

▶ Hair accessories

▶ Zip lock bags, Tupperware® or RubberMaid® containers. Pack your suitcase with everything in them and then leave them after washing them out when you leave. Stuff cracks in your suitcase with the plastic bags. Make sure some are large enough to put in your wet and dirty clothes.

▶ If you are going to do medical work, medications for the hospital or clinic work you are going to perform are sometimes a problem. There is a worldwide awareness program pointing out the dangers of outdated drugs. Most countries will not allow outdated drugs into their borders and some require that the expiration date is at least six months later than the date of entry into the country. Sometimes the official policy and roadblocks to importation of those drugs does not seem consistent with the fact that you can buy any medication over the counter at the pharmacy or from a little lady at the market who has piles of various shapes and colors, unmarked, unidentifiable and who prescribes by color. It is very tempting to collect all the sample drugs that you are given and "repackage" them to save room. If you do, do so with the knowledge that they might be confiscated if you get the wrong person in customs on the wrong day. At the very least, make sure you put in the drug inserts and at least one package with a clearly identifiable expiration date. If you get the drugs in bulk from one of the wholesalers or ministries mentioned in the back, it is safest not to repackage them until you have gone through customs. Make sure you take your proper paperwork with you. Many people doing short-term outpatient clinic work will create a dose pack for the commonly used medications. This saves time but you do run the risk of having your drugs confiscated because they are not properly labeled. If you create a label for these dose packs, make sure the name, manufacturer and expiration date are clearly spelled out. Get advice from someone who has done it before in this country and from your in-country professionals. Narcotics and controlled drugs are another issue beyond the scope of this discussion, but make sure you have properly gone through all the channels and have all of the needed paperwork.

► Taking surgical, medical, laboratory or imaging supplies can sometimes be a problem. It seems to help if you carry a signed and sealed letter from your organization stating that these are gifts for the work and for the people of the country. Also a letter of invitation from a person at a recognized institution, governmental office (local or federal) or known ministry within the country can often smooth the way. If the goods are confiscated, get a detailed receipt and leave it to your in-country contacts to solve the problem later. Do not pay a bribe.

Gifts for the nationals are sometimes a little trickier if you want to prevent the "Santa Claus" syndrome. Many missionaries are very leery of visitors with gifts. They understandably want to avoid creating the perception within the nationals' minds that every visitor bears gifts and that the nationals with whom you are most likely to interact have somehow received favored status with the missionaries because they have received gifts from many visitors. Always clear it with the missionary before you give any gift worth more than a few dollars. Remember, in many of the countries where you will work, a full day's wage for a workingman is only a dollar or a dollar and a half. What you perceive as a minor gift may not be perceived in the culture as a minor gift and you do not wish to precipitate a major cultural and employee rift.

► Gifts of yourself are always the best, both at home and there:

• Take a musical instrument if it is not too big or accompaniment tapes if you want to sing special music. Guitars are not uncommon in most third world countries, so you may be able to borrow one.

• If you are an artist, take your sketchbook, pencils and pastels. If you start drawing nationals, you will have an instant audience. Your artistic skills may be appreciated elsewhere, as you design and execute wall murals, give art lessons and add beauty to the locale.

• If you have skills in puppetry, take your puppets or the materials with which to make them. Teach the nationals how to make them and how to use them. Help them build sets and screens.

• Balloons–kids love them. They are cheap and a guaranteed hit. Buy a book on how to make animals out of them. It is not hard and with a little practice, you will be a superstar.

• Magic tricks. Anyone can learn some simple tricks with some practice and especially if you can combine them with a gospel message, you will have a great ministry.

• Take a folding pocket parafoil kite and fly it with the children.

► Work with the children:

• Sunday school materials, especially visual ones, can allow you to tell the Bible stories.

• Craft supplies.

• Coloring books (especially with Biblical themes), crayons.

• Bible stories and small gifts of the type usually given for Sunday schools and Vacation Bible Schools. Your local Christian bookstore is a good source and there are many companies selling over the Internet that sell appropriate little novelties and gifts.

• Tooth brushes, toothpaste, combs, brushes.

• A roll of shiny American pennies makes 50 great gifts and souvenirs of their visiting American.

• Candy and chewing gum is never a bad choice for children the world around (again with the possible exception of gum in Asia).

- Make wordless gospel books or bracelets and teach them its message.
- Puppets, coloring books, etc.
▶ Other gifts that are for adult nationals could include:
- Bibles (especially reference types) or Bible study helps for pastors and laymen, if they speak English or some other language that you can get Bibles written in.
- Writing paper and pens (in bulk, paper is heavy!). Ballpoint pens are very popular gifts, especially the retractable type
- Wall calendars
- Hand towels
- Tee-shirts
- Bookmarks
- Small U.S. flags
- Lapel pins
- Used clothing and shoes as gifts for house helpers and other nationals you meet
- Cassette tapes, CDs or DVDs of music from your church or favorite musicians (be sensitive to cross-cultural tastes in music)
- Cheap watches (often obtainable for as low as $5 each at discount stores)
- Solar (dual) powered calculators
- Pictures of yourself and your family. Bargain photo deals like those available through discount stores may be ideal. One option is a mini-prayer card the size of a business card with your picture and description of your ministry on one side and your contact information on the other.
▶ For the hospital or medical personnel:
- Surgical scrubs, surgical dresses, caps, white coats
- Penlights, reflex hammers, stethoscopes, blood pressure cuffs
- Surgical instruments and equipment
- Oximeters and other hand-held instruments.
▶ Here are some things to also take with you that weigh nothing and very useful. You will be glad you brought them:
- A sense of humor when you get uptight over situations and people.
- A teachable attitude toward those you are working with.

- A desire to learn from God, missionaries, and nationals.
- A flexible spirit when things don't go as planned.
- A willing heart to do whatever you are asked to do.

CHAPTER 8

STEP BY STEP—PREPARING TO GO

In the chapter entitled "Travel and Documents" and in the chapter on health, there were many things that needed to be done in the months before your trip. In this chapter, we will focus on the actual processes of leaving your home, arriving at the airport, the plane trip itself and the arrival at your destination and back again. We will try to break it down into small parts that are easier to handle in the confusion of your impending trip:

Two Weeks in Advance

▶ Make sure that you have received all of your necessary passports, visas, tickets, seat assignments, and that airlines have been notified of special dietary needs, special arrangements for infants, extra luggage, and asked for waiver of extra charges where needed.

▶ Check with telephone (both land and mobile) companies, cable companies and other utility companies to see if you are eligible for vacation rates. If you hope to use your mobile phone overseas, check on that as well.

▶ Go over your financial records and check register to see what bill payments, estimated tax payments, premiums and infrequent periodic payments might come due in your absence. Pay in advance, automatically debit, or have a family member handle the payments. If you use a program like Quicken® or Money® with Internet banking capabilities, you can program it to pay your bills automatically at the right time. Also, make arrangements for deposits from pensions, employers, or dividends to be made directly into your account.

▶ If not previously done, execute a power of attorney so that someone can handle your affairs if necessary. Execute health power of attorneys for the guardians of your children. Execute regular power of attorneys and health power of attorneys for each other if both you and your spouse are traveling together.

▶ If not previously done, make sure your health insurance company will cover you for any bills engendered for care out of the country. Some do not. If they do not, make sure you have applied for and received supplemental insurance. Consider medical evacuation insurance and insurance for expatriation of mortal remains.

▶ Call your credit card company and your bank (ATM) to give them your itinerary—otherwise a credit request from some strange place may raise suspicion that it was been stolen and they may refuse it. It is very hard to restore your credit from another continent.

▶ Get your international driver's license if you will need one.

▶ Begin planning your meals to use up what you can in the refrigerator and freezer.

▶ If you haven't done so, order any special meals (children's, diabetic, vegetarian, etc.) from the airline. Your travel agent may help you with this.

▶ Make arrangements to make your arrival less stressful and safer. If you do not know each other, e-mail a picture of yourself or your group to the person picking you up; ask them to do the same in return. If you have the picture in hand, then you will not be fooled by scam artists. If that is not possible, make sure that the person picking you up knows a "password" that you have given them so you can confirm that you are being picked up by the right person. All of that is to make it easier on you in a crowded airport but also to prevent abduction for ransom. In some airports in Africa, some arrivees have been abducted because they saw their name on a handheld sign and they went with the person without confirming the person's identity. What had happened is that the scam artist had seen the newcomer's name on another person's sign, quickly replicated it and then abducted them. The pictures are valuable because some airports have now outlawed the signs because it was such a problem.

One Week in Advance

▶ If you have children that you are leaving under the care of others, make sure those guardians have your health insurance information and complete medical information on each of your dependants for whom they are caring (including significant health conditions, immunizations, medications, allergies and the names and contact information of your regular physicians). Make sure the guardians have a health power of attorney for those dependants so they can authorize care in the case of a need for urgent medical care. You may wish to talk to your physicians to explain the situation and your wishes for care if something were to come to up.

▶ Identify a neighbor, friend or relative to check your house while you are gone. Be aware that some home insurance policies are not valid if you don't have someone watching your home while you are away. Show them where the shut-off valves for water and electrical boxes and circuit breakers are to your house. Tell them which companies supply utilities. Ask them to periodically start your cars and let them run for 20– 30 minutes to recharge your batteries. The frequency depends on the temperature and the state of your car battery. Give them the security code and any information necessary to talk to the monitoring company if they accidentally set it off. If they can make daily visits, have them open and close curtains to suggest that someone is there. Have them water plants, check the function of any freezers, look for water leaks, pick up any newspapers or flyers left on your door, etc. Leave a list of people who you like to work on your house if something happens (plumber, electrician, heating repairman, etc.) and of your insurance agent number (with your account number). Make it clear whether they can or cannot drive your car if the need arises. If your car is being driven while you are gone, most insurance companies will not cover any rental car you are driving. If someone is driving your car, you must take the supplemental insurance policy available from the car rental company. Check with your agent to make sure what rules apply.

▶ Notify your neighbors and the police department of your planned dates of absence and tell them who they can contact if there is a problem.

▶ Mail: have your mail forwarded, pickup arranged, or have the postmaster hold your mail. If you are expecting something important, for example packages, bills,or checks, make sure you give your agent permission to open that mail. Give him directions of how to handle it or notify you of its contents. You might want to tell him or her to open unexpected mail from certain sources, e.g. IRS, your law firm, your accountant, your bank, etc., depending on your circumstances, and give him directions of how to handle it.

▶ Call the circulation department of your newspaper and stop delivery.

▶ Security system: make sure there is someone to respond to any real or false alarms. Notify the monitoring service of your absence and alternative numbers for them to contact. Review the system with your family or friends who will cover problems. Show them how to turn it on and off, bypass portions if necessary and give them the account number, password, and security codes.

▶ Arrange lawn care and garden care so your house doesn't look unkept, which is an invitation to burglars.

▶ If you know that you will be using your credit card to withdraw cash and you don't want to pay interest, make an extra payment in the amount of cash that you expect to withdraw.

▶ Use the packing checklist you can download from www.S3Ministries.com or create your own checklist to make sure you have everything you need or plan to take. Make a shopping list and acquire what you need.

A Few Days in Advance

▶ Arrange care for your house plants. If the weather permits, put them in a suitable place outside. Two long term watering techniques are to set plants in a kiddie pool filled with a few inches of water or use use the automatic watering sytems (spikes that go into inverted soft drink bottles are available at discount stores and gardening centers). Even if you have the person checking your house come in to water your plants, these techniques will minimze the number of times they are required to care for your plants. Another option is to give them to someone you trust.

▶ Turn off, cover, and winterize (if necessary) whirlpool spas and swimming pools. If necessary, arrange for someone to care for your pool, adding chemicals and cleaning it.

▶ Purchase automatic timers for house lights to give an appearance that someone is home

▶ Arrange to have someone drop you off and pick you up at airport

▶ Leave with relatives, close friends, and the person watching your house your itinerary, field contact number/fax/address or stateside contact information of parent group with whom you are serving.

▶ Seventy-two hours before your flight, call and confirm your tickets with your airlines. International flights, especially those that originate in developing countries, may be cancelled. This gives you time to arrange alternative ticketing. Also, overbooking is common and failure to confirm your ticket may give the airline legal right to cancel your ticket.

▶ Begin packing those bags with items that are not needed any more. Make a careful inventory of the contents and label the bags so you can tell them apart. A copy of this inventory can help you make a record for tax deductible items you leave with the misisonaries.

The Day Before

▶ Empty your refrigerator of any thing that will spoil, giving it away or throwing it out.

▶ Take your pet to a guardian or kennel.

▶ In cold weather, fill up the fuel tanks of your vehicles so water condensation will not be a problem. If you are going to be gone for a long period of time, add fuel stabilizer.

▶ Leave keys to house and car, security codes.

▶ Weigh your luggage to make sure it doesn't exceed the weight requirements. If you insist on trying to carry overweight luggage, be ready to pay the sometimes stiff surcharges (check, cash or major credit card), or make sure the person who has taken you to the airport has not left so if you get caught, they can carry home the items you need the least.

▶ Do advance check-in using the Internet. Make sure your seats have been selected and print your boarding passes. Paying for any luggage fees on the internet they day before usually results in a lesser charge than that charged at the airline counter.

▶ Call friends to bid good-bye.

Day of Departure
▶ Lower heat or raise the thermostat on the air conditioning. Keep temperature where plants and water pipes won't be harmed.
▶ Water your plants.
▶ Decide whether to leave automatic lawn sprinkler systems on or off.
▶ Lower water heater temperature to save energy or shut them off. Make sure all faucets (taps) are completely closed.
▶ Turn off anything electrical that heats or cools or collects water: iron, coffee makers, automatic dehumidifiers, fountains. Unplug electronics (stereos and televisions) and computers to avoid lightning damage.
▶ Clean out your refrigerator of perishables and turn off ice makers and their water supply.
▶ Put 1or 2 lamps in various rooms on timers and set them to mimic your usual usage of light.
▶ Make sure each piece of your luggage has easily visible ID tags, all padlocks are in place, and all questionable latches have been secured with tape or luggage straps. Make sure you have the inventory with you.
▶ Last minute phone calls to family to bid good-bye.
▶ Lock the doors and windows. Set your alarm system.
▶ Before you shut the door: Check for everyone's passport, tickets, visa, immunization certificate, money, traveler's checks, personal meds, keys to your luggage, health insurance cards or records, and driver's license. Be certain to carry with you the contact telephone number(s) of the local mission personnel in the event that your schedule is changed after you depart from the U.S. or the unlikely event that your arriving flight is not met.

ON YOUR WAY!
___

Arrival at the Airport
   The best advice is "Arrive early." Traditional advice is to arrive at the airport for international flights 2 hours in advance. Since the events

of Septermber 11, 2001, planning on even more time may be wise, especially during times of high security alert. The extra time is required for check-in, handling the excess baggage, and document formalities. Arriving early also has the advantage of having a better chance of getting better seats or an upgrade if you want them or need them. You will need a photo ID and on international flights, you must present your passport and visa for your port of destination. You will need a photo ID for every member of the party over 18 for even the domestic portions of the flight. The name on the ID and on the ticket must match. Put these IDs somewhere you can find them again easily. They may ask you to present them again along with your boarding pass when actually boarding the airplane.

Checking Your Luggage

Double check the ID tags and put TSA-approved padlocks on each bag. Do not leave your luggage unattended at any time. Make sure that the desk agent has checked your luggage through to your final destination. Tell him or her at the beginning and then double-check the code for the final airport on the claim checks that she hands back to you. On international flights, you often must claim all your luggage at the first port of call in the destination country, clear that country's customs and then recheck your luggage through to your final destination. If that is the case, do not be surprised if they will check it only through to the first airport in the country, even though you must travel on to another in-country destination. If you have to pay extra surcharges for extra numbers of bags or for extra weight, keep in mind that your testimony as a Christian is at stake as well as your wallet. Having someone whose luggage and comments mark them as a missionary pitch a hissy fit is not becoming to the name of Christ.

Be aware that if you have a stopover in another country and take your luggage from the airport, you are likely to be subject to the much more stringent international weight requirements when you check your luggage again to continue your trip. You are likely to have to pay excess baggage charges at that time. This can get to be expensive, but can usually be charged to a major credit card. Some people decide to wait to do any visiting in transit countries until they are on on their way back home when their luggage is usually much lighter.

Security Checks at the Airport

They aren't kidding! It is their ball and their rules. Be cooperative, good-tempered and don't make silly jokes about the contents of your luggage. Sometimes, random checks of the luggage (x-ray and/or hand-searching) is performed at the check-in counter. Sometimes, all luggage is x-rayed and/or hand-checked. Do not carry anything in your carry-on luggage or on your person that can even remotely be viewed as a weapon, even one of self-defence. If you have a metal prosthesis (e.g., hip or knee joint, rod in a fracture site, a pacemaker), obtain a letter from your physician to show to security personnel since you may set off security alarms. Sometimes, they will pull someone out of line and randomly do a repeat search of someone as they board the plane. Just go along with it. The plane won't leave without you.

Security of Your Luggage

Do not leave them unattended at any time (we sound like those airport announcements, don't we?). If you are concerned about the radiation effect on your film or other sensitive recording media, you can request a hand-search of the items in question. The x-ray dosage is carefully monitored in developed countries but in the developing countries, the radiation may exceed recommended dosages. Carry your film in a lead-lined bag (available from your camera supply store) if you are particularly concerned. There is one trick that thieves use that must be guarded against. Do not put your valuables (especially computers) through the x-ray machine until you, or another member of your party, had gone through the metal detector and is ready to collect it on the other end. It is very easy for someone to walk up while you are held up in line and walk away with your things without being questioned.

Checking with Customs

Most people do not need to check with customs before you leave the country. However, there are two cases where it might be advisable. The first is if you are taking a relatively new foreign-made camera or other item that may be subject to duty upon your return, get the item registered at customs before you leave or carry the original purchase receipt with you. The second is that it is illegal to take more than $10,000 in cash or other liquid forms without registering it with customs and filling out the appropriate form. From their web site, "You may bring into or take out of the country, including by mail, as much money as you wish. But if it's more than $10,000, you'll need to report it to Customs. Ask the Customs officer for the Currency Reporting Form (CF 4790) (It can be downloaded from www.unclefed.com/IRS-Forms/1996/F4790.PDF. The penalties for not complying can be quite severe. "Money" means monetary instruments and includes U.S. or foreign coin currently in circulation, currency, traveler's checks in any form, money orders, and negotiable instruments or investment securities in bearer form."

Boarding the Plane

If you hope to sleep on the flight, eat in the airport before you board the plane so you can sleep through any meal service. When flight boarding time gets near, remember your mother's advice and use the toilet before you board. This will minimize the number of times you have to crawl over fellow passengers on the flight. With the prospect of a 10 hour or longer flight ahead of you, it is tempting to wait until the last minute to board the plane. However, since most short-term missionaries will be carrying the maximum allowed carry-on luggage, there is the risk that you will have no place to place your larger pieces in the overhead bins. Boarding as soon as you are allowed will help this

"The saying 'Getting there is half the fun' became obsolete with the advent of commercial airlines."

—Henry J. Tillman

problem and give you a better chance of
obtaining a blanket and pillow from the
overhead bin or the steward if you want
one. On overnight flights, the pillow and
blanket may already be on your seat.

"An airplane is a
great place to diet."
—Wolfgang Puck

On most flights in North America,
you are boarded by priority and then by
row or group number. Those with mobility problems, those traveling
with small children, those in first or business class and those with a
priority frequent flyer status from that airline board first. The rest will
board by row or group number. However, be aware that in many countries and on many airlines, there is just a mass boarding call. It seems
that these are often the airlines that seem to have no restriction on the
amount of carry-on luggage, so you may have to board early to have
any chance of a place of storing your luggage.

When flights are full, they have the right to restrict the amount of
carry-on luggage and may be very fussy about the weight and size of
the piece. If you are carrying valuable electronics, cameras and similar item, tell them and they may exclude you. If they are adamant, try
to take your valuable things with you even if requires that the two of
you carry only one piece between you and check the other less valuable things in the other case. It is just exactly for that reason that we
carry TSA-locks on our carry-on luggage and/or use cable ties as a
cheap and easy lock (but you may have trouble getting the cable tie off
on the other end since you can't carry anything sharp!) Thievery in
baggage handling areas can be a notorious problem at some airports
and you don't want to check what you can't afford to do without.

If the plane is not full, move to other more desirable seats as soon
as the plane has left the ground and the seat belt sign has gone off.
Some airlines provide complementary socks, eye masks and ear plugs.
Take your sleeping pill if you want one, take off your shoes, pull on
warm socks, put on your eye mast, put in your ear plugs and get comfortable. The sleep is usually of more benefit to you than the movie!

During the Flight

The changes in altitude during take-off and landing bring changes in the surrounding barometric pressure that can cause ear pain if you do not compensate for them. During departure and landing, chewing gum, sucking hard candy or making frequent swallowing motions will cause the ear to "pop." If necessary and other maneuvers fail, another maneuver can help but should be done very gently. Pinch the nose shut and blow gently until the ears pop. Little children, especially infants, are not capable of doing this voluntarily and it is often wise to make sure that the baby is taking a bottle during departure and landing. This forces the child to swallow and will prevent most of the problems. Some people who know that they have sinus congestion or a cold may find that taking an oral decongestant or a nasal spray decongestant prior to take-off and landing can prevent much of the problem.

The dry air of the recirculated airplane air can be uncomfortable. Drink plenty of fluids. Do not hesitate to drink because it may cause another trip to the lavatory. The benefits outweight the inconvenience. If you are wearing contact lens, use a wetting solution or artificial tears frequently to prevent corneal irritation. Some people like to carry a small bottle of saline nose drops to moisten their nasal mucosa during the trip.

Eat lightly and when it is safe to do so, move around the plane during flight and/or do isometric exercises in your seat at least every hour. Avoid alcohol and drink plenty of water to prevent dehydration. The so called "economy class" syndrome has recently received more attention. The sitting position and forced inactivity can predispose to the formation of deep venous thrombosis ("blood clots"). Those who have a predilection for such problems (obesity, on birth control pills, previous history of blood clots, history of leg swelling, history of congestive heart failure) should pay especial attention. Many peoples' ankles swell on the long flights and this does NOT necessarily represent a dangerous condition. In fact, it is common enough that one should plan on it and wear comfortable, loose fitting shoes. Those that are slip-on are best unless you enjoy the contortions necessary to slip your shoes on and tie them with the tight constraints of the allowed seat space. For those people to whom this leg swelling is a common or severe problem, heavy-duty or prescription strength support hose may be of some help. Airlines have been concerned enough about this that you might find some recommended exercises listed in your inflight magazine.

Arrival in Your Destination Country
Often, the airlines will give you the necessary forms before you land. If not, they will be available inside the terminal. Fill out custom and immigration forms completely and accurately. Dishonesty can be punished severely with fines, jail sentences and at the very least, marked inconvenience. Sometimes one form per family is sufficient and sometimes they require one form for each person with a passport. They usually ask for your name, home address, age, marital status, occupation, traveling companions, the purpose of your visit, where you are going to stay (have the address easily available with your paperwork), the flight number and your passport number, as well as place and date of its issue. Be sure to honestly report how much money and liquid financial instruments you are bringing with you. Failure to properly claim them will allow them to confiscate them. You will have no recourse for you have a written record in your own hand that you never had them in the first place! Keep the form inside your passport on the appropriate visa page in preparation for your visit to immigration.

> *"Airplane travel is nature's way of making you look like your passport photo."*
>
> —Al Gore

Disembark the plane as soon as you can and walk rapidly to get near the front of the immigration line. The purpose for being near the front is that it can take a long time and luggage carts at the baggage claim before customs can sometimes be hard to come by. If you already have a visa, immigration is usually a mere formality and patience is the only needed item. If you do not have a visa, ask where the office is and get in line. Look for the forms to fill out before you get to the clerk. Usually the fee can be paid in United States or other major currency.

Many countries now require that you be photographed and/or finger-printed upon arrival in the country. Just go along with it.

After you clear immigration and your passport has been stamped, you will have to collect your luggage. Grab luggage carts if they are available. In some Third World airports, there are skycaps who are working for tips, and they will help you if you wish. Sometimes, they are the only ones with luggage trolleys, so you have little choice. They may or may not be dressed in any sort of uniform. Work with only one, refusing offers from others to help (you will be expected to tip everyone who even touches a bag unless you make it clear). Since often all incoming baggage is x-rayed, it may take a long time before the luggage appears. Position yourself or someone next to the carousel so you can see all the luggage as it comes out. This will insure that someone else does not pick up your baggage by mistake. When you have all of your luggage, proceed through Customs with your passport and the filled-out Customs form in hand. Answer all questions honestly but don't volunteer information. Have easily accessible your inventory list and any letters or recommendation or credentialling from your sending agency, but do not show them until absolutely necessary. A long list of potentially valuable (or confusing) materials can actually slow you down if you show it too soon.

In some countries, it is possible for a national or missionary you are working with to meet you at the baggage carousel. It is very helpful and less stressful for you if you have someone who can speak the language and assist you through Customs. Plan on taking up to two hours to clear customs. Do not become alarmed if customs officials at some point take your passport. Just be certain that you receive your own passport in return and that it is in your possession when you leave the customs area.

A couple of situations may come up for the short-term missionary: if you have something for which Customs wants a large amount of duty (e.g. a requested piece of electronics for a missionary or supplies for the hospital), leave it in Customs, get a receipt that describes in detail what was left and let the missionary deal with the problem later. Never pay or offer to pay bribes. Explain that you are coming to volunteer your help for the less fortunate, you are working for free and these are donated materials for the people of their country. It is best to get approval for bulk medicines before you arrive by sending list ahead containing brand and generic name, strengths, numbers and expiration dates. Your missionary will be able to help you with this approval before you come. Leave plenty of time to accomplish this since this may take months to get all of the necessary approval.

Arrival Hall

There is seldom a greater sense of vulnerability than there is when you first arrive in any country and push open those doors leading out of Customs. You are assaulted by sights, sounds, smells and languages shouted by a wall of people. All are unfamiliar. It is painfully obvious that you are the visitor and at someone else's mercy until you figure out what to do. You are very aware that you have all your cash, cards, documents and anything else valuable on you right at that moment and you have too much luggage to handle by yourself. You will often be mobbed by eager taxi drivers and tour operators as you officially step into the country, all offering to "help." Politely but firmly decline their offers until you get your bearings and know exactly what your plan is. Be cautious and think your problem through before acting. Every precaution you take will help to avoid any potential problems. Keep careful track of your belongings. After all, you do not want someone to "help" themselves, especially when you have just arrived.

The first thing to do is actually best done before you leave your own country. Try to get some prior information as to the rough layout of the airport where you will be arriving. This will help, for you will then have a vague sense of where you should be going and where the taxis are located etc. If you are being met by someone, find out where in the airport they will meet you. If possible, have them send you a picture over the Internet of the person who will meet you and you can send a picture of yourself to them. They may look alike to you, but you certainly look alike to them as well.

If possible, exchange your currency in your home country to get at least enough money for the first day or two. Exchange only the amount you will reasonably need in the next few days. You will need sufficient for the ride into town, a phone call, a tip (perhaps) and a little for unforeseen needs like toll ways or a bottle of water. Ask for small bills or coins in amounts suitable for tipping. Keep the small amount of this local currency easily accessible in a pocket or something and not with your other money, to avoid giving clues to a potential thief where it is. If you were not able to get local currency beforehand, see if there is someplace to exchange money (an exchange bureau or preferably an ATM) and follow the same rules. Be careful that you do not flash a large bankroll or make it obvious where you keep your money. Change cash or travelers' checks to local currency. Keep your wallet and valuables safely secured in a handbook, passport pouch or in a front pants pocket to prevent pick-pocketing. Ladies should keep the strap around their shoulder or neck and their hand on the clasp.

If you have not been able to find anything out about the airport where you landed, then ask one of the airline staff, or the government tourism booth (if they have one at the airport) for some assistance, or tips on the best way of travelling. Many guide books will have good discussions about the airports and the best way to get around.

Whenever possible, especially in certain countries, take either the airport limousine, or a hotel pick up. Never take a taxi that seems just to be hanging around, offering its services (especially when there is a proper taxi queue available). They may be illegal or you may find yourself in the middle of a raging battle between this interloper and the taxi drivers who have waited in line. If you do need to use a local taxi, remember to settle the price before stepping into the cab.

If you need to make a phone call, many telephones in developing countries do not take coins and cannot be depended upon to take major credit cards or telephone cards from the large North American telephone companies. They require a telephone card issued by the local company. If you find yourself in this fix, usually one of the boutiques in the airport will have the cards for sale or will be able to tell you where in the airport you can purchase one. If you brought a tri- or quad-band phone which uses SIM cards, often the SIM cards and phone usage cards are available in the airport.

Jet Lag

Travelers are divided into two main groups: Those who have jet lag and those who lie about it. Seriously, some people never seem to be bothered very much and for others, it can be severe and make several days of your time "vanish"—or make you wish they would vanish. Some say it is worse for them flying east and others say it is worse flying west. Some people claim that the body takes a full day to recover for each time zone that you cross. For a long trip and a short stay, you may not be recovered before you have to recover from your return trip. Ouch! Nobody ever dies from jet lag and everyone recovers from it, but obviously, prevention is better than the cure. So how do you prevent it? Here are some things to help.

Schedule your flight so you can arrive at the right time of day. Intercontinental flights usually leave in the early morning or in the evening. Obviously which flight you should schedule is affected by how well you sleep on a plane. If you are going to land in the morning, you would like to be able to sleep on the plane during the trip. If you land in the evening, you don't want to sleep on the plane. If you have to stay awake, make sure you have brought enough to keep your attention. It helps to know whether can you use your laptop (batteries and if you are lucky enough to fly business or first class, adapters are necessary if they have power outlets), are the movies ones you would like to watch, and do you have enough good books or CD's to keep you entertained? If you can sleep, a nice hot shower in the morning should allow you to hit the ground running. Some international airports have showers that you can rent and you can be fresh as a daisy before you leave the airport or get on that next flight.

Schedule your time carefully for the first few days: Particularly if you are someone who is hit hard by jet lag, make your schedule and responsibilites light for the first few days if your time-frame permits.

Setting your external clock: Change your watch to the local time early in the flight and try to sleep and eat on your trip according to that new schedule throughout your stay. It takes some willpower to wait to eat or sleep when you now "should," but if you rationalize what you want to do with a statement like, "Well, it is really so-and-so o'clock back home and that means I would ordinarily do so-and-so," it just delays your adaptation. Regular scheduled exercise also seems to help.

Setting your internal clock: when you do arrive at your destination, and it is daytime, try not to go to sleep, no matter how tired you are. Instead try to go outdoors and into the sunshine if possible. This exposure to light helps to alter your body clock, and you will be back to normal a lot quicker. Attempt to get early morning sun if traveling east and evening sun if traveling west to help reset your internal clock. Melatonin has been found helpful by some travelers but it must be taken days in advance in order to "reset" your clock. Take 2–4 mg each day for a week or two before you leave. Take it at the time of day corresponding to bedtime in your new time zone.

> *"Travel is only glamorous*
> *in retrospect."*
>
> —Paul Theroux

Sleeping pills and naps: consider use of a sleeping pill for the first few nights. However, be aware that you will often have a "bad" night at some point when you stop the pills. One of the first hotels to offer a jet lag service was the Okura Hotel in Tokyo. They would offer the guests a special bright light in their rooms, special food designed to help the body clock, massages and a whole load of other things, all so that you could be refreshed and ready to go as soon as possible. If you are anywhere else and if you can't resist and your eyelids are drooping, and you feel more and more tired, then set your alarm for four hours time, have a very hot bath, and jump into bed. Awake and make the most of the rest of the day.

HEADING BACK

My, where did the time go? Even if you are eager to get back to home and hearth, it is still difficult to leave new friends and come down from the emotional and spiritual high that has sustained you for the past few weeks or months. That emotional let-down can be severe. The spiritual let-down can be equally difficult to handle. See Chapter 16 on reentry for some ideas on how to best handle it.

It is time to pack to go home. Now it suddenly strikes you that what you bought, you actually have to get home! The breakable things will have be packed well or carried by hand. You may decide to ship some things home to comply with weight limits or just to make your return trip easier. Shipping gifts home to various friends and family members can avoid the problem of paying custom duties if you are over the limit but has to be weighed against the cost and uncertainty of mail originating in a foreign country. Remember, U.S. citizens may bring back $400 worth of goods duty-free. I hope that you were very careful in what you purchased to take home but check again. Be aware that seeds, plants, food and other such items may be of restricted entry in order to avoid the introduction of foreign diseases into the U.S. U.S. customs will confiscate items made from endangered animals. Items that are considered vital to cultural heritage or history may be confiscated by the customs on either end.

Gather up or obtain any receipts any mission-related expenses that you incur overseas if you desire a tax deduction or reimbursement by your agency upon your return home. This includes taxis, groceries, departure taxes, other local transportation, etc.

Just remember four things: first, your weight limit going home may be much smaller than when you came. Some people begin to give away all of their clothes and any supplies that they brought with them: batteries, medications, cosmetics, books, etc. Secondly, confirm your ticket at least 72 hours before you leave. This can be done by phone or sometimes by Internet. If neither is available, consider sending an e-mail back to your travel agent or family in N. America to ask one of them to do it for you. If you are making an in-country call and if there is a language barrier in the country where you have served, asking one of the nationals or missionaries to make the call for you is more effective. Thirdly, confirm your ticket at least 72 hours before you leave and finally, number four, confirm your ticket at least 72 hours before you leave.

Show up early at the airport. It can be bedlam. Some people arrive very early, check in their luggage, get their boarding passes, fill out the necessary forms and then eat.

Most countries have a local airport departure tax. Be sure to ask about it before you go to the aiport so you have the right currency in the right amounts. This is payable in local or U.S. currency at the time of departure from that country. This may or may not be included in the price of your ticket. If you pay your departure tax in U.S. currency, you will want to pay the exact amount so that you do not have to accept foreign currency as change. You may not have a choice of what currency to use—it may be required in either the local or U.S. currency.

Remember, many countries have strict regulations about how much of their currency (paper and coinage) they allow to be taken out of their country. It is often a great souvenir or token to give to your prayer team and supporters, but be sure to comply with the regulations or risk having it confiscated as you "donate" it to the government.

U.S. Customs

On your return flight, you will usually receive the necessary arrival forms including custom declarations. Fill them out accurately. Passports are now required for all American citizens returning to the U.S. The same ways of doing thing discussed in the section of foreign immigration and customs officials apply here as well. Remember, you are not on American soil until you have passed these folks. They have a job to do and are there to protect your homeland, your job, your freedoms and your health. Give them cooperation and respect. Do not expect "favors" because you are an American if you try to break the rules and regulations. An aside: Cellular phones are not permitted in Immigrations, so call your family before you get there or after you leave there.

One last thing . . . Welcome home and thanks for serving!

CHAPTER 9

TRAVELING WITH CHILDREN

Why take your kids at all? That is a question that is often asked. The answer is that sometimes if you are going to answer the Lord's call on your life, you have to take them with you. But there is a side of you (and often to a deafening chorus of disbelieving and non-encouraging families, friends and even church members) that screams all sorts of objections and questions: Aren't there all sorts of diseases and dangers? Isn't it too expensive? Do you have a right to disturb their schooling (soccer, friendships, cheerleading, etc)?

To understand better, let's listen to the words of a "veteran" short-term missionary wife: "At first, I was apprehensive about all of us living in such primitive conditions. I found my fears were overstated and nothing I really worried about ever came to pass. On the other hand, my husband and I saw tremendous growth in our children. They prayed more than they ever had, and the neat thing was that they could see a real and sometimes immediate direct correlation between their prayers and the effect of the prayers.

"Our family time was very good and very enriching. My children had a chance to work with my husband and make rounds with him. They developed a new understanding and appreciation of what my husband's medical career is all about. They could never do that in the U.S., and their relationship grew stronger

> *"To bring up a child in the way he should go, travel that way yourself once in a while."*
>
> —Josh Billings

because of it. The kids also joined me in ministering to the patients, the staff and the surrounding people. It was a sweet time for me. We all found out through these experiences that our true hope and strength comes from Christ. I think that when we remove the supports of the familiar, we all saw where the strength really came from. As a family, we could explore the Great Commission without the negative effects of peer pressure, media and conflicting demands on our time. They came away with more of a world view about God's extended church, not just about our little church back home in comfortable North America.

"From a purely 'selfish' standpoint, it was a great adventure with our family. We have bonded with shared experiences that will never be taken from us. I wouldn't have missed it for the world."

Even with such glowing testimonies, it must be admitted that traveling with children adds a whole new dimension to the trip. Taking your children can be a blessing but it requires special planning in many areas.

Passports for Children

Passports, ticketing, and seats were discussed in Chapter 4. To briefly summarize, in the U.S., every child now needs a passport. Children can no longer travel on their parent's passport. A few hints about applying for their passport: it is now necessary in the United States that both parents sign the application in the presence of the person taking the application. This regulation was enacted in response to concerns about abduction of a child by one parent in case of custody battles.

Another hint about passport photos for infants: take a white sheet or blanket for a background and put it between the infant seat and the child. No part of anyone or anything extraneous is allowed to be seen in the picture. If it is, they will require you to have new photos taken. This stratagem with a blanket allows you to support the infant without being seen in the picture.

A Child-friendly Itinerary

Planning your itinerary when traveling with children brings a different set of priorities into play. Given the almost universal experience of some previous frustrating time on much shorter family trips, one of the first concerns often raised is how the kids will tolerate the long trip. One of the questions to be answered is whether you should arrange a layover? Well, that depends on whom you believe and how well you know your own family. There are good arguments on both sides of the question. Proponents argue that direct flights are more expensive and also that children often do not tolerate the long trips to remote destinations well unless the traveling is broken up into more manageable sections. They would suggest that you should consider deliberately scheduling a long layover in a hub city so that you can get a day room or a regular room in a hotel. Use this time to let them nap, blow off steam and stretch their legs.

If you are going to do that, consider using connecting hubs that are known to be especially "children friendly." Many airports worldwide have children's lounges that permit play under parents' supervision. Examples are Kidsport at Logan Airport in Boston; Denver's Stapleton Airport; KLM's Junior Jet Lounge in Amsterdam provides a haven for children awaiting connecting flights; O'Hare Airport in Chicago has another great children's play area; and so does London's Gatwick Airport. When you plan your itinerary, be sure to ask your travel agent about what is available in the hubs where you will be or search the Internet.

Opponents of layovers (and any non-direct flight) make the following arguments against longer layovers:

▶ It is just one more place that is strange to you and in which you have to try to figure out the layout, to transport children, to transport a pile of luggage, and to exchange money into a confusing and unknown currency so you can buy snacks and drinks.

▶ If you have to pick up your luggage, it is one more hassle with yet another opportunity for someone to lose your luggage, to argue with you about your passport and visa, to give you a hassle about customs, and last but not least, to have you pay extra baggage charges. This is especially true if you had to pick up your luggage at the airport and are now subject to the lower weight allowances of many international and in-country airlines for the next leg.

▶ Your obligation to amuse, entertain and referee your children does not stop just because you are in a hotel room instead of being on the plane. One of the adults will still have to stay awake if the children can't sleep; perhaps both of you!

▶ Layovers mean the actual trip will take even longer from door-to-door. Why would you want to do that?

▶ So, what to do? We will leave the decision strictly up to you! No matter what you decide to do, allow the children to take regular walks about the airplane during long flights. It is good for your own circulation as well.

▶ For long trips, seriously consider getting each child a ticket for a seat. It used to be that children under the age of 2 years traveled free on most airlines, but this is usually no longer the case. They will often make some charge (e.g., 10% of the adult rate) even if the child sits on your lap. To provide your children with their own seat, the price is usually 60–75% of the adult rate but at least this is partially offset by a full luggage quota for the child. Check with your agent regarding the airline you will use and their policies for children.

In addition to the points listed above, consider the following:

▶ If you can, schedule your flight to avoid the busiest times of day at airports (8 to 10 AM, 4 to 7 PM). This is especially helpful when you are traveling with children who must sit on your lap. When you make your reservations, try to avoid a full flight even in the "non-busy" hours.

▶ Give yourself plenty of time—arrive at the airport and check in early so that you can get the baby settled before others board the plane.

▶ If you have to change planes, be sure to schedule adequate time for the connection.

▶ Airplane food being what it is and children being what they are, you might want to consider ordering special meals for the children. Many airlines have special meals designed for children. If you have strong feelings about your child's nutrition, you might ask exactly what food they are likely to serve, and then decide if you want to take up your valuable space with a picnic lunch of more wholesome foods.

Seats and Child Restraint Systems

As also discussed previously in Chapter 4, every type of seat location has its benefits and drawbacks. Select the seats that will best serve your needs. Since, as a parent you are concerned about safety for your children on the ground once you have arrived at your destination, it makes sense to take a child restraint system (CRS) with you if it can be used both on the plane and in a vehicle when you land. Ask your airline if they can provide a CRS—if so, they may require you to check your own as baggage (you will still need one for the car trips to and from the airport). Be sure you know the difference between a CRS and a child safety device. A child safety device is an FAA-approved alternative to using a hard-backed seat and is approved only for use on aircraft. It is **not** approved for use in motor vehicles. For example, the FAA has approved a new harness-type device (CARES™) appropriate for children weighing between 22 and 44 pounds. It is light and easy to pack, but is not safe for children riding in a car however. Not all airlines approve their use—and they will have the final say, so check ahead of time. Here are some tips for child restraint systems:

▶ Proper use of an approved child restraint system on an aircraft enhances child safety in the event of an accident. A CRS also provides protection for a child during turbulence. The FAA strongly recommends that all children who fly, regardless of their age, use the appropriate restraint based on their size and weight.

• Children less than 20 lbs should be in a rear-facing seat.
• From 20–40 lbs use a forward-facing seat or booster.
• Children over 40 pounds use a regular seatbelt.

▶ Place the infant seat in the window seat or on wide-bellied jets, the center seats of the center section, so they do not block egress in the case of an emergency. Let the airline know you intend to use a child restraint system to see if it is permitted. Only ticketed children are guaranteed a seat and therefore only they have the right to use a child-restraint system. Make sure you have reserved two adjacent seats. Some, but certainly not all airlines, will allow you to use one if the seat next to you is empty even if fare for the child has not been paid, but you can't count on it.

The CRS must be FAA approved. It must have "This restraint is certified for use in motor vehicles and aircraft" printed on it. Otherwise, you may be asked to check the CRS as baggage. A harness system must have ""FAA Approved in Accordance with 14CFR 21.305(d), Approved for Aircraft Use Only" on it. In Europe and the

UK, a car seat must be ECE approved (take a restraint meeting the R44 standard), but not all airlines allow them. The use of an FAA-approved seat in the UK (or Europe) or an ECE approved seat in the U.S. may not be permitted. This is more an insurance liability issue than a safety issue. Ask your travel agent or the airlines to check about current regulations and alternatives. British Airways and some other airlines now have toddler seat (and carrycot) facilities. Some foreign airlines will not allow the use of any child restraint system.

Check the width of your CRS. While airline seats vary in width, a CRS no wider than 16" should fit in most coach seats. A CRS wider than 16" is unlikely to fit, even if the armrests are moved out of the way.

Always follow the manufacturer's instructions regarding use of the CRS. Do not place a child in a CRS designed for a smaller child.

If you need to change planes to make a connecting flight, it can be very challenging to carry a CRS, a child, and other items through a busy airport. Most airlines will help parents make the connection. Request that the airline arrange for assistance in your connecting city.

For more information, call: 1-800-FAA-SURE (1-800-322-7873), 1-866-TELL-FAA (1-866-835-5322) or check the web at www.faa. gov/passengers/fly_children/crs/.

Clothing and Diapers

Your proposed itinerary, the expected weather, the amount of time you are willing to dedicate to washing and the need for packing light are all factors in what you choose to bring. At the very least, you can get by with two sets of clothes: one to wear and one to wash. Also take extra socks, underwear, a hat, a jacket, nightclothes, and perhaps a dress if you have a girl. Make sure they are mix-and-match, don't show dirt easily, and are easy to maintain. If your itinerary requires a lot of time in a crowd, make sure they are brightly or distinctively colored, and throw in a whistle that they can wear on a lanyard or pin. It allows them to signal you when they get lost (don't give it to them on the plane!). Since they are going to be wearing them frequently, it helps if they like the clothes you have selected. Remember, the longer a term you are serving overseas, the more important it is to remember that children grow. You may need to bring the next sizes with you.

Babies are another matter because of their need for more frequent changes. Diapers (nappies) are a major decision. Disposable diapers can be both hard to find and expensive, but can't be beat for easy disposability while traveling. Check ahead with someone in-country to find out whether the diapers are available and how costly it will be. Cloth diapers can be difficult to find anymore in the United States, given the predominant use of disposables, but may be equally difficult to find in foreign countries, so you can't automatically assume they will be more available. Cloth diapers do have the advantage of doubling as towels and bibs in a pinch. Take a minimum of a dozen if you are going to use them. Safety pins may also be hard to find easily in some foreign countries, so you may wish to take them with you. A collapsible camping bucket, available at camping stores or on the Internet, may be good to take in order to soak the dirty diapers before laundering them. Plastic pants can be hard to find in Third-World countries and in warm climes they can precipitate a nasty diaper rash. Cotton over-pants will not keep everyone else dry like plastic does but they "breathe" better and are sometimes better tolerated by the baby.

If you opt for the use of disposable diapers with plans of purchasing them in the country, consider taking a roll of masking tape to use in case the adhesive or fasteners fail. Diapers available overseas are often made with lower quality, especially the adhesive used on the tabs. A warning–don't carry the roll of tape in your carry-on luggage or you are likely to have it confiscated.

A good compromise is to take as many disposable diapers from home as you have room for (fortunately, they are not heavy and make great packing material) and use them for traveling, saving the reusable cotton diapers for more stable conditions.

As a protection against insect bites and cool weather, also consider a sleeping bag for baby's nightwear. This refers not to the camping type of sleeping bag but rather the lightweight cotton bags that are put on like a nightgown but with a closed bottom like a bag. Cotton, flannel or woolen ones of various weights can be used depending on the climate. Pajamas with feet as a part of them are another option.

Other Accessories

Port-a-cots or the combined bed/playpen combinations are sometimes a good choice. Often the airline won't charge for this as a separate piece of baggage, but you will want to call ahead to make sure. The extra baggage charge is often about equal to the price of the accessory, so one alternative is to buy one in country. This obviously requires a bit of detective work ahead of time to find out if and where such an accessory could be purchased in your destination country. Another alternative is to have something made by a local craftsman for the baby to sleep in when you get there, but with that alternative, you either have to arrange to have it done before you get there or wait until it is finished. In any event, leave it in the country. It will save you baggage charges and the missionaries or people you worked with may love to have it.

A stroller, or perhaps some other form of baby carrier discussed in the next section, is the one almost indispensable accessory. There are three types to consider: a good collapsible travel stroller, a true travel system (which combines a car seat and a stroller), or a collapsible, wheeled frame that that will carry a number of different models of infant seats. The travel system is the most flexible but often the most expensive and can be rather bulky. The travel stroller is suitable for the largest span in age and weight groups. The infant seat stroller system is only suitable for smaller infants and only for use with certain models of infant seats. Usually, any of these options for strollers can be used right up to the airplane door where they are then checked. Make sure you understand whether the stroller will be returned to the airplane exit at the next destination or whether it is then handled like regular luggage to be picked up at the baggage carousel. The latter can be a problem if you absolutely have to have the stroller to schlep all the children through a large airport.

Strollers have the relative disadvantage of being easy to use only when the terrain is not too steep and is relatively smooth. In order to get around those limitations, baby-carriers (where the infant is carried in front of the adult) and infant backpacks (carrying the infant behind you) are alternatives. There is a modification of the backpack that is a combined collapsible stroller and backpack. The model you decide upon depends largely on how comfortable the design is for you, the weight of the child, the amount of time you expect to carry the child, and the type of terrain you expect. The wheeled backpacks are neither particularly good strollers nor particularly comfortable backpacks, but are great if you do not plan to do too much of either mode of transportation. Before you purchase one, see if you can borrow one from someone and carry your child for a few hours. It may well point out the need for another more comfortable model. If you do not expect to have to carry a child in a backpack, but once you are there you find you wish you could carry a child that way, you always have the option of "going native," carrying the child next to you using a sarong or similar piece of cloth.

Admittedly, a booster chair or some sort of portable highchair is somewhat of a luxury, but either is sometimes very nice thing to have. There are also table-mounted chairs that lock onto any table but most are limited to children who weight no more than 35 pounds. Lightweight plastic booster seats that are good for travel when you have a slightly older child are also available.

If your child is toilet-training, a small plastic potty chair or a training lid that fits onto a regular commode may be desirable for you to carry along. For smaller children who are already toilet-trained but who have small capacity bladders, having one of these along can be a blessing, especially if you are taking long car trips as part of your journey.

Feeding Your Baby Overseas

Formula can be hard to get overseas and is often expensive. Breast-feeding, continued until you return if at all possible, has the advantages of easy availability, easy preparation, low-cost and sterility. If you need to make up powdered commercial formula, ALWAYS prepare it with boiled water to prevent the passage of intestinal pathogens that can make a small infant very ill. Remember at altitude, you may need to boil the water as long as ten minutes. Since refrigeration may be hard to come by, make up only what you will use at the time. You may want to take along a hand-operated breast pump in case you need to express milk for some reason. Travel packs are available but remember that you will have to have one that works on the local voltage.

Plastic baby bottles are better for travelers. They are lighter than glass ones and cannot break. The American Association of Pediatrics has stated that sterilization of baby bottles is not necessary if you are using a (safe) municipal water supply; however, that is not a given in the Third World. Your alternatives are to wash the bottles, nipples and caps with warm soapy water, then rinse with previously boiled water and air-dry (completely). A possibly safer option is to sterilize the bottles by boiling (5–10 minutes depending on altitude and water quality). If you chose the latter option, try this at home before you go to make sure your plastic bottles do not melt or distort with the heat.

Pre-processed baby foods can be hard to get and you may need to be able to produce your own. Processed baby food is often not available where you are going. Buying a blender in country is one alternative but in any event, we would recommend that you take a small hand-powered mulcher/grinder. If you have the ability to process a whole can of fruit or vegetables at once and have a freezer, you can freeze the puree in the

CHECKLIST FOR FOOD PREPARATION AND FEEDING EQUIPMENT

❑ Bottles, teaspoon, or baby spoon
❑ Small travel kettle to boil water for feeding
❑ Plastic dish with a lid that snaps on securely
❑ Strainer (tea strainer)
❑ Food mulcher/grinder that allows you to prepare food for your toddler
❑ Ice cube trays
❑ Bibs
❑ _____
❑ _____
❑ _____
❑ _____
❑ _____
❑ _____
❑ _____
❑ _____

ice cube trays. This makes a convenient way to store the food and make it easy to warm up and mix and match portions.

Bedding

For baby, take two cotton sheets, a warm blanket, a square of plastic (for changing), and a waterproof undersheet (for those with bedwetting problems). Consider taking a lambskin. The lambskin can serve for something to cuddle against, something to keep the child warm on cold nights and when used as something to sleep on, can keep the child cooler on warm nights. *Where insects are a problem, especially in malarious areas, a mosquito net is mandatory.* These can usually be purchased in country and that is easier to do than hauling them from the home. However, if you want custom-fitted mosquito nets for playpens and strollers, you will most likely have to buy them in the U.S. or spend time making them when you get there. Remember, prevention of mosquito bites is ALWAYS better than chemical prophylaxis.

Screening at the Airport

Sadly, in these days and times, everyone must be screened at the airport. Even babies must be screened. Before you go, you should explain to the older children what will happen and help them practice the event. You cannot keep the child in the infant carrier, which must go through the x-ray machine, along with all carry-on bags, strollers, booster-seats, etc. If your equipment cannot fit into the machine, they will inspect it by hand.

If your child can walk without assistance, they will ask the child and you to walk through separately. If the child must be carried, you may not pass the child to another person behind or front of you during the process and the security officer is not allowed to hold the child. You may be asked to help the officer screen the child if it is necessary.

You are probably aware of the 3:1:1 rule—all liquids, gels and aerosols must be in a 3.4 ounce (100 ml) or smaller container (rolled up toothpaste tubes or partially-full bottles that are larger are not allowed). Those must all be placed in a single, quart-size, zip-top clear plastic bag. Large bags are not allowed and you may only have one. The bag must be x-rayed separately from other things. But what about baby formula, medications, breast milk and juice? Relax. The TSA states that these things "are allowed in reasonable quantities exceeding 3.4 ounces (100ml) and are not required to be in the zip-top bag. Declare these items for inspection at the checkpoint." (www.tsa. gov/travelers/airtravel/children/)

Before leaving home, give thought to how the children are dressed and how their shoes are fastened—collecting all the stuff, tying lots of shoes and trying to get them re-dressed on the other side of security is not fun!

And a final warning: Remind your child that it's illegal to make any kind of jokes about bombs. According to the FAA website, even a child's jest can result in fines and delays.

The Airplane Trip Itself—Ascent and Descent

For takeoff and landing, if the baby is sitting on your lap and does not have a ticket, put the seat belt around just you and hold your baby on your lap or put it in a front carrier. Don't place the seat belt around the baby unless it is one the special ones that is designed for that. If the baby has a seat and you have a child restraint system, be sure to use it according to manufacturer's instructions.

Remember that your baby's ears may plug up or hurt on takeoff or landing due to the change in cabin air pressure. Landing is usually more likely to cause trouble than ascent. Swallowing helps equalize the air pressure. You can help keep your baby's ears clear by nursing or feeding when the plane is climbing and descending. Because sucking on a pacifier does not always stimulate swallowing, feeding is a better option than a pacifier. Sometimes getting the child to feed requires some manipulation of your feeding schedule during the flight. Older children can chew gum, use a bottled drink, suck a lollipop or use a spout cup to drink as they ascend and descend.

Using antihistamines and decongestants for children to prevent this problem is a point of great debate. If the child is having a great deal of discomfort, having a liquid painkiller for the child may make

things easier. Over the counter preparations of antihistamines and decongestants may prevent the trouble and
encourage the baby to sleep. If you
decide to use it, it must be given at
least thirty minutes before it is needed to have maximum effect. If your
children have nasal congestion and
signs of a cold when they fly, it is
something to consider very seriously
because such pressure build-up can
make the children very uncomfortable. Be aware that some children
have adverse effects to these medications and become more irritable.

**Keeping Children Occupied
in Flight**
    Most carriers provide in-flight
coloring books and small playthings
with a travel theme to help occupy
time. Airlines restrict the use of
portable video games (please—only
use with headphones!), tapes, MP3,
and CD/DVD players. There are indications that these items may interfere
with aircraft communications and nav-
igation systems. Check with the airline before boarding. Usually, you can
use them while the plane is in the air.
    Have each child wear his own
daypack that contains his own items
for entertainment, snacks, and drinks.
What you pack is obviously very age-
dependant. Smaller children require

CHILD'S OWN PACK

❑ Stuffed animal of choice
❑ Pack of crayons
❑ Coloring or activity book
❑ Stickers
❑ Small cars, plastic animals,
  or dolls
❑ Chewy sweets for take off
  and landing
❑ Spill resistant cup
  (or spout cup)
❑ Inflatable neck cushion or
  pillow
❑ Wrist or waist reins
❑ Cassette, CD, DVD, or MP3
  player with earphones
❑ Electronic video games
❑ Batteries
❑ Wet wipes (travel pack)
❑ _____
❑ _____
❑ _____
❑ _____
❑ _____
❑ _____
❑ _____
❑ _____

more thought and attention since they are often least successful at
entertaining themselves. Pack a few surprises in there for them. It is
very dry in a plane, so have lotion handy for your hands and theirs. Be
sure to pack batteries if you expect the electronic gizmo to keep them
occupied for the whole flight. If you pack crayons, make sure they are
the non-rolling kind in case they fall off the seat tray. Bringing toys is
something that mothers either swear by or swear at. It depends on the
age of the child. If your child is at the stage of playing the game of
throwing something on the floor to let you retrieve it, do NOT bring
small toys. Cramped seating makes this game painful for you. Select
their favorite toys and plan to bring them out only one at a time. You
may want to have a few favorite toys disappear a few days before
departure so he will be extra happy to see them and play with them on
the plane. Remember—hold some back for the flight home, too. Make
sure your toys for babies have a string or ribbon tied on them so you
can easily retrieve them. Make sure they are cheap, so you can leave
them if it isn't worth crawling under the seat two rows back! Do not
take musical toys unless you want everyone to hate you. There is also
always the risk that forty-two straight choruses of "It's A Small World
After All" will cause you to go berserk. For older children, have them
help pack the backpack to be carried on with them.

Babies in Flight

The first bit of advice is to the mother: forsake fashion and pursue
comfort. Dress as comfortably as you can. Go in comfy shorts/pants,
shoes, and shirt, remembering what the weather will be like at your
destination! Given the tendency of babies to spill and sling food, you
might wish to have a clean top in your carry-on to change into before
landing. Dress your little one in as little as possible, perhaps only an
onesie and socks. If you are concerned about the baby's warmth,
remember that you are usually allowed to board before the others, so
grab a blanket before they are gone. Pack a couple of changes of clothing for the baby because they are likely to soil their clothing.

Diapering can be a hassle on the plane. No airplane lavatory is
overly spacious and many smaller domestic lines do not have a chang-

ing table in their lavatories. Change the baby just before you board. Try to double-diaper or use ultra-absorbent disposable diapers, put on just before you board the plane, and then change in the airport bathroom after the flight arrives. Bring along a changing pad (or piece of plastic) and if push comes to shove, you can change small infants on the tray table or an empty seat next to you. Please have consideration for your fellow passengers and do this only if the baby is wet and not if he or she is distinctly malodorous!

If you do change diapers on the plane, remember that flight attendants, because they need to deliver food to the rest of the passengers and for their own health, cannot handle the dirty diapers unless they are wrapped in a plastic bag. Even then they will sometimes refuse to do so. Do everyone a favor. Bring plastic bags in your diaper bag and take care of them yourself without asking the stewardess to do it for you. If you forgot the plastic bags, you can use an airsickness bag to dispose of the diapers.

The flight attendants can warm baby food and bottles for you. Some airlines have baby meals that you can request in advance. If you use formula, pre-measure the amounts you need and bring disposable plastic bags, add warm water, seal the bag, mix by repeated squeezing and then pour it into the bottle. Also, be sure to bring small snacks your baby can nibble on and play with: Cheerios®, bagels, etc. Be sure to clean up your seat area before you deplane.

Given all the equipment you have to carry when you travel with a baby, it is easiest to let other passengers deplane before you.

Children in the Airport

▶ Do your homework ahead of time and head toward the children's play area.

▶ Allow extra time at the airport—both for arrival and for the layovers. As you know, everything takes l-o-n-g-e-r when traveling with kids.

▶ Give your older child safety rules, such as what to do if you become separated. Should she stay where she is and wait for you?

▶ One way to pass time in the airport is to give your older child a little "airport allowance." Visiting the shops in search of the perfect snack or a magazine can keep kids happy and busy for extended periods.

▶ Even if you don't ordinarily use a child tether, consider using one just in the airport. Remember, you will be distracted when checking in and claiming your luggage. There may be moments when you have to let go of your child's hand.

HEALTH ISSUES[1]

Please check with your child's physician and with the latest CDC recommendations (www.cdc.gov) and look for the sections about traveling with children to get up to date information about vaccinations, malarial prophylaxis and treatment of traveler's diarrhea. There is a wealth of good information available at the other sites listed in the article entitled "Helpful Web Sites" which can be downloaded from www.S3Ministries.com.

What are discussed below are general guidelines to preserve your child's health and are not to replace the specific directions of your physician. Remember:

▶ Prevention of exposure beats any vaccination

TO CARRY ON WITH YOU IF TRAVELING WITH CHILDREN

❑ Medical kit
❑ Supplies for feeding baby
  ❑ Bottles for baby
  ❑ Insulated bottle bag
  ❑ Jars of baby food
  ❑ Jars of baby juice, baby cereal
  ❑ A couple of plastic baby spoons and a bowl with a tight-fitting lid
  ❑ Formula (pre-measured in sealable plastic bags)
❑ Snacks and water for emergencies
❑ Bottle of fresh drinking water (for mixing formula in overseas airports and other emergencies)
❑ Entertainment surprises for the older children

(cont'd on p. 171)

---

[1] The material in this section is presented for your information but it not meant to take the place of an informed consultation from your physician or healthcare provider.

▶ Careful attention to water and food beats any treatment for diarrhea.

▶ Children are not small adults.

▶ Routine childhood immunizations should be up to date or accelerated prior to travel.

▶ Most water-borne diseases (especially typhoid, cholera and most bacterial diarrheas) can be avoided in infants by breast-feeding and in children up to two years of age by careful reconstitution of their food with boiled or treated water.

Take along a pediatric health kit. Special devices, added to those mentioned for adults in the chapter on health, might include a thermometer (contact type), something to accurately dispense medications (the nipple pacifier type, syringe, or spoon measurer), aspirator, and pediatric nail clipper. Medications for baby might include anti-diaper rash crème, an antifungal (anticandidal) crème, and a pediatric formulation against the use of any anti-diarrheal medications in children, several bottles of a fever-reducer, and an antihistamine. Saline nose drops, band-aids, and antiseptic ointment may be desirable. Pediatric formulations of prescription drugs may be hard to get overseas. Taking some, if your child is known to have recurrent problems with middle ear infections, bronchitis, asth-

(cont'd from p. 170)

❑ Resources to change diapers
❑ Diapers
❑ Disposable or ordinary bibs
❑ Diaper pins
❑ Plastic bags for disposal of diapers
❑ Travel pack of wet wipes or washcloth and soap in plastic bag
❑ Cotton cot sheets if a sky-cot will be available
❑ Security blanket or cuddly toy for baby
❑ A change of clothes for you and your child
❑ Front pack for carrying a small baby
❑ Purse or fanny-pack containing your personal items
❑ Passport, tickets, money, credit card, ATM card, frequent flyer card
❑ Something to read
❑ Lipstick and mirror, tooth-brush and toothpaste

ma, etc, is probably wise. A packet or two of oral rehydration solution may help you.

Traveler's Diarrhea in Children

This is one of the greatest risks of traveling for two reasons. First, children do not tolerate dehydration well and secondly, many of the medications commonly used for diarrhea should not be used in children. Most pediatricians would recommend that antibiotics, e.g., ciprofloxacin or other fluroquinolones, and tetracyclines, are contraindicated. Talk with your child's doctor about treatment regimens before you leave on the trip. If, despite your precautions, the diarrhea begins, begin treatment to prevent dehydration before it sets in. Soups, thin porridges, and other safe beverages are advised. Milk should be avoided both because of a possible lactose intolerance induced by the infection and because it may aggravate the situation by causing an osmotic diarrhea. Infants with diarrhea who exhibit signs of mild dehydration, such as thirst and restlessness, should be given an oral rehydration solution (ORS) to drink. This is a packet of salt and carbohydrates that should be prepared following the package instructions and using boiled or treated water. It is widely available abroad. If it is not available, in an emergency, make up a solution with 8 teaspoons of sugar and half a teaspoon of salt to a liter of water. With either ORS solution, continue to have the child drink even if the child initially vomits the fluid back up. Much of it will have been absorbed. If bloody diarrhea, dehydration, fevers in excess of 102° F and chills, or persistent vomiting occurs, seek immediate medical help.

Vaccinations

There are some general CDC guidelines specifically for vaccinations in young children but the schedule should be reviewed with your physician as far in advance of your trip as possible. Some vaccinations can be given earlier than recommended or on an abbreviated schedule. Your physician can seek advice from the CDC if the routine recommendations do not fit your situation. Diphtheria, tetanus, pertussis, measles, mumps, rubella, polio, hepatitis A, hepatitis B, Haemophilus influenza (h.flu), rotavirus and varicella should be given per the routine. Girls at the appropriate age may be a candidate for the human papilloma virus vaccine. Discuss the appropriateness of pneumococcal and meningococcal vaccine with your caregiver. Additional information on typhoid, meningococcal and yellow fever vaccine are given below.

Typhoid Fever: As mentioned above, small children are most easily protected by breast-feeding and careful preparation of their food. There is no vaccine now approved in the U.S. for children under the age of 2 years of age. The injectable ViCPS typhoid vaccine (Typhim Vi, Sanofi Pasteur) is recommended for children between 2 and 6 years of age traveling to areas where there is questionable sanitation. It is given as a single injection but the child must be vaccinated every two years. It must be given 2 weeks before exposure.

The oral vaccine (Ty21a, Crucell/Berna) is not recommended for children under 6 years of age. It consists for four capsules taken every other day and is good for five years. It should be completed 1 week before exposure. Do not give within 72 hours of any antibiotic agent.

Meningococcal Vaccine: The first dose is usually at 11 or 12 years, but can be administered earlier in patients who are high risk (ask your your provider for advice). Protection may not be completely effective in children vaccinated between 3 months and 2 years, especially for vaccination given before 3 months of age. It is usually only given in children 2 years of age or older. The vaccine may be given to infants safely, but it may be less effective than in adults. If the child was originally vaccinated with MPSV (meningococcal polysaccharide vaccine) three years or more earlier and remains in a high-risk area, the child should be revaccinated with MCV (meningococcal conjugate vaccine).

Yellow Fever Vaccine: Infants less than 4 months of age: not recommended.

Infants 6–9 months: give if travel to area of risks is absolutely necessary and there is not a high level of protection from mosquito bites. It is advised that your physician contact 800-CDC-INFO for further advice.

Infants greater than 9 months: as required for travel to areas where the vaccination is required (South America & Africa)

Malaria Prophylaxis for Children: Please remember that there are many other diseases that are insect borne besides malaria and the best prophylaxis for all of them is not to be bitten at all. See the section in the chapter on health tips to review the things you can do to avoid insect bites and to get a good general background in mosquito-borne diseases. For children, use something approved for children with the following CDC-recommended repellents:

- Repellents with DEET concentrations no greater than 30% to 35% (including, but not limited to: Off!, Cutter, Sawyer and Ultrathon)
- Picardin (including, but not limited to: Cutter Advanced, Skin-so-Soft Bug Guard Plus, Autan (the last available outside the U.S.)
- Oil of Lemon Eucalyptus (PMD). Products include but are not limited to: Repel
- IR3535 (including but not limited to: Skin-so-Soft Bug Guard Plus Expedition)

The effect should last about 4 hours with one application if the concentration of the active ingredient is >10%. It will need to be reapplied if the child stays out longer, sweats profusely or gets wet. Use according to label directions, wash it off when the child returns indoors, avoid applying to wounds or broken skin, avoid breathing or swallowing it, and avoid use on the hands (where it might get transferred to the eyes or mouth). Use permethrin treated mosquito nets for sleeping.

When you visit your health care provider before you leave on your trip, be sure to discuss malaria prophylaxis. Here are some general tips:

▶ Buy your drugs in North America: the reliability and availability of generic drugs in other countries cannot be guaranteed.

▶ Some medications have scored tablets and the prescribed dosage may mean you can use a half or a fourth of a tablet. For children who require dosages that do not easily yield to such a method, or who do not easily swallow tablets, have the prescription filled at a full-service pharmacy that compounds drugs. The pharmacist should grind the tablet, weigh each dose, and store the powder in a gelatin capsule. This service usually takes 3–4 days.

Since mefloquine, chloroquine, and Malarone taste very bitter, prepare the child's dose of medication by breaking open the gelatin capsule and mixing the drug with something sweet, such as applesauce, chocolate syrup, or jelly.

The dosage, contraindications and appropriate drugs are listed at the web site www.cdc.gov/malaria/travel/drugs_children_public.htm. The recommended drugs for chloroquine-resistant malaria are mefloquine, doxycycline and Malarone® (atovaquone/proguanil). Primaquine has some limited applicability as well. Chloroquine and hydroxychloroquine are recommended only if the malaria in the area is known to be chloroquine-sensitive. One drug combination, used for prophylaxis in some countries for children because it is tasteless, is not available in the U.S. This is a combination of pyimethamine and dapsone (Maloprim). Resistance is increasing to this drug. It has a small risk of wiping out your bone marrow's production of certain white cells (granulocytes) and is less effective against *P. vivax*. It is not a recommended drug.

These drugs have the same indications for usage in children as listed in the malaria section of the chapter on health but have some differences in the pediatric age group and they are listed by drug below. As always, leave the final decision up to your health care provider.

Mefloquine: Can to be taken by children of all ages and weights who are not allergic to it, who do not have seizure disorders, or conduction abnormalities of the heart.

Prophylaxis should begin 2 weeks before departure, continued weekly on the same day of the week and taken for four weeks after leaving the malaria-risk area.

Take on a full stomach to reduce nausea, the most common side effect. Nausea and vomiting usually do not require stopping the drug. If the child vomits the drug within 30 minutes, the parent should give the child another dose of the drug. Remember to mix it with something sweet. If the child vomits after 30 minutes, he or she has absorbed enough of the drug and a second dose is not required. The incidence of neuropsychiatric symptoms has not been well documented in children, but appears to be low. It is contraindicated in those children with documented depression or other neuropsychiatric diseases and in those with a history of non-febrile seizures.

Doxycycline: Do not give to children under the age of 8; teeth may become permanently stained. Since children have the tendency to play outside, the photosensitivity of tetracyclines is an important side effect. Children should avoid the midday sun, use a high-SPF sun block, and wear long-sleeved shirts, long pants, and a hat.

Parents are advised to give doxycycline on a full stomach, for example, after dinner, to minimize nausea. Do not let the child lie down for 1 hour after taking the drug to prevent reflux.

Malarone: Do not give to children less than 11 pounds (5 kg) in weight or who have severe renal impairment. Although the CDC states that it may be used for infants and children who weight between 5 and 11 kg, it also notes that this constitutes off-label use in the United States.

Prophylaxis should begin two days before arrival in the country and, because of its mechanism of action against the malaria parasites, can be stopped seven days after return. It is given daily after a meal or milk.

Although side effects are rare, abdominal pain, nausea, vomiting, and headache may occur.

It is expensive.

Chloroquine & Hydroxychloroquine: Use if, and only if, traveling to areas where chloroquine-resistant malaria is NOT a problem.

It can be given to young infants with dosage based on weight.

Start 1 week before entering the country and continue for four weeks after leaving the country. It is taken weekly on the same day.

Although side effects are rare, nausea and vomiting, headache, dizziness, blurred vision, and itching have been reported. Give the drug on a full stomach to minimize the nausea. Both drugs may worsen the symptoms of psoriasis (not a common problem in children). Hydroxychloroquine may be better tolerated than chloroquine.

Primaquine: Children *must* be tested for G6PD (glucose-6-phosphate-dehydrogenase) deficiency and have a documented normal G6PD level before use. Primaquine can cause a fatal hemolytic anemia (bursting of the red cells) if the child is deficient in G6PD.

Dosage is based on the child's weight. The first dose is given 1–2 days prior to travel, continued daily at the same time each day and continued for 7 days after leaving the risk area. Do not share the drug with others! The most common side effects are stomach cramps, nausea and vomiting.

Self-treatment for a Presumptive Diagnosis of Malaria

Malaria can be fatal, especially in small children. Malaria symptoms will occur at least seven to nine days after being bitten by an infected mosquito. Fever in the first week of travel is therefore unlikely to be malaria; however, travelers should be advised to have any fever promptly evaluated. It is always better to treat the flu like malaria than to treat malaria like the flu. With this in mind, if the child develops fever or other flu-like symptoms, and professional medical care is not available within 24 hours, a self-treatment dose of Malarone™ is recommended. Parents should be advised to seek professional medical care as soon as possible after treating their child. Dosages are available on the CDC website (search for malaria in children).

Fansidar is considered by some to be a second-level option if you *know* that the malaria in that area is Fansidar-sensitive). Fansidar resistance is known to occur in the Amazon basis of South America, Southeast Asia and the African counties of Kenya, Tanzania, Uganda, Malawi, Mozambique, and South Africa. Use Fansidar® only if the child is NOT allergic to sulfa drugs.

Use Malarone™ if your child is not taking Malarone for prophylaxis. Children on Malarone prophylaxis who take presumptive self-treatment should use Fansidar if they are traveling to an area without Fansidar resistance. Consult the CDC Malaria Hotline (770-488-7788) or consult your physician for advice for children who cannot take Fansidar or Malarone for presumptive self-treatment.

If the child becomes ill during the first year after your return from a trip, always consider the diagnosis of malaria and make sure your health-care provider knows where you have traveled.

YOUR CHILDREN IN-COUNTRY

Once You Are There

As a spouse, you too have a big job on the mission field. The success of the trip depends as much upon you as it does your spouse who seems to have the more "glamorous" role. How is that? You are settled into your new place. You have learned the truth of the axiom that it takes a lot of time just to live on the mission field. Your family is safe from water borne diseases, well-fed and clothed in clean clothes. But there is still more that falls to your shoulders: keeping them emotionally content, spiritually fed and adequately educated. Don't worry; you can do it with God's help!

Preparing Them for the Trip and Helping Them Document It

The amount of preparation to get the children ready for this change in their routine varies on both the age of the children and the health of your relationship with them. Small children do not need to be consulted about whether you go, but woe to the parents who uproot their teen-agers without having previously discussed it with them in detail. Educating them about the trip and your goals and motives is probably the most important thing and it may take some time to help the children work their way to the point that they are excited about going.

Before you make the final decision, let them know about the mission field you are interested in and why you might be interested in going there. Use videos and pictures from the mission agency or the mission agency itself as a point of discussion. If possible, have someone from that mission field in your home for a visit. Be honest with them about your own motives, hopes and fears as you go along.

Do some homework yourself and know what the missionaries are doing in the country, what needs are present and how the whole family might help. Concentrating your information on the plights and problems of families and individuals helps personalize the problem.

▶ Encourage the children to research a specific problem, people group, or country in order to encourage them to understand better what they will see and to get a better emotional "buy-in."

▶ Involve them in the planning. Make an itinerary of each day's plans and include a couple of activities that are flexible and optional. Make time for free time and for fun time as a family. Stopping off in some country you have always wanted to see on the way to or from the country may be a special treat for all of you.Encourage them to prepare information and present it to their class, Sunday school class, AWANA, children's mission group and other groups.

▶ For smaller children make a calendar and mark off the days each day during your prayer time. Pray specifically for your trip and for each of the members of your family. Be sure to include them in the spiritual preparation for the trip.

▶ Present books, toys, animals and other items with a focus on the upcoming adventure. For small children, plastic zoo animals might help them understand the country and its fauna. For older children, a book or ViewMaster™ with slides about your country may help.

▶ Let the children chose their favorite items to take with them. You give them a basic list of what must be included in their suitcase, but let them choose their outfits.

▶ Each child can pack his own bags to carry on with him. They can be small knapsacks or wheeled carry-ons, depending on the age of the children. The contents of their bags will depend on their age, but be sure to include items that have good entertainment value over a period of days or weeks. Pack hard candies, gum, snacks, pre-moistened wipes, a journal and pen, etc. If you decide to include something that runs on batteries, be sure to include extra batteries.

Before departure, discuss safety and security rules. Be sure they know what to do and where to meet if you get separated and who to call if the adults become ill.

Discuss rules about spending money and reinforce your rules about ordering food in restaurants and from room service.

▶ Documenting the trip can help to build and refresh memories from your great adventure. Here are some ideas, but it is by no means exhaustive. Let us know what has worked for you by e-mailing us at info@S3Ministries.com.

▶ Talk about what they have seen each day and their reaction to those events, peoples and places. This is a great way to help them interpret what they have seen and in doing so, you may change how they look at other people for the rest of their life. Children in particular may have lasting impressions of the poverty, harsh conditions and deprivation often seen in the mission setting. Talking about (and living out) how a Christian should respond can be very powerful in this setting.

▶ Buy a cheap camera. A cheap digital camera or several disposable cameras are options. Don't worry about how good the pictures are. They will be meaningful to the children.

▶ Take tape recorders to record their journal and any special sounds or music. Extra tapes and batteries are advised.

▶ Create a project book: blank and lined pages for a journal, recording interesting trivia, pasting in souvenirs, etc; plastic pages with a resealable top can help organize small items. Save ticket stubs, brochures, leaves, napkins and paper placemats from restaurants to paste in your scrapbook. Don't forget to pack the glue stick.

▶ Have the children write serial letters to people at home and keep a copy of them for a scrapbook. If you have a laptop and access to the Internet, send serial e-mails and your copy is automatically saved.

Older children may use a laptop computer to create a web site for posting once they get home.

▶ Identify some theme: animals, flowers, stamps, children's books in other languages, and have the children collect a sample from each place they visit.

▶ Have your children write a report about each place they visit. Share them by mail or e-mail with their schoolmates, Sunday school class, scouting troop or children's group. This has the added bonus of possibly solving their "What I did this summer" theme problems when they return to school.

Emotional Support

Be aware of the stresses of culture shock. This will not only affect the adults, but will affect everyone in the family in some way or another. Be prepared, there may be a reversal of roles if you are the one who handles the culture shock better. This can cause some marital relationships to be a little rocky for a while. This is particularly evident if the doctor-spouse, who whizzed through advanced scientific training, gets too discouraged at language study. Languages are a real gift and sometimes the spouse, who may not have achieved anything else that the couple considers particularly noteworthy, has a fluency in language that the more accomplished partner does not. Anger, jealousy, frustration and discomfort at these new and extremely uncomfortable personal and relationship dynamics can be a problem. Most ultra-short-term missionaries don't face this but may recognize this dynamic at work in the lives of relatively new career missionaries with whom they are working. Be sure to extend sufficient grace, and pray for them as well. Other more common sources of frustration for the short-term doctor-spouse can include all of the stressors that are somewhat unique to the practice of medicine in the Third World. It may help both the spouse and the healthcare provider to read the chapter on the challenges of short-term medical missions in *Medical Missions: Get Ready, Get Set, GO!* before you go and at least once or twice after you are there a short time.

Homesickness can be a problem for both the adults and children. Education before you come and involvement after you get there are the best solutions. Don't let the "Back home we…" syndrome get a foothold. Make a game out of it with some silly penalty to the first one who starts saying it. One thing that works well for adults is a selection of pictures of important people in your life. For children, a special pillowcase that has been painted with fabric paints (names, hand- or pawprints) can bring a sense of connection and familiarity in a strange place. It has the additional advantage of being useful and easy to pack.

Educational Support

You have basically two choices in educating your children overseas, both of which require a fair bit more parental involvement than you might have at home. This is because you may have to be both teacher and coach. There is actually a third alternative called summer vacation but not everyone can do their short-term mission experience during school vacations! The first is to work some sort of accommodation with your children's school. Contact their teachers before the children go to get homework and make sure you can help them with it. Try to minimize the amount of books they have to take (consider scanning and putting the material in the computer on a disk). See if they can submit homework by Internet but make sure that the teachers understand the frequent problems with third world Internet service (and the possible delays in meeting deadlines that would result). The second choice is some sort of online or home schooling alternative. For longer stays overseas, this is the only practical alternative, but there can be significant choices to make. Start your self-education about alternatives and your selection very early in order to give you time to make wise choices, order appropriate materials, and do the necessary paperwork. See our list of web sites or use any Internet search engine to identify the hundreds of resources that are available to you. If you have certain skills or knowledge in certain areas, you might be able to share teaching duties with other missionaries who are home schooling. For example, if you are great in science and math but so-so in English and history, you might find someone to whom the whole field of algebra is one big unknown but is excited about split infinitives and dangling participles. You teach what you know and they teach what they know, and you both get some time to yourselves.

One bit of advice from a veteran home-schooling mother, "Establish and keep a routine." Easier said than done but good advice, nonetheless.

Family Time

Without the boob tube, some families find themselves at somewhat of a loss when they actually have to communicate with each other. This is a great time to communicate with each other in a way that you may have not done before. Family game times can become a very special memory in progress. Given the realities of limited luggage space, games, especially card games of various sorts, are a mainstay. Some board games are suitable for travel and, with imagination; some can even be made out of easily found items. Some board games and other types of games are specially made for travel using magnets, sealed dice, and other ways to minimize the loss of pieces. Decorating your house for holidays, making ornaments and decorations with limited resources, can stretch your imagination and be good fun. A packet of colored construction paper, tape, glue and scissors are always helpful. Look your calendar and note any special holidays or events that you should celebrate. This is true for those who are left at home as well as those you are traveling with. Arrange for cards and gifts to be delivered to your loved ones at home. Give careful thought to taking along with you gifts to give for birthdays and anniversaries. You may want to bring along flags, banners, decorations, candles and paper goods to give some gaiety to the occasion. Even a special cake mix can be carefully packed and hoarded for a special surprise. If you are carrying your laptop and have access to a printer, software for making greeting cards and other announcements can be immensely popular, not only with the family but with the nationals and missionaries.

Perhaps one of the greatest benefits will be the spiritual times together just as a family. If you are not used to having regular family devotions, here is the perfect time to begin. Meals on the mission field tend to be more regular and less hectic and it is a great time to talk with each other bringing in spiritual applications as they come up. Having regular family Bible studies and teaching can be a daunting concept. If you are concerned about the challenge, there are now many resources available for you. As a suggestion, use the search engine on a Christian Bookstore site and type in "devotions" and "children" as key words. A long list of readily available resources will appear.

Some suggested ideas are below in the suggested readings but there are dozens of options you can find if you go to www.christian-books.com or other sources and search for "family devotions".

Consider taking along a translation of the Bible aimed at children of your children's ages. Read from it regularly.

Good resources are available at either of these two sites: www.heritagebuilders.com or the Focus on the Family web site (www.family.org). Look for the Family Nights Tool Chest books that may also be available from your local Christian bookstore. These are great pre-planned evenings that will help you and your children communicate about spiritual truths.

Don't forget that audiotapes or CDs of children's radio programs (the Odyssey series from Focus on the Family), audiotapes or CDs of Christian radio dramatizations of books (e.g. the CS Lewis tales for children), or other similar types of media may give a good time of entertainment and lead to questions of a spiritual nature.

For the more dramatically inclined, puppet shows or dramatizations of Bible stories can take up a great deal of creative time and energy as they combine the use of their imagination and their knowledge of the Bible stories.

Summary

Take your children. You won't regret it.

SUGGESTED READING

Bree, Loris, M. Bree. *Kid's Trip Diary: Kids! Write About Your Own Adventures and Experiences.* Marlor Press, 2007, ISBN: 1892147141

Briscoe, Jill. *Renewal on the Run: Embracing the Privileges and Expectations of a Ministry Wife.* New Hope Publishers, 2005, ISBN 1563098490

De Francisco, Fawzia Rasheet. *The Rough Guide to Travel with Babies and Young Children,* Rough Guides, 2008, ISBN: 1843537044

Franklin, Sarah (ed.) *How to Fit a Car Seat on a Camel: And Other Misadventures Traveling with Kids.* Seal Press, 2008, ISBN: 1580052428

Hawkins, Susie. *From One Ministry Wife to Another: Honest Conversations about Ministry Connections.* Chicago: Moody Publishers, 2009, ISBN 0802460305

Hoekstra, Elizabeth. *Keeping Your Family Close When Frequent Travel Pulls You Apart.* Wheaton, IL: Crossway Books, 1998, ISBN 0-89107-975-0

Hughes, Barbara *Devotions for Ministry Wives: Encouragement from Those Who've Been There* Grand Rapids: Zondervan, 2002, ISBN: 0310236320

Kalb, Rosalind and Penelope Welch. *Moving Your Family Overseas.* Yarmouth, ME: Intercultural Press, 1992, ISBN 1-877864-14-5

Lanigan, Cathy. *Travel with Children, 4th ed.* Victoria, Australia: Lonely Planet Publications, 2002, ISBN 0-86442-729-8

Miller, Jamie. *10-Minute Life Lessons for Kids: 52 Fun and Simple Activities to Teach Your Child Honesty, Trust, Love.* HarperCollins, 1998 ISBN: 0060952555

Nappa A, and M. Nappa. *52 Fun Family Devotions.* Augsburg/Fortress, 1994 ISBN: 0806626984

Piet-Pelon, Nancy J, and Barbara Hornby *Women's Guide to Overseas Living, 2nd Ed.* Yarmouth, ME: Intercultural Press, Inc., 1992, ISBN 1-877864-05-6

Rivoli, Shelley. *Travels with Baby: The Ultimate Guide for Planning Trips with Babies, Toddlers and Preschool-Age Children.* Travels with Baby Books, 2007, ISBN-10: 0615159257

Wiliford, Carolyn. *More Devotions for Families That Can't Sit Still.* Wheaton: Victor Books, 1991, ISBN0-896930-252-4. She also has the first book in the duo: *Devotions for Families That Can't Sit Still.*

Williams, Joyce. *Quiet Moments for Ministry Wives: Scriptures, Meditations and Prayers.* Beacon Hill Press, 2006, ISBN: 0834122618

CHAPTER 10

ADAPTING TO A DIFFERENT CULTURE CAN BE PAINFUL

"What is wrong with me?"

"I swear that I will go nuts if they do that again.
Why don't they think like me?"

"Don't they understand the value of (fill in the blank)?
These people always . . ."

"Why, back in the States, we . . ."

"The answer is obvious. Just do it like we do it back home!"

"What is wrong with our mission agency?
Why did they let this happen? Didn't they know that . . ."

Back before vaccination for the disease became available, almost no one could avoid catching the common childhood disease of chicken pox. It was so inevitable that sometimes your mother would take you to expose you to someone in the neighborhood so you could catch the disease at a "convenient" time. You could not avoid it; you could only hope you did not get it too severely.

The condition known as "culture shock" is very much like that. Virtually nobody avoids it completely. You can only hope and pray that you are not too miserable while you grow through it and that it does not leave you scarred. Even if you survive relatively unscathed, you will see those on your short-term mission trip who are having a really rough time—and the most affected may even be the career missionaries you are going to work with.

Like most significant "diseases," there are great scholarly tomes written that tell you more than you could possible want to know, and at the end of the chapter, we have listed some references that you

---

[1] One of the best is Kohls, L. Robert. *Survival Kit for Overseas Living, 3rd edition.* Yarmouth, ME: Intercultural Press, Inc., 1996, ISBN 1-877864-38-2 Much of the material in this chapter is adapted from his book.

might like to read more.[1] There is no vaccine, in fact, no medicine, nor any completely effective prophylaxis against it. Your family doctor probably cannot even discuss it intelligently. Rest assured however that you can get through it. A realistic set of expectations and a prepared heart go a long way to ameliorating the symptoms. Before we mention some coping mechanisms, we will review the natural history of the condition. Like Kübler-Ross' stages of grief, not everybody goes through them in the same order or necessarily in any order at all, but it helps to simplify the stages so we can understand better.

"When you travel, remember that a foreign country is not designed to make you comfortable. It is designed to make its own people comfortable. "

—Clifton Fadiman

Culture Shock is a term used to describe the more pronounced reactions to the psychological disorientation most people experience when they move for an extended period into a culture markedly different from their own. It can cause intense discomfort, often accompanied by hyper-irritability, bitterness, resentment, homesickness, and depression. In some cases, distinct physical symptoms of psychosomatic illness occur. For some lucky people, the bout with culture shock is brief and hardly noticeable. These are usually people whose personalities provide them with a kind of natural immunity.

In a sense, one has to be willing to suffer through culture shock as the occupational hazard of overseas living in order to have the pleasures of experiencing other countries and cultures in depth.

Culture shock has two quite distinctive features:

▶ It does not result from a specific event or series of events. Rather it comes from the experience of encountering ways of doing, organizing, perceiving, or valuing things which are different from yours and which *threaten* your basic, unconscious belief that your culture's customs, assumptions, values, and behaviors are right.

▶ It does not strike suddenly or have a single principal cause. It is cumulative. It builds up slowly, from a series of small events and frustrations that are difficult to identify.

Culture shock comes when you are:

▶ Cut off from the cultural cues and known patterns with which you are familiar.

▶ Living and/or working over an extended period in a situation that is ambiguous.

▶ Have your own values brought into question or have your moral rug yanked out from under you.

▶ Continually put into positions in which you are expected to function with maximum skills and speed but where the rules have not been adequately explained.

THE PROGRESSIVE STAGES OF CULTURE SHOCK

Culture shock progresses slowly. One's first reaction to different ways of doing things may be "How quaint!" When it becomes clear that the differences are not simply quaint, an effort is frequently made to dismiss them by pointing out the fundamental sameness of human nature.

"Everyone carries his own inch-rule of taste, and amuses himself by applying it, triumphantly, wherever he travels."

—Henry Adams

After all, people are really the same under the skin, aren't they?

Eventually, the focus shifts to the *differences* themselves, sometimes to such an extent that they seem to be overwhelming. The final stage comes when the differences narrow down to a few of the most troubling and then those are blown up all out of proportion. (For Americans, standards of cleanliness, attitudes toward punctuality, and the value of human life tend to loom especially large.)

By now, the sojourner is in an acute state of distress. The host culture has become the scapegoat for the natural difficulties inherent in the cross-cultural encounter. Culture shock has set in. Following are some of the symptoms that may be observed in relatively severe cases of culture shock:

▶ Homesickness

▶ Boredom

▶ Withdrawal (e.g., spending excessive amounts of time reading; only seeing other Americans; avoiding contact with host nationals)

▶ Need for excessive amounts of sleep

▶ Compulsive eating and/or drinking

▶ Irritability

▶ Exaggerated cleanliness

▶ Marital stress

▶ Family tension and conflict

▶ Chauvinistic excesses (in both the jingoistic and sexual sense)

▶ Stereotyping of host nationals

▶ Hostility toward host nationals

▶ Loss of ability to work effectively

▶ Unexplainable weeping

▶ Physical ailments (psychosomatic illnesses)

Not everyone will experience this severe a case of culture shock, nor will all the symptoms be observed in any given case. Many people ride through culture shock with some ease, only now and again experiencing the more serious reactions. Nevertheless, many others don't. Some sufferers will be in denial, stating categorically that they do not now have nor did they ever have culture shock. For you who suffer a great deal, it is important for you to know (1) that the above responses can occur as part of culture shock, (2) that culture shock is in some degree inevitable, and (3) that your reactions are emotional and not easily subject to rational management (i.e. you are not crazy!) This knowledge should give you a better understanding of what is happening to you and buttress your resolve to work at hastening your recovery.

Before we examine what you can do to counteract culture shock, let's spend a few minutes finding where it fits into the whole overseas experience. There are distinct stages of personal adjustment, through which virtually everyone who lived abroad went. People call us "Ugly Americans" when we manifest these behavior patterns, but it is true that anyone from any culture may demonstrate them when their usual props are knocked out from beneath them while on a trip or relocation. These stages are:

▶ Initial euphoria
▶ Irritability and hostility
▶ Gradual adjustment adaptation and biculturalism

People on short-term trips will see two common reactions. The first is typified by comments that over-idealize the national people; the second is typified by overly critical comments. Neither is correct and they represent the first two stages of cultural shock. When team members or family members are at different stages, it takes a bit of understanding and grace not to lash out at the other person for his "obviously wrong" interpretation of events.

1. Initial Euphoria. Most people begin their new assignment with great expectations and a positive mindset. If anything, they come with expectations that are too high and attitudes that are too positive toward the host country and toward their own prospective experiences in it. At this point, anything new is intriguing and exciting, but usually it is the similarities that stand out. The arrivee is impressed with how people everywhere are really very much alike. This stage can be artificially lengthened if you have people who serve you (hotel staff, guesthouse staff, etc) and buffer you from the realities of life. This period of euphoria may last from a week or two to a month, but the letdown is inevitable. You have reached the end of the first stage.

> *"The most important trip you may take in life is meeting people halfway."*
>
> —Henry Boye

2. Irritation and Hostility. Gradually, your focus turns from the similarities to the differences. These differences, which now suddenly seem to be everywhere, also become troubling. There may be endless complaining, constant carping and faultfinding. You blow up little, seemingly insignificant difficulties into major catastrophes. This is the stage generally identified as culture shock. Some unfortunate souls never get out of this stage. For people who are staying a long time, the "Little Americas" arise in an attempt to isolate themselves from these annoyances.

This process can take months and even years to resolve. Short-termers may, with luck and perseverance, get to the third stage but often flounder around between one of the first two steps, because they never have the time to achieve the adaptation and biculturalism. Their battles with this process can and have given short-termers a bad reputation among career missionaries who have forgotten their own struggles. You may find yourself in a situation where the career missionaries are in culture shock as well, albeit the more chronic variety. Their complaints may be directed against the mission board, the field executive committee, or the colleagues who put the relative newcomer (themselves) in this intolerable situation. They may express bitter feelings about real or imagined injustices. Policies are bitterly attacked. Their blame their own personal failures on a lack of proper orientation, on the fact that nobody had warned them it would be like this, or on the fact that nobody has protected them from this suffering. They may demonstrate marked criticism of others in the work who do not feel the way they do.

They may turn this rejection inward. For many relatively new missionaries to the field, the failure to identify an established ministry or a role in a ministry that is a comfortable fit can cause backlash against those in authority. They do not know what they are supposed to do or what they must do does not fit their image of themselves or their understanding of their calling. They will think that they are failures, that they had no business going overseas, that they cannot possibly make good. All the money, time and training has been wasted on getting them and their families to the field. They blame themselves for every mistake and feel utterly defeated when they are not an instantaneous success in everything they try. Their awareness that this is "not spiritual" and their comparison of themselves to others who have worked through this may only compound the situation. Ultimately, there may be a time when they reject God. Ultimately, they feel, God is at fault for all of this.

Interestingly, there may be a variant of this reaction where, rather than rejecting the new country, there is a rejection of the home country. The visitor may go native, embracing the life styles and mores of the new country. They may reject their own moral rules. In Christian works, this can cause tremendous damage to the missionary community and to the name of Christ.

This stage may also be manifested by an excessive homesickness and consequentially falsely elevated opinion of all things familiar at home. For some, it may manifest itself as an excessive concern about germs and illness, with compulsive hand washing and refusal to eat anything that is not absolutely safe. In a less significant way, it is manifested by a refusal to seek anything but American medical care, American educational systems, etc.

3. Gradual Adjustment. The crisis is over and you are on your way to recovery. This step may come so gradually that, at first, you are unaware it is even happening. Once you begin to orient yourself and you are able to interpret some of the cultural clues and cues that passed by unnoticed earlier, the culture seems more familiar. You become comfortable in it and feel less isolated from it. Gradually, too, your sense of humor returns and you realize the situation is not hopeless after all.

4. Adaptation or Biculturalism. Full recovery will result in an ability to function with confidence in two cultures. You will even find there are a great many customs, ways of doing and saying things and personal attitudes that you enjoy. Indeed, you have in some degree acculturated, and you'll miss these ways of doing and saying things when you pack up and return home.

The interesting thing about culture shock is that there is routinely not one but two low points (or even more). Interestingly, they seem to accommodate themselves to the amount of time you spend in the host country. They will spread themselves out if you are going to stay for a longer period or contract into a shorter period if your initial assignment is for a shorter time. How long culture shock lasts also depends to some extent on you and your resiliency. You can expect a let-up after the first dip, but be prepared for the second downturn that will probably be somewhat more severe.

SKILLS THAT MAKE A DIFFERENCE

Some people seem to take to another culture more naturally than others do, and some foreign countries seem to be easier for Americans to adjust to than others are. However, there are certain skills or traits, which you may have or which you may develop with a little effort, which will facilitate your rapid adjustment.

Here are the skills that experience has shown to be the most important:
► Tolerance for ambiguity
► Low goal/task orientation
► Open-mindedness
► Non-judgmental
► Empathy
► Communicativeness
► Flexibility/Adaptability
► Curiosity
► Sense of humor
► Warmth in human relationships
► Motivation
► Self-reliance
► Strong sense of self
► Tolerance for differences
► Perceptiveness
► Ability to tolerate failure

One of the largest international cultural exchange organizations in the United States (American Field Service) uses *a sense of humor* and the *ability to tolerate failure* as principal selection criteria for the thousands of people they choose for international exchanges.

Our choices for the three most important traits are in agreement but we would add one more: *low goal/task orientation.* In other words, if you have low expectations, fail at those and can laugh about it, you will do okay! *A sense of humor is* important because there is going to be much to weep or get angry, annoyed, embarrassed, or discouraged about. It does not matter how many of the other desirable traits you have; the ability to laugh things off will be the ultimate weapon against despair.

> *"If you reject the food, ignore the customs, fear the religion and avoid the people, you might better stay home."*
>
> —James Michener

Americans abroad too often undertake tasks that are unrealistic and set goals for themselves that are unattainable. That is one of the major causes of failure. To the extent that you set your goals too high and refuse to accept the realities of what you will truly accomplish in a foreign environment, you are going to be disappointed. Experience shows that Americans who are less goal-oriented or task-driven and more able to relax and ride with events tend to be more effective and enjoy themselves overseas.

The ability to tolerate failure is critical. If you have virtually never experienced failure and/or have very little tolerance for it, you are likely to have trouble as are those who work and live with you.

How do you prevent or treat culture shock? There is nothing foolproof but try the following things. Do them consciously, as early and as frequently as possible. Prayer—your own, from your fellow traveling companions, and from folks back home—is your most important secret weapon.

▶ Travel with an open mind. Leave your North American mentality behind.

▶ Plan to make your schedule a reasonable one and keep a margin in your plans for the unexpected. Do not arrive or just survive in an exhausted state of mind. Any stresses loom much larger when you have no reserve left. If possible, take a day or so at first to just walk around and to get a feel for the place, the smells, and the sounds. Fully savor the mystique of the new land you have just discovered.

▶ Know everything you can find out about your new country or service. This starts by trips to the library, searches on the Internet and in guidebooks. Read voraciously. Learn what the country is like, what life is like under the governmental regime that is there. Try to learn some words and phrases of the language before you go. Ask the missionary to send you the proper pronunciation and spelling for the common phrases in everyday living. You will not really understand fully until you are actually in the country mingling with the locals, but it is a great foundation.

▶ Seek to understand and give grace where you do not understand. Consciously begin to look for logical reasons and basic cultural assumptions behind everything in the host culture that seems strange, difficult, confusing, or threatening. Take every aspect of your experience and look at it from the perspective of your hosts. Mission compounds often have resources that they use to help the career missionaries understand the culture and religious climate. Ask to borrow them.

▶ Get to know the people. Despite your own problems show you care. Turn the focus of your life from yourself to others. Look for new experiences. Allow yourself to receive their hospitality. Give hospitality and invite them to your new home. Learn some of their language and their common greetings. Ask questions, ask questions, ask questions. Get to know the national people in their environment: their church, their home, and their marketplace.

▶ Avoid unhappy Americans and other expatriates. Try to avoid "Little Americas" as much as possible. It is contagious.

▶ Refuse to participate in any bashing of the national culture and inhabitants. Resist making jokes and comments intended to illustrate the stupidity of the natives.

▶ Try to remember that whomever it is that frustrates you did not wake that morning with the express desire to make you miserable. Have faith in the essential good will of your hosts.

▶ Identify a host national (a neighbor, coworker, friendly acquaintance) who is sympathetic and understanding, and talk with that person about specific situations and about your feelings related to them.

▶ Keep a sense of humor. There is something funny in everything, even if you have to dig to find it. Do not point your humor at people or the culture because that kind of humor can become destructive quickly. Be known as the foreigner with the big smile!

▶ Be positive and optimistic. A little bitterness poisons the whole group. Expressing that bitterness will not make you any happier either. Learn to thank God for the little things: There is power today! The e-mail finally came through! The roaches are smaller today!

▶ Stay flexible. Get used to disappointment and incredible blessings. Everything takes longer to do and nothing goes as planned. Your experience will be what you make of it. Expect the unexpected but do not let it warp your whole life. Focus instead on people and relationships and not the achievement of goals and compliance to a schedule. Sometimes you have to remind each other with little catch phrases designed to help you

"Tell me about your family."

"Tell me about the work you do."

"How did you come to know Christ?"

"What do you enjoy doing the most?"

"Tell me the history of your people."

"Can you teach me a little of your language?"

both remember the humor and stress of your situation: "Flex," "Cope," "WAWA (West Africa Wins Again)," "China 1 and Visitors 0," "Why me Lord?" "Punt," "Ah so!" "Your shot," "Isn't it great to be an American?"

▶ Stay in touch with home and other important people in your life. E-mail and telephones are widely available and even if they may be a little more expensive than at home, it may be the best money you spend. The occasional phone call or e-mail reassures both you and your loved ones that you are still a family, no matter how many miles separate you. It can also reduce the stress of readjusting to home life after the trip is over, since you are not so out of touch. There is nothing more relaxing than asking the kids how they did in the track meet or what they did over the weekend. By the way, never ask how your kids performed in their exams. The answer to that question may not be relaxing.

"When you come to a fork in the road, take it."

—Yogi Berra

▶ Control homesickness. Some homesickness is inevitable but you must keep it under control. Bring pictures and something that makes you feel connected to home and stay in touch as possible, but do not let it control your life. Don't try to live with one foot in both worlds. Do not let the "back home" stories begin. You might need to make this a game with some penalty. For example, the first one to mention something "back home" does the dishes for the day.

▶ Reward yourself. Take a few minutes to pamper yourself each day in some small way. Take a few days off to visit the country or do something you have always dreamed of doing. Even if you have to shoehorn it into a busy schedule, just the act of taking care of yourself will make a world of difference.

▶ Keep a journal. Writing down your feelings in a diary may help relieve stress and serves to reinforce an invariably faulty memory. Those things that seem to be so clearly etched on your mind slip from your recall disturbingly quickly. Write down the blessings and the answers to prayer. It is also great self-therapy. A study done at Johns

Hopkins over a decade ago showed that people who wrote down some of their adventures, be they positive or negative experiences, showed improved mental health and were able to cope with stress better. Sometimes just the experience of writing everything down and reading it a few days later gives you a new perspective on your own faulty reactions. It can also serve as a written prayer to God and His peace can follow.

▶ Establish little daily rituals. The establishment of certain rituals can provide predictability in an otherwise chaotic environment and reassure us that no matter how bad conditions may get, some things will remain constant. For the Christian, the time of Bible study and prayer is one of the most effective. If your family is with you, the establishment of regular meal times and regular family devotions can be a real blessing.

▶ Request accountability. Make a checklist of the symptoms and have someone check you out every so often, so you can make the proper diagnosis and realize the true problem in your life. You may run into others who are in various stages of culture shock; learn to recognize the signs and give grace.

▶ If you cannot do it "right," fake it! Copy a reliable model of someone who has made it through. Using your best insights, go ahead and act! Do not let the fear of offending prevent your involvement.

▶ Serve hard! Do more than your share. Look for opportunities to volunteer. Have a servant's attitude. Look for some task that will lighten someone else's load. Always look for a way to help.

▶ Remember, you *do* make a difference in the lives of those in need, but perhaps on a measurably smaller scale and in painfully slower ways than those of which you had dreamed.

▶ Remember, too, God is on your side and always willing to listen!

People on short-term mission efforts commonly see certain struggles repeatedly and those bear further comment:

Cultural "Do's and Don'ts"

This is a common place to stumble. Almost by definition, things in this category are things about which you would not have any clue unless you are told about them. Failure to comply however can mark you as uncouth, rude or deliberately offensive. You can have a problem in this area with both sins of omission and sins of commission. There are things that are proper at home but may be improper there. In various cultures, you should never: Speak in a loud voice or yell. Sneeze aloud. Point at someone with your finger. Shake hands with or even touch a member of the opposite sex. Give the "OK" sign.[2] Touch anyone or hand anyone something with your left hand. Eat with your left hand. Show them the bottom of your foot when you cross your leg. Squeeze into a row of seats with your bottom facing the people already seated. A woman should not look a man in the eyes. Wink. Blink deliberately. Cross your fingers. A woman should not sit with her knees facing a man. A woman should not wear slacks at the risk of being thought a prostitute. The list is almost endless.

Conversely, things that are improper here may be proper there and take a bit of getting used to for us: Two men holding hands. Hugging a stranger. Belching loudly after a meal. Various states of dress (or undress). Encroachment on personal space.

These lists can be endless. The only way you can handle this is to ask the missionary or national for advice. Ask what the more serious blunders are and try not to make those. If the national is not used to foreigners, he may not know what to tell you until after you have erred. Ask for topics of conversation that may be unwise. If they cannot help you or you need more help, the only things you can do is to carefully watch someone of your own sex and mimic their behavior, and when that fails, laugh about your mistakes.

Trying to Deal with a New Culture

You can solve most problems with common sense and the Golden Rule administered with Christ's heart of servanthood. Therefore, it is understood that you should not yell at the nationals no matter what your level of frustration. You should not disrespect them in front of

---

[2] Axtell, Roger. Gestures: *The Do's and Taboos of Body Language Around the World.* New York: Wiley and Sons, 1991.

their peers. You should not not make fun of people and their culture. There is one rule that goes a long way: "Greet everyone." IN North American, you are not considered rude if you ignore some of the people around depending on the situation, social status, occupational status, etc. However, in most developing countries, relationships are above efficiency and time. Take time to be involved in chai (tea) breaks. Do not pretend you will ever completely cross the cultural barrier, but try. You are a guest and must adapt to their culture. Do not expect it to go the other way. They will not change easily or necessarily even give you any slack.

However, it is easy to make a blunder and not know it. It is also easy to make a well-intentioned error that can have major repercussions for the rest of the group or the career missionaries. If in doubt, please ask the missionaries for advice and put off making a decision or doing something until you have had a chance to discuss it with someone more experienced in that culture. The most common problems arise in the areas of employer-employee relationships, gifts to nationals, promises to nationals, and decision-making.

For most North Americans, the problems of household servants and knowing how to pay them are major. Most of us are not used to having servants and feel sensitive to charges of colonialism, paternalism and snobbery. We feel there is something vaguely non-Christian and un-American about it. Occasionally, our discomfort spills over and it causes trouble when we as short-termers criticize career missionaries who have decided that having house help is the only way the family caretaker can get free enough to have his/her own ministry. As Americans, we want to be egalitarian, treating everyone like equals and guests. Yet this may well conflict with the local understanding of the position of a servant in the house and with what the servant finds comfortable.

We can cause a major cultural disruption when we do not treat house help according to that society's expectations. As an example, at one large mission hospital, the short-term missionary's wife felt too guilty about paying her household help the going wage of approxi-

mately $2 a day. Instead she paid her $10 a day. It was certainly a wage
that was still a bargain by North American standards and still low
enough that she felt guilty. In a flash, the news of the national worker's
good fortunate spread widely over the compound grapevine. It had the
predictable result. All of the other women working as house help
demanded the same wage from the expatriates and national employers
alike. Most of the nationals who worked at the hospital and hired
house help could not afford that wage and the career missionaries
knew it was unwise as a matter of principle to pay something so far out
of line with the norms. This well-intentioned effort on the part of a
wealthy visitor ended up with most of the national women unemployed. They wouldn't work because they now had their pride on the
line. In addition, the missionary caretaker spouse had to cut back their
own ministry because now her day was taken up with the business of
taking care of the family, and the national employers were angry that
an "uncaring" American had been so thoughtless. It was almost two
years before things got back to normal on that compound.

On the other hand, even if the expatriate realizes that this is considered a good job for someone or that they need the help to be effective in that country, Americans have a heavily built protective wall of
personal privacy as part of their cultural norm. The presence of servants can mean an invasion of privacy. Emotionally, it is an intrusion
and they feel exposed. This can cause significant stress for some people.

In much the same way and for the same reasons, gifts to nationals
can cause significant problems. The best advice is to ask for guidance
from the missionary before mentioning or giving any gifts to nationals. In a culture where you can hire a man for $2 to work all day in the
blazing sun, a gift of a soccer ball or a pair of old jeans may represent
a gift of a month's salary. Electronics such as a portable radio or tape
player can be very expensive in those countries. The desire to give a
gift must be balanced against the concern that giving gifts to just one
or two can breed jealously, cause others to jockey for a position to
manipulate the next visitor to give gifts to them, or can make good
national Christians become materialistic. This does not mean that you

should not give. Just be very careful. Small gifts given sporadically are probably the best way to give. Also, spread the gifts around. There are some times when gifts are customary and culturally expected. In many countries, a gift is customarily given when you visit someone's home and they may give you a gift in return. It is usually best to give a locally available gift: tea, sugar, flour, fruit, etc., although a small gift from your home country may be appropriate. Ask your missionary hosts for guidance in the nature and amount of the gift.

Promises to the nationals can also be a point of major contention. As a rule, it is best not to make what seem to be insignificant promises without consulting with your career missionary. Even if you can keep the promise, it may not be an appropriate promise to give. If you cannot keep that promise, it will hurt your witness as a Christian and by extension, the reputation and witness of the work that you came to help. Be careful what you promise or half-promise. One of the most common things facing you will be the request for help with school fees. If, after you have consulted with the missionary you have promised to do it, the national will often think that you have therefore agreed to pay for all of that child's education until the end of his scholastic career, perhaps for all the other sibling's education and for every incidental they may need. This might have been far beyond your original intent. Make sure that when you give the gift, you are explicit about the terms of the gift. Also, remember that a gift once given no longer belongs to you. Do not be upset if it is not used the way you had intended or even if it is sold.

Often nationals will ask you to help get them or their family to the U.S. For example, if someone wants to go to school in the U.S. and you say, "I will see what I can do," they may believe that you have promised to find the school, pay for it and even offer to pay for lodging. Be aware that few missionaries or their organizations endorse nationals going to the States for training, and then only under very clear guidelines. Many nationals that have come to North America do not return to their homeland, or when they do return, they may no longer fit into the culture or church. In addition, sending someone to the U.S. is very expensive for the national church. It will inevitably be asked to help financially. It also splits families. If asked to help with advanced schooling, tell a national that you cannot help them, or that you will consider helping if you receive a formal request from the national church and mission and have time to discuss it and pray over it.

One last bit of advice: Be careful about giving out your address. There is a natural tendency to want to keep in touch with your new-found friends and that is laudable; however, you may receive many requests for financial help long after you leave. Many short-termers will feel obligated to help. When the requests continue and build in scope and frequency, it becomes annoying. Failure to respond proper-ly by their standards can hurt your testimony and the testimony of the work you went to help.

The last topic is the role you as a short-termer play in a chronic situation. Many national workers will see you as a new way to address an old grievance. You, of course, want to help, but precipitous action can cause major problems. Even if you are able to do something, be very conscious of the way decisions are made in that society. Do not discuss with your staff any problems concerning the hospital, inter-personal relationships, the mission, church, etc. In some cultures, you must involve everyone on the staff in any hospital issues that need to be resolved, and in other cultures you must involve the big men of the village and church and then those decisions are handed down. Again, the best decision is to ask for advice from the missionary and be very careful not to overstep your bounds.

Not Everyone Is As Impressed with You As You Are

Recognize other cultures may see the American traits that we are proud of as negative and undesirable ones. American social structure emphasizes the core family and there is generally a lack of emphasis on wider kinship bonds. For an American, convalescent homes or insti-tutions for the emotionally disturbed or mentally retarded are consid-ered a reasonable solution; for many Asians and Africans this is a scan-dal, and they do not understand our calloused attitude. Americans also emphasize associations and a differential social class structure. Movement through these various social structures is rather fluid and expected. It is a sign of ambition. These emphases within social classes are virtually unheard of in most African and Asian cultures.

American culture is based on many presuppositions that are not valued in the rest of the world. We emphasize a romantic individualism. We consider it moral, just, and even an individual obligation to be competitive and to better ourselves. This means we generally are not in favor of governmental regulation of our personal or business lives and generally believe that an individual is responsible to face the consequences of his fate without expectations of forgiveness or help.

We also have an amazing dedication to romantic love; no arranged marriages or concerns about family origin, social class, ethnic origin, public pressure or anything practical for us. It does facilitate the movement between social classes that we believe so strongly in.

We couple our emphasis on individuality with a distrust of authority. We are a nation of law-keepers but do not like to be told what to do. A sign of our distrust of the essential goodwill of authorities is the principle of limited terms of office. There is respect for parents and elders but not to the extent that is traditional in many developing countries where a grayed head alone is sufficient cause for respect and obedience.

Progress dominates almost everything an American does. New is always better. Other cultures may perceive this as dangerous and disrespectful to tradition and custom.

Optimism is another characteristic of Americans. We consider pessimism bad manners. In many cultures, this is seen as a deliberate affront to the gods and to fate and if not that blatant, at least in poor taste.

Activism is therefore a logical part of American lifestyle. If we see something that "should" be changed, then we must do what we can to change it for the better (progress) and we are fairly sure we can do it (optimism). The more uncertain the situation, the more the American "must do something." A nation of immense practicality, we are looking for ways to improve things. If we cannot actually accomplish what we hope to accomplish, at least "doing something" has a virtue in and of itself.

Success is a major factor in life. We perceive success to be potentially within the reach of everyone and if not actually achieved, one should certainly strive for it. Failure to compete is seen as a sign of shame and inadequacy. Education is important because it is a tool for success. Humor and witty repartee is part of our mobility through various social strata, and the sensitivity and gentility so prized in many cultures is not widely valued in ours.

Conformity to others is a marked characteristic of Americans, even with our emphasis on individuality. We have a right to be different, but only within certain circumscribed limits.

Our views on health and cleanliness, our obsession with time and punctuality, and our passion about financial accountability puts us in conflict with much of the world. For many North Americans, to be kept waiting 15 minutes is the ultimate of insults; for much of the world, arriving "only" 15 minutes late is remarkably considerate and punctual, if not disturbingly early. The American will spend much of the time fuming and expect an apology. The other person has no clue what is wrong. He or she only knows that the meeting is not going well. In many cultures, the view toward financial matters is different. In one example, a group of Americans and Ugandan pastors were asked what a man of integrity should do in the following situation. An American gives a man $50 with clear instructions as to how it should be spent and for what purpose. On the way, the Ugandan finds out that his mother is ill and needs the $50 for medical treatment. What should he do? To a man, the Ugandans said he should use the money that belonged to the other man to take care of his mother and then explain it to the first man. The Americans were flabbergasted that they would consider taking the money that belonged to another a Christian attitude; the Ugandan's could not believe that a Christian would do anything else but take care of his mother.

Avoid a Superior Attitude

This is a problem that is sometimes tied up with the cultural shock issue but can be a problem all of its own. It is very easy to assume that your theology is somehow superior to the "uneducated native."

Do not talk about how great things are in your home country or compare the host country to yours. Do not speak badly of the country or the people who live there. The less you talk about yourself the better. Your goal is not to build yourself up but point people towards Christ. Remember that your comments to those who came with you can be overheard. Some people will understand more English than you think. Do not talk about how wonderful things are in your home country. People already know it is. On the other hand, do not criticize it. They will not understand what they perceived disloyalty, and you may lose face for all of your witness. Do not criticize the local or national government of your new country. Criticism accomplishes nothing and at times, you can get in big trouble

Racial Issues

    Cross-racial ministry can have some unexpected emotional impact. Before they go, African-Americans returning to Africa and people of Asian heritage returning to the Far East may feel a sense of identification with the people of the area were they are serving and a sense of homecoming. To their surprise, the culture shock they feel is often more than they expected and this can be unsettling. This is due to more than the language barrier. While they may feel a sense of unity and oneness with the national people, those people will not often accept them in a reciprocal fashion. They may be judged and be received not by the color of their skin or their racial genetics but rather as a member of the culture they came from. The story is told of an African-American missionary in Africa who did not find the plate of singed caterpillars particularly palatable but he was offended when the woman of the house picked them up and carried it off muttering under her breath, "White man." One can only imagine his internal conflicts to that remark. Another African-American missionary tells of the frustration of constantly fielding questions about whether he belonged to one tribe or another. Others then treated him as they would treat the members of that tribe and the loss of identity and prestige as an American was unsettling to him. This can be good or bad depending upon the situation, but can be downright dangerous if there is serious animosity afoot.

Accepting and Rejecting Offers

We Americans take things at face value and in cultures where it is impolite to accept an offer at first offering, we often do not read the cues that tell us that this was not a serious refusal. We can get a reputation for being insincere and shallow in our offers when all along we thought we were respecting their decision. There is the tale of one American who offered a ride to a woman along the road. She refused and so he drove on, only to find out later that she was furious at him for leaving her standing along the road. In her cultural view, he should have known that she was just being polite and he should have persisted in his offer of a ride.

Relations with the Opposite Sex

The best rule when in doubt is "No PDA," no public display of affection. Most foreign cultures frown on men and women demonstrating affection in public. It is inappropriate in some cultures for even married couples to hold hands publicly, hug, kiss, or touch. Despite the obvious contradictions and problems created by the promiscuity that you may see, most cultures frown on those of the opposite sex being alone together unless married. Western style dating is an unknown (and immoral) concept to them. The best advice to you is to avoid getting romantically involved with nationals of the opposite sex. Even if you have, or would like to have, a relationship with someone on your own team, wait until you return home to express it.

Dress

Most missionaries are not fuddy-duddies even if you think they dress that way. They are adapting to the local culture. In many places, pants, sleeveless blouses, short skirts, excessive jewelry, noticeable makeup, and other things may be a bad witness. It is not a legalistic issue but rather a question of Christian liberty as Paul talks about. Do not harm your Christian brother or sister through your actions or become a stumbling block to them. You gave up your rights at the cross. Adapt to what is proper locally.

Local dress may be a point of trouble for you. Please understand that just because someone is immodestly dressed by your standard, that does not mean that they are immodest by his or her own standards, or that they are not a follower of Jesus. For example, in some cultures, a bare-breasted woman does not draw a second glance but a woman who shows the shape of her thighs is considered highly provocative. In our culture, we would consider the bare breast highly erotic but a woman dressed in slacks or shorts would ordinarily not draw a second glance. Mark Lowery, the Christian comedian, often makes the comment that he learned many things in Bible school that he didn't read in the Bible! Modesty is definitely a Biblical concept but the definition is not given.

Habits

In many foreign cultures, the church body forbids alcohol and tobacco use; in Islamic countries, alcohol is banned in any amount and breaking the law can land you in jail. You should refrain from using either alcohol or tobacco while you are on your trip and that includes the time you are traveling or away from the mission. Obviously, drug use is in the same category, and in almost every country of the world, possession of illicit substances may land you in jail for a long time without access to your American rights. Do not even carry unlabeled prescription drugs: those jails are not fun.

Whether rightly or wrongly, others will see as a missionary from the time you leave home until you return. They will scrutinize your actions with that assumption firmly in mind. Again, the use of alcohol and tobacco is an issue of Christian liberty. Are you being an obstacle to the spiritual development of others? Certainly, in the few weeks you have, you will not make a sweeping impact for change by arguing and demonstrating your idea of Christian liberty. However, you can destroy a lot if you persist in selfish behavior.

Smells

The smells may be indescribable. You will get used to them. One frustration you will find when you get home is that none of your pictures will be quite the same without the accompanying odors.

Missionary presentations will never be the same once someone perfects "Aroma-Vision."

Language

Language, or more exactly the inability to communicate verbally, is one of the biggest causes of culture shock. As previously recommended, it will make an enormous amount of difference to you if you learn a little or as much as possible of the local language before you leave. Take up classes and practice it as much as you can; if you are studying Thai, eat out at Thai restaurants and try to practice your Thai. This small step will make your life a lot simpler and will give you immediate respect when you arrive in the foreign country. Just a few words can open many new doors. If you show an interest in the other person's language and culture, they will show an interest in you.

Even if you learn only a few phrases, it is worthwhile. However, the short-termer must remember that even the use of his or her native English has its own problems in the foreign culture. An obvious warning to the short-term missionary is avoid the use profane language and be careful about using slang. The use of profanity may ruin your testimony and the use of slang or idiom may cause you to be misunderstood. Be careful about comparing anyone to any animal, even in jest. "You are acting like a monkey!" will not be interpreted as a joke in many cultures. "Eating like a pig" would be very offensive in others. In general, do not speak or laugh loudly to draw attention to yourself in an inappropriate way. Remember always to guard your tongue. More people than you think often understand the uncharitable observation, the biting comment, and the smart-aleck criticism. They may understand English better than they let on and such inopportune comments can ruin your witness.

For most short-termers, there is not a serious attempt to learn the local language, largely because the short time does not warrant the effort. For those staying longer periods, language barriers and the difficulty of language school can be a major source of culture shock and is perhaps the one thing that can shake their confidence down to the bedrock. The newcomer to a culture knows no language and that ignorance strips him of his primary method of communicating with people. He is subject to constant mistakes, often laughed at and placed on the level of a child—and sometimes treated accordingly. After weeks and months of study, he can perhaps discuss the price of a poke of potatoes but certainly not physics. He cannot display his own education and intelligence, the symbols that gave him status and prestige at home. He meets intelligent and educated people but he responds like a child or idiot because he can do no better.

> *"You can learn more from a missionary in half an hour than you can pick up yourself in a couple months of travel."*
>
> —William Borden

The process of language study itself can be highly stressful. Many people do not like to practice or work at something they don't understand, but they can't understand without practicing. If they cling to the crutch of translation, they will spend their time desperately trying to find out how to translate the things they want to say into a local language. This is a poor substitute for the true knowledge of the language, for even if they can preach a fully translated sermon, it does not mean they know the language. Parroting is the not the same as understanding. To understand a language is to understand a worldview and the underpinnings of a culture.

The language learner has the uneasy feeling that people are laughing behind his back—and often they are. The study is tiring, boring and frustrating. It is not logical to him because the new language is based on entirely different paradigms of thinking than he has used before. It is easy for the learner to blame the teacher, the study pattern of learning, and the techniques of teaching. To avoid the stress, the learner can demonstrate psychosomatic illness, or become so involved administrative work or trips that it justifies the claim that he is too busy to learn the language.

Language training can also cause the shock of self-discovery. Most relationships have defined roles and the study of language can disrupt those. The "airhead" spouse may find he or she has a real gift for language and finds it easy. The highly erudite partner can't put three words together after weeks of study. It begins to interfere with their self-esteem and the perception of their relationship. For the person who usually has a long habit of success, such failure can be devastating. For the person with a long habit of failure, such success can be exhilarating and change his/her whole life. Emotional frustration can be evident and the mechanisms for psychological support, which would have worked in their old environment, may have been totally removed.

While the short-termer is unlikely to undergo these dynamics for the reasons mentioned, it may be obvious in your dealings with the newer career missionary. A better understanding of their stress may facilitate your relationships.

Other Hints

▶ Stay out of prison. You have no rights in most countries and being an American helps very little, if at all.

▶ Be aware of local curfews, especially in some Asian countries. They mean them.

▶ Do not spit or chew gum in most Asian countries. It will get you jailed in Singapore.

▶ Avoid exchanging money on the black-market. Even if the rates are more attractive, it is called the black-market because it is illegal and therefore both carries some risk and is against Christian principles of honoring the law. There are some "gray markets" and whether to use those is a personal decision. Look into it very carefully and get advice from the missionaries.

▶ Do not buy inappropriate souvenirs. Fully understand the regulations of the country you are visiting regarding what may be removed from their borders. In general, items made from endangered animals or species are forbidden and the removal of "national artifacts" is illegal. Icons, archaeological relics, historical relics, fossils, etc. may fall into this category. Also understand what items may be restricted for import into your home country and any countries you may stop in on your itinerary. Import of vegetables, fruits, seeds, some wooden objects, and the sort of thing discussed above is usually forbidden to prevent the introduction of disease, the destruction of species or the destruction of cultural integrity.

There are three rules to remember that may help:[3]

Remember, you are not a tourist. Everyone is familiar with the concept of the "ugly American." Like many stereotypes, there is often enough of a kernel of truth to perpetuate the stereotype. Tourists are overall self-centered. They have come to get their money's worth in sights and sounds. They want everyone to know how important and wealthy they are. They want to be comfortable and pampered and take home pictures and curios to brag about their trip. If you act like a tourist, they treat you like a tourist. Nationals will be looking to see what money or things they can get out of you. There may be a time on your scheduled trip when you can do everything that is not recommended in this book and act just like a tourist—when the men can break out the Bermuda shorts, undershirts, wing tips and knee-high socks and the women can wear something inappropriate for the local culture—but the time is probably not now.

Remember, you are a missionary. Act like one. Since this is written largely to medical professionals and their family, most of you have strong memories of the first time that you put on the accoutrements of your profession. The starched white coat or uniform made you feel something like an impostor, but in assuming the role, you assumed and gradually accepted the new perceptions of others toward you. As a missionary, you are an ambassador of your church, your country, and your King of Kings. You should act accordingly and the best model is Christ Himself. He traveled from God's throne room to serve—not to be served; to love—not to be loved; and to be humble—not to exalt his self.

The obvious conclusion is that if you walk like a duck and quack like a duck, people will think you are a duck. If you are working with missionaries, nationals will automatically think of you as a missionary.

---

[3] Modified from the CMDA *Mission Survival Kit.*

They expect the same conduct and witness out of you as they do a long-term missionary. Do not jeopardize the standing of the hospital, mission, church, or of the Lord by insisting on locally and culturally unacceptable behaviors. For example, you may feel you have the liberty to smoke or drink and not have it compromise your Christian standards, but most cultures find those two behaviors incomprehensible for a Christian. Criteria for modesty and appropriate behavior between the sexes are other common areas in conflict. As Paul wrote in Chapter 14 of Romans, there are differences among Christian brothers and sisters, but "make up your mind not to put any stumbling block or obstacle in your brother's way." (v. 13)

Remember, you are a guest. You are a guest in the missionary's home, in the host church, in the host hospital, and in the host country. Make your mother proud. Be grateful and be appreciative. Do not complain. Look for opportunities to help, no matter how menial the task. Remember, you do not know anything about living and working in that culture. Assume the missionaries and nationals have figured out the best way of doing things from the options available. What works at home, likely is not available there or does not work in that culture. Remember that many missionaries think there should be an immediate death sentence to anyone who utters the words, "You should do it this way," or asks the question, "Why don't you do . . . ?" Such statements and questions can be demoralizing and insulting.

In summary, culture shock is real and there are certain people who can handle it better than others do. There are coping mechanisms that can be learned by anyone, but the Christian has a powerful helping mechanism if it is taken advantage of. There must be a renewed commitment to Christ. Cultural adaptation gets at the true meaning of Biblical self-denial. It involves a conversion, a discovery of one's true self, and a change in that self. Instead of symptoms of rejection and insecurity, there comes an objective knowledge of ones strengths and weaknesses. With that knowledge comes a relaxed acceptance of one's self, a determination to do one's best without pretense. This is added to God's promise that "I can do everything through him [Christ] who gives me strength." (Philippians 4:13)

To be well adjusted is to live sensibly, adapting to local patterns as far as is practical, to feel a creative sense of identification, but not to have lost objectivity in selection of the life and values you are to follow. Adaptation is not based on pathological rejection but on wholesome selection of what is valuable from all cultural streams with which you come in contact.

Luke 10:1–2 reads, *After this the Lord appointed seventy-two others and sent them two by two ahead of him to every town and place where he was about to go. He told them, "The harvest is plentiful, but the workers are few. Ask the Lord of the harvest, therefore, to send out workers into his harvest field."* He gave some other instructions about how they were to handle their reception. They too were probably apprehensive about their experience, but in verse 17, it says they "returned with joy." May you too follow Christ's commands for your life, and return with joy!

> "The traveler sees what he sees, the tourist sees what he has come to see."
>
> —Gilbert K. Chesteron

CHAPTER 11

FEEDING AND WATERING THE FAMILY— AND YOURSELF

Everyone who goes overseas needs to read this chapter. However, it is aimed particularly at the spouse who becomes the primary care taker of the family. In the chapter on health, we talked about traveler's diarrhea and the other sorts of diarrhea that can come from parasitic infestation (amoeba and Giardia). How to avoid such things is largely a matter of great care in what you eat and drink.

WATER

According to the U.N. World Health Organization (WHO), contaminated water is the largest health problem in the world. Waterborne gastrointestinal infections account for 80% of all disease in the world, and more than 50,000 people are killed each day by waterborne pathogens.

Waterborne pathogens (disease-causing organisms) fall into three categories: protozoa (including the cysts), bacteria, and viruses. Protozoa, one-celled animals varying in size from 2 to 100 microns (one micron is one-millionth of a meter, or 0.00004 inches), live in many insects and animals, and survive in cysts (protective shells) when outside of an organism. They include *Giardia lamblia* and *Cryptosporidium*, both common contaminants in almost any surface water and many other sources. Because protozoa reproduce so rapidly inside a host organism, ingesting only a few can cause disease. Symptoms include severe diarrhea, abdominal cramps, bloating, and fatigue and weight loss. They can be hard to diagnose and are responsible for many chronic cases of diarrhea.

Protozoa can be considerably larger than some bacteria. Bacteria may measure as little as 0.2 microns. We live in symbiosis with many bacteria, but other types cause a variety of infectious diseases, including typhoid, paratyphoid, dysentery, coliform diarrhea and cholera. Once in water, they can survive for weeks, or even longer if frozen in ice.

Viruses are the smallest agents of disease, and perhaps the most problematic. Because they are as minute as 0.004 microns, they can pass through the smallest filter. Waterborne viruses that can cause serious problems frequently in the developing countries include hepatitis A and E, Norwalk virus, rotavirus, echovirus and poliovirus. Viral diarrhea is a common problem, especially in children, but is usually self-limited. The hepatitis viruses and polioviruses are potentially life-threatening. Since there is no good treatment for viruses, they are particularly dangerous, especially among immunocompromised populations.

Water is a major concern. Much of the world's drinking supply is contaminated and you must be on constant guard to avoid becoming sick. Nothing like a few days of nausea and diarrhea to take the edge off your mission experience!

What are your choices in obtaining clear and safe drinking water?

1. Carbonated bottled (or canned) water is perhaps the safest option but many people don't like the carbonation or the taste. It also has the disadvantage of being expensive and often is hard to obtain. The idea of rushing your teeth with carbonated water is often more than you can stand the first thing in the morning! Even if you use this, be careful that the area of the can or bottle touching your mouth is dry and clean.

2. Bottled water: in terms of practicality, availability, and convenience, this is often the best choice. However, be forewarned that quality assurance programs in the developing countries are not always what they are in the developed countries. Before they go, one mission agency routinely checks bottled water in the country where they are going to undertake short-term building projects and have found as many as 50% of the samples they have taken are contaminated with coliform (fecal) bacteria. Bottled water is widely available in urban settings and is not too expensive. However, it may not be available if you are in rural areas or in the bush. A hint: in a restaurant, always

open the bottle of water yourself or watch it being opened to make sure the seal is intact. There are rumors of entrepreneurs reusing these bottles and refilling them from local water sources.

3. Tap water: it is rare outside of North America and Europe that tap water is safe to drink (potable)—and not always safe in those two continents! The best advice is to avoid even brushing your teeth with the tap water. Even be careful about getting the water in your mouth when you take a shower. There are several options available to purify your tap water (or rainwater from a cistern). Ranked in increasing efficiency in terms of both turbidity and microbiological safety, they are filters, chemical decontamination, boiling, and purifiers.

Filter bottles & systems do exactly that. They filter. They are relatively inexpensive but there is no germicidal activity. These have some sort of ceramic, charcoal or cartridge filter and come in various sizes from individual bottles to larger multi-gallon ones capable of filtering water for the household. The size of the filter pore determines the efficacy in filtering both sediments and infectious agents. There are regular filters that are effective against protozoa and some bacteria. There are micro-pore filters that can filter many bacteria (but not all and certainly not viruses). Virtually all will improve the clarity by removing the sediment, but obviously, the more sediment in the water, the shorter the life of the filter and the sooner the filter will need to be replaced or cleaned. Micro-pore filters clog with sediment or silt more easily. Maximum safety can be achieved by either adding a form of chemical decontaminant (iodine or chlorine drops or tablets) before or after the filtering, or by boiling the water before or after it is filtered. If you decide to boil the water before you filter it, do NOT pour the hot water through the filter. It can ruin the filter and destroy its effectiveness.

Chemical decontamination is achieved by the use of iodine or chlorine to decontaminate the water. These are effective against virtually all parasites, bacteria and viruses if you let it work long enough. Use chlorine in solution (4–6% concentration). Two drops of the concentrated solution are used per liter. For disinfection with iodine, use either tincture of iodine or tetraglycine hydroperiodide tablets, such as

Globaline®* and Potable-Aqua®. Use iodine as the tablets per the package instruction or as a 2% tincture, using 5–10 drops per liter. If the water is cloudy, double the contact time. Other forms of iodine tablets are used to purify the water and should be used as the label directs. Many sports and camping stores carry these tablets. Enough for 25 liters will cost $5–6. Chemicals, if used properly, have the advantage of making the water safe from the standpoint of biological agents but it is impossible to always be sure you have used enough. These chemicals may taint the taste of the water and there is some concern about the long-term (over many months) use of iodine. Obviously, this technique does not remove turbidity or sediment. Letting the water settle and using only the clear water is one option. As mentioned above, filtering it is another option.

Boiling is perhaps the best method from the standpoint of biological decontamination but obviously does nothing for silt and sediment. Filtering before or after is an option to make the water clearer. It is somewhat inconvenient, requires large kettles or pots, a heat source, and must be done frequently to keep enough water available for your use. It does have the advantage of being able to make larger amounts of water available for larger numbers of people. At sea level, bring water to a vigorous boil for at least 5 minutes (10 minutes is better). At higher altitude, you must boil even longer because water boils at a lower temperature than it does at sea level.

ELEVATION	WATER BOILS °F	WATER BOILS °C	MINUTES TO BOIL WATER
0	212	100.0	5
500	211	99.4	6
1,500	209	98.3	8
2,500	207	97.2	10
5,000	202	94.4	15
6,000	200	93.3	17
7,000	198	92.2	20
8,000	196	91.1	23
9,000	194	90.0	27
10,000	192	88.9	32

Pressure: Pressure water at 15 pounds for 5 minutes. Pressuring is more efficient than boiling, especially above 7,000 feet.

Purifiers are devices that have both some sort of micropore filter that removes sediment and larger microbiological agents as well as an iodinated resin that purifies the remainder. The model mentioned below also has a carbon filter as the last step to remove the iodine and other undesirable taste in the water. This also improves its effectiveness against certain other contaminants like lead, arsenic, asbestos fibers, and pesticides. It is the size of a sports bottle and has the advantage of portability and easy use from a variety of potential water sources. Unlike filters, purifiers must be registered with the U.S. Environmental Protection Agency to demonstrate effectiveness.[1] This certification does NOT help you judge between the effectiveness of the various models. Claims are made that penta-iodide resins are more effective than tri-iodide resins but we have not been able to find good scientific comparisons between the two. There are also claims that one type of system is more effective at removing residual iodine from the water than the other. Again, direct comparisons between available systems under rigid testing protocols are lacking. They are effective in treating from 100–500 liters depending on the quality of the water. The Katadyn Extreamwater bottles (penta-iodide resin) are available from www.tealbrook.com or many other retailers and are approximately $44–$52 retail for a 26 ounce system. Be aware that the iodine is radiodense (i.e. blocks x-rays) and often security procedures at the airport which use x-rays will show the unusual rectangle and will cause your bag to be searched. Putting it in the x-ray basket where its nature is obvious may stop unnecessary searches but it may still be questioned since these systems are not common.

---

[1] Unlike water filters, water purifiers sold in the United States are required to be registered with the United States Environmental Protection Agency (EPA). To receive such registration, a product must demonstrate that it meets strict EPA standards under a rigorous testing protocol. The EPA protocol requires that to be registered as a "microbiological water purifier," a device must remove, kill or deactivate all types of disease-causing microorganisms from the water, including bacteria, viruses and protozoan cysts, so as to render the processed water safe for drinking. The device must perform under a broad range of pHs, flow rates and temperatures in water containing added organic carbon and particulate matter.

The relatively new SteriPEN® (manufactured by Hydro-Photon) uses C wavelength ultraviolet light to automatically purify clear water. It works rapidly (48 seconds for 1/2 liter and 90 seconds for 1 liter) and is effective. Used as directed, it has been shown to destroy over: 99.9999% of bacteria, 99.99% of viruses and 99.9% of protozoa (i.e. Giardia and Cryptosporidium). These levels of destruction exceed the requirements of the U.S. EPA's Guide Standard and Protocol for Testing Microbiological Water Purifiers. Water with significant discoloration or particulates can reduce effectiveness of UV sterilization by inhibiting the penetration of the light through the water. The sediment should be filtered (a 4 micron accessory filter comes with it) or allowed to settle. The approximate cost is $60–$100 depending on the model. It fits into your pocket and is battery operated. Cleaning it is easy and the light bulb is good for several years. It is cost effective compared to the iodine/charcoal filters if you will use it for multiple trips, multiple people or a combination of both, but does not have the benefit of activated charcoal in removing undesirable taste in the water and does not remove sediment.

At a couple of the mission stations where we have served, there was enthusiasm for putting your drinking water in clear plastic bottles (empty soft drink bottles) and leaving them in the sun for a full day. If an unlabeled PET bottle is used, this system is 99.9% effective for bacteria and viruses if the water is greater than 40 degrees Celsius for six hours or more, but parasites are less sensitive to sunlight. While giardia cysts are rendered inactive within 6 hours, cryptosporidia cysts must be exposed to direct sunlight for at least 10 hours before they are neutralized. Amoebas do not die until the water temperature has been warmer than 50°C for over an hour (www.sodis.ch). The other methods are easier.

When do you start worrying about these things? From the time your plane leaves a developed country. If you plane's catering service was done in one of the cities where you would not drink the water, do not drink the water on the plane unless it is bottled and do not use ice in your drinks. Once you are at your station of service, make all of your ice with purified water. Freezing does not reliably kill bacteria or viruses.

FOOD

The old saw for travelers is "If you don't cook it or peel it, forget it!" Obviously, there is going to be a difference on how you approach things if you are doing your own food preparation, eating at a restaurant or at someone's home.

Let's take eating out at a restaurant first. What kind of restaurant should you choose? Find out where the expatriates eat. That is often a good choice but not invariably failsafe. Think about what kind of food you want (or are likely to get) and how it might be prepared. Chinese restaurants are often a good bet because of the fact that is everything is cooked to order (therefore it is hot and hasn't sat around), food is rarely served raw or fresh and the restaurants are amazingly ubiquitous. What about your menu choices? Don't eat fresh salads or anything with uncooked vegetables, raw meat or shellfish. Be aware that some fish can be toxic at unpredictable times. Some fish are not guaranteed to be safe even when cooked because of the presence of toxins in their flesh. Tropical reef fish, red snapper, amber jack, grouper, and sea bass can occasionally be toxic at unpredictable times if they are caught on tropical reefs rather than in the open ocean. The barracuda and puffer fish are often toxic, and should generally not be eaten. Highest risk areas for those toxins include the islands of the West Indies, and the tropical Pacific, and Indian Oceans. Other possibly unsafe foods and beverages include: moist food at room temperature (sauces, salads, buffet offerings), dairy products (including milk unless ultra heat-treated or reconstituted milk made with safe water), and never forget tap water and ice cubes can be dangerous. Generally safe food and beverages include: steaming hot foods, dry foods including breads, high sugar content foods (jellies and syrups), thick-skinned fruits you peel yourself, bottled drinks in their original containers (be sure to clean the top of the container), and coffee and tea, if served steaming hot.

If your food is cooked, make sure it is hot and fully cooked. Fruit is okay if you peel it with clean hands or instruments, but may possibly be contaminated if peeled by others. Wash the outside of the fruit before peeling (this may be hard to do in a restaurant. Avoid food sold by street vendors, even if the missionary is eating it, unless it is piping hot. The missionary's gut has become used to many of the bacteria he or she sees in that country and therefore he or she won't get sick. You might. One short-termer related that he thinks the most dangerous words he ever hears on trips is "Go ahead, eat it. I eat it all the time."

If you are invited out for a meal, there is only one thing to do—accept! Please don't let the concerns about disease prevent you from experiencing their hospitality. Friendship and hospitality involves food and the sharing of meals the world over. Eating together is very important. The word for "friend" in the Wahgi language of Papua New Guinea literally means "one who eats with another." Don't let this become one of the things you wished you had done. Check with your missionary friends to see if there are any rules about eating that you need to know. For example, in many cultures, your left hand is considered unclean because that is the one you use for your intimate self-care. Therefore, you should never touch food or a dish of food with your left hand. Find out if there are any other cultural habits that apply. In some places, it is rude to leave any food on your plate and in others, cleaning your

COOKBOOKS WE'VE FOUND HELPFUL

Bideshi Baburchi II—Western Cooking in an Eastern World
200 recipes in English and Bengali

The Four Ingredient Cookbooks
Coffee, Linda and E. Cale,

The Fannie Farmer Cookbook: Anniversary Edition
Cunningham, Marion, et al

Easy Chef's One Million of the World's Best Recipes
CD-ROM

Make-A-Mix
Eliason, Karine, N. Harward, M. Westover

Grandma's Wartime Baking Book
Hayes, Joanne Lamb

Grandma's Wartime Kitchen
Hayes, Joanne Lamb

(cont'd on p. 223)

plate means you are still hungry. In those cultures, you signify your satiety by leaving a bit of food. In some cultures, belching at the table is unbelievably rude; in others, it is the highest compliment to the cook. In some cultures, they serve the males first, women second and children last.

Most of the nationals you will meet have an understanding of water-borne diseases. They will often stretch their budget to buy bottles of water or soda that you can drink. They are not usually offended if you ask if the drinking water you are offered has been boiled, especially if you make some sort of comment that you have a "delicate stomach" and have to watch certain things. They have grown up in a culture of gastrointestinal disease and are understanding of such problems. In many cultures, they will offer you a basin and water to wash you hands before you eat. Carrying a small bottle of waterless cleaner as a backup is a good idea if you can do it unobtrusively. Carrying your purifier sports bottle (unobtrusively) is also an option.

As far as the food itself, use the same principles in someone's home that you would use in the restaurant, at least as far as propriety and good manners will allow. Try everything unless you absolutely know you can't handle it. Remember the old missionary credo,

(cont'd from p. 222)

Jungle Camp Cook Book
Summer Institute of Linguistics

More-with-Less Cookbook
Longacre, Doris Janzen,
    Mennonite Central
    Committee

Extending the Table: Recipes
and
    Stories from Argentina to
    Zambia in the spirit of
    More-with-Less
Schlabach, Joetta

The Wycliffe International
    Cookbook, 4th ed.
Williams, Gaylyn, T. Whalin
(ed.)

Download the full bibliography from www.S3ministries.com for full details.

"Where He leads me, I will follow. What He feeds me, I will swallow." Try praying Dr. Bob Pierce's famous prayer, "Lord, thank you for this food and protect me from it." In a more serious strain of thought, if you are seriously concerned about what you may have ingested, a single tablet of doxycycline or a fluroquinolone when you return home can minimize your risks of getting ill.

Cooking at home on the mission field has three steps and each can be problematic: acquiring the food, making the food safe, and cooking it. For something you took for granted at home, it is amazing how stressful food preparation can become when you are on the field. Grocery shopping in the third world has four problems to overcome. You must face the strangeness of the market itself, deal with the lack of familiar brands, improvise when faced with the lack of whatever you actually need, and figure out what you should do with foods you have never seen before.

Commonly, shopping is done in two ways. In some areas, most staples are available in stores that will be familiar in concept to you. They may be small and carry only a few items of a limited inventory, but you will know how to shop there. The remainder of your groceries, especially the green groceries, will be available in an open market. In other locales, everything is available at the market and you just have to wander and look for what you need. As a general rule, items in the stores are at a fixed, predetermined price. Items in the market may either be fixed or open to negotiation. Ask your advisor which system prevails where you are. With time, you will find that you can pick up a fair bit of the language or do very well with just pointing and using a calculator to show the price you are offering. They may then take it from you and punch in their counteroffer. It is fun! See the chapter on bargaining for some more hints.

If the price is flexible where you are shopping, always realize that there is likely a dual-pricing structure. This is not a deliberate strategy they learned in Business 101 but it is real nonetheless. There is missionary (expatriate) pricing (often laughingly referred to as a "skin tax") and there is pricing for their friends and neighbors. With time, the difference will get smaller and smaller and it is a sign that you have (1) learned to bargain and (2) become accepted. Just accept it and have fun with it. It is never enough money that you will go broke or go hungry. If it is too high, just laugh and refuse to buy.

Since you probably don't want to face this experience of shopping alone for the first time, take someone with you and let them be your guide to the "dos and don'ts" of the market place as well as serving as your interpreter. Before you go, have a pocketful of small coins in the size you are likely to need. You don't want to flash large bills out in the market (for your own safety) and secondly, they are unlikely to have enough to break the bill in the first place. Secondly, check with your missionary friends to see if you need to carry your own shopping bags. In some places, they are provided or can be purchased for a small sum and in other places, you are expected to bring your own. If you have a protracted shopping trip planned, consider hiring one of the nationals you are familiar with to sit and watch your car and goods to prevent thievery while you continue to shop. Also, consider borrowing a cooler from the missionaries to put your foods in to keep them from wilting in the tropical sun.

When shopping for fruits, vegetables (and sometimes eggs), ask your shopping companion which foods may be delivered to the door to be purchased there. That may affect your decision on how much to buy. Try some of the more exotic appearing fruits and vegetables. Use this as an opportunity to get to know one of the national women later when they show you how to use and prepare these items. Often in the marketplace, a little child will offer to carry your things for a tip. This can be a nice service if you are carrying a lot. Most of all enjoy the experience! It sure isn't like home and that is why you came.

In buying dairy products, be sure that milk, cheese, and other dairy products have been pasteurized. In the developing countries, much of the milk is available as UHT (ultra-high temperature) and is packaged in bags or boxes that do not have to be refrigerated until opened.

In buying meat, freshness is the major thing. If you have access to stores that handle frozen, prepackaged meat that is perhaps the safest way to buy it. However, such stores may be few and far between where you are. Ask the missionaries where they buy meat and what times of day or the week are the best to buy it. Here are a couple of hints: much of the meat is rather tough. The use of a meat tenderizer (either the hammer type or the ones with dozens of tiny blades) may help. Powdered papain ("meat tenderizer" or green papaya) may be helpful as well. Pressure-cooking is another way to handle these cuts and make them a little easier on your jaws. Also, since contamination of the meat is always a concern, be sure you clean your cutting boards and utensils very carefully. Wiping them down with the bleach water or other disinfectant is a good idea to prevent cross-contamination with something else.

It would not be honest if we didn't mention that you will find yourself with strange cravings for foods that you might never have had back home. Don't worry, you are probably not pregnant! Some of the cravings will be predictable and do your best to bring the food with you or find recipes to make them. Other expatriates will share some of those cravings. Ask them. They may already know where to find what you need to satisfy the cravings! Make a point of trying some new local delicacies. You may find yourself craving those when you return home!

Preparation of Your Food

The idea of putting bleach on your food probably never struck you as a desirable thing to do back in North America. However, it is a wonderful disinfectant and allows you the luxury of having foods that you might otherwise have to forswear until you get home. Put a small amount of tincture of iodine or sodium hypochlorite (bleach) in water. An ounce is enough for several liters. An older alternative is potassium permanganate (two small crystals dissolved in the water to make a light. Scrub your vegetables and fruits with a vegetable brush to remove all visible dirt. Disassemble heads of lettuce and stalks of celery and then soak the food for 30 minutes in the bleach water (or potassium permanganate). Rinse copiously with safe water (boiled or treated, not tap water). If your vegetables wilt with this technique, soak them with safe water to restore their crispness (the refrigerator might help here). Only scrub what you will use that day. Scrubbing the protective layers off some vegetables and fruit will cause them to spoil sooner. Wash your hand frequently but rinse with safe water. Wear an apron to protect your clothes from bleach splashes.

Use purified water for all ice, beverages, all uncooked foods or foods that are cooked for less than 15 minutes or baked less than 30 minutes. Use purified water to wash all foods to be eaten raw as described above.

To wash your dishes, add one tablespoon (15 milliliters = 1/2 ounce) of household bleach to the detergent and dishwater. Pour boiling water over the washed dishes and allow to dry rapidly. Store in a covered area.

Cooking

Often the guesthouse where you are staying has been the recipient of an odd collection of pots, pans and utensils. Check with the station hostess by phone, letter or e-mail before you arrive and ask what is available. If you have enough room in your luggage, you might consider getting a basic set of pots and pans, utensils, plastic mixing bowls, plastic storage bowls and the like and bring them with you. You can pack things inside these containers to take up less room. If you do not have adequate luggage room, see if it would be possible to buy some after you land, or see if the missionary can get them for you. Be sure to reimburse them for their trouble. In either event, when you return home leave them in the guesthouse for future use. As mentioned above, a pressure cooker is a nice thing to have and often not available in developing countries.

Before you leave, consider collecting a series of simple recipes that your family likes and that do not use esoteric ingredients. There are some cookbooks listed in the sidebar on pages 222–223 that are helpful to have. They make great gifts to your missionary hosts, as well. Also, talk with the other missionaries and find out what recipes they use. They are more than willing to share the recipes, especially if you swap them some of your own. When you review these recipes, make a list of the recipes and flavorings that you need and either take them, or check with the missionaries to see if they are easily available in country. Liquid extracts such as vanilla, almond, and maple flavoring are always good to have for baking (and making homemade syrup). Italian seasoning, poultry seasoning, beef and chicken bouillon, taco mixes, envelopes of powdered sauces, cinnamon, nutmeg, rosemary, thyme, mixed herbs, cumin, dried garlic, dried onion, ginger are all things to consider. In some countries, these spices and mixes are readily available and in others, not available at all.

Storing your food

Ants, roaches and bugs galore await you. The only way to control these is the judicious use of insecticides and the compulsive use of airtight containers—and the first doesn't work too well, because there are more of them than there is of you! Starving them out is the only reasonable approach. Eat only at the table, wipe up all spills immediately and store your food in airtight containers. Plastic bags and twists (or rubber bands) are available most places you will serve. Resealable bags of various sizes are not always available but are easy to pack, and you will be glad you did. With careful washing and re-use, they can last an amazingly long time. Resealable plastic containers (e.g. RubberMaid® or Tupperware®), especially those of square or rectangular shape, are inexpensive in North America, easily packed, do a great job of keeping your small items together in your luggage and make much appreciated items when left or given as gifts. All food, including flour, sugar and various mixes, needs to be carefully stored, all spills cleaned up and cereal and bread either stored in airtight containers or in the refrigerator. Instruct your family how important this is and if necessary, make it a game with penalties for failure to comply. If you are lucky, it may even carry over to when you get home. One other hint: Some folks put the feet of a cupboard in pans of water or water with a little kerosene in it to keep ants from getting into the cupboard.

CHAPTER 12

BARGAINING, BUYING,
BRIBES AND BEGGARS

There are some things that are ubiquitous in many, if not most, of the developing countries and how you adjust to them will in large part affect your experience. You might with care never have to face a situation calling for a bribe, but it is hard to get by without ever buying something and almost impossible to avoid all beggars on your trip. These are things that North Americans do not handle well.

In some cultures, shopping for anything, from a bolt to a car, involves bargaining. We are the first to admit that fortunately God in His grace seems to match up couples in this regard so no one ultimately starves. Either the husband loves the haggling and his wife hates it, or she loves it and he hates it. Bargaining has its own rules, often attended by little hints and clues to which you must be culturally attuned to understand. Knowing that you may never be a great bargainer, you certainly don't want to offend either. Your options are: take a national with you who can bargain for you, take a missionary with you, or just sally forth realizing the worst thing that can happen to you is that you will pay too much. Oh, be sure to take along your patience and your sense of humor. You will need both.

Not all cultures bargain, as you already know. Some will bargain in certain situations but not in others. For example, in some cultures, you always bargain in the market place or at your door, but never in traditional shops. In others, you never bargain in the market but always at your door. If you are uncertain, ask your hosts or watch the others around you. If they are having lively debates over the cost and value of items, you are free to do so as well. If you don't see anyone bargaining, it is never improper to ask, "Do you give a discount?" or "Is that your best price?" Sometimes, yes means yes and sometimes it means yes until you begin to walk out the door and they come after you. There are some rules that will serve you well in almost any market:

▶ Remember, they will not sell you what they cannot afford to sell no matter what protests they make.

▶ Prices are usually not marked. Don't ask unless you are seriously considering buying. If you ask, you will be pestered to buy everything. It is obvious that you are a Rich American. Be polite when you refuse.

▶ If you are uncertain whether you are paying much too high a price, ask a national friend or expatriate. Avoid overpaying. Paying a ridiculously high price makes it harder for the next expatriate to pay a more reasonable price.

▶ Their first offer is often 200–300% of what it is worth. In the negotiation, never name the first price unless you know exactly what it is worth. You will either overpay (if they accept it), or you will be accused of insulting them (usually as a bargaining ploy but sometimes in earnest). If you don't know the item's worth, try a counter-offer of 1/3 of the price they named.

▶ Buying in quantity gives you an edge in any bargaining.

▶ Be prepared to hear frequently one of the opening gambits: "Special price for my friends," "First sale of morning good luck so offer you a special price." Anyone who truly believes those statements needs to watch out for someone selling a bridge or a nice piece of swampland.

▶ Walking away increases your bargaining power.

▶ If you see something you are interested in, do not keep returning to it. Obvious desire gives them leverage.

▶ Have fun, joke, smile and above all, be polite and do not show anger. Try to enjoy the experience.

▶ Bargaining does not commit you unless you mutually agree upon a price. If you have agreed upon a price, it is a "gentlemen's agreement." They will not push the price back up but you *must* buy at that price. Further attempts to push it down or reneging on the deal will break the trust relationship and give you (and by extension, other expatriates) a bad name. This is poor intercultural behavior.

▶ A repeat: Remember, they will not sell you what they cannot afford to sell no matter what protests they make.

There is nothing that is more frustrating and less clear than the area of bribery. The big question is always whether it is a gift, a tip or a bribe? Someone who puts out a hand or asks for a monetary consideration in exchange for what they should otherwise do seems to be a clearly defined situation but it is often not clear cut.[1] The best thing to do is to ask your missionary friends whether a request is likely, and if so, when and where you might expect to face such problems. The most important answer to get from them is what you should do if asked. Does the mission have any written or firm policies on such matters?

How do you create your own philosophy? First of all, not all "bribery" is bribery. The expatriate must realize that sometimes the lower-level officials with whom you deal literally do not have the budget that it takes to comply with your request. For example, once we needed a social worker to fill out reports in order to facilitate the court's handling of our requests for commitment of orphans to the orphanage. It was his job, but he asked for money before hand. Rather than rejecting his request as a matter of course, we asked questions and got to know him better. It turns out that what he was really asking for was money to cover the cost of fuel for his scooter so he could do the necessary travel. He really wanted to do a good job for us but couldn't do it without his scooter. To reject him with a misplaced sense of self-righteousness would have prevented the accomplishment of our request. It is not to suggest that the ends justify the means, but be very careful not to jump to premature conclusions.

Also appreciate that many cultures routinely give gifts to each other in appreciation of services rendered. Where the dividing line is between such gifts and outright bribes is sometimes hazy. To help focus their thoughts on the subject, some missionaries use the question, "Is this a gift I would have given with or without the performance of the requested service?" If they can say that it is, they will go ahead.

---

[1] One veteran missionary who read that felt that the situation described was not a bribe at all. Her definition of a bribe was money given to someone to make them do something they should *not* do and giving money to have them do what they *should* do was just a culturally expected gift of appreciation.

Many petty officials in these countries do not make an adequate salary, often because the government itself is bankrupt. Taking gifts (or bribes) from those they serve is the only way they and their family can survive. Some missionaries quote the Biblical admonition of Deutoronomy 25:4: "Do not muzzle an ox while it is treading out the grain." Whether that applies to a recalcitrant official requires Solomonic wisdom.

What then should you do when you feel you are being shaken down for a bribe? This is one time where being a dumb foreigner is helpful. Use your ignorance of language and customs to your benefit. Pretend not to understand what they are asking for. Use a stoic hands-folded-on-a-counter stance, expressing friendliness and a willingness to comply with any reasonable request. Do *not* reach for your wallet. Use calmness and patience as your primary tools. If you have time, try a calm sit-down "strike" by offering to wait for the mythical "bossman who has to sign the papers and won't be in today." With time, your calm, quiet presence causes a loss of face and becomes an embarrassment for them. One example: One short-term missionary we know was the brunt of a racket being run by the police in the country he was serving. They pulled him over because of some alleged non-compliance with some regulation regarding his truck. To put fear into him and to encourage compliance with their ultimate request, they told him they would have to take him to the magistrate. On the way, they acknowledged that they knew he had much to do and if he paid a certain amount, they would forget the whole thing and take care of the ticket. Knowing he was being indirectly asked for an illegal bribe, he brightly said with a naïve tone that it was only right that if he had broken the law, he should face the magistrate because he wanted to be seen as a welcome guest in their country even if that took paying the fine. He went on in that vein for a while. He remained delightfully and politely obtuse, refusing to understand, until they gave up on him and took him back to his vehicle, citing a sudden change in heart toward this expatriate who was here to help their people. He had depended the whole time on the fact that they would never take him to a magistrate because he knew he was in compliance.

As with any stand for a Biblical principle, you may pay a price. Keep this in mind and keep the matter in prayer. This situation will not have caught God by surprise.

Given the poverty often found in developing countries, the poorest of the poor may break your heart.[2] We often ignore them in the United States, felling that our social service net will take care of most of them. In many countries, begging is the only method of survival open to certain orphans, the disabled, and the displaced. Social programs do not exist. Your experience in the Third World begins to show you that Americans are truly rich in comparison to any of them. Beggars, both those who must beg to survive and those who are "professional" beggars, are ubiquitous in the developing countries. It is not always easy to decide how to act toward them, and it is sometimes harder to handle our emotions and sort out our duties to them. Encourage them and you may be swamped with requests every time you walk outside the door. Be overgenerous, and some have found themselves in the middle of a mob and even suffered injuries. Be too miserly, and your heart keeps you awake at night.

You need to develop a personal philosophy about what you will do. Before you carry out anything, know your mission group or mission station's established policy about giving money to nationals. DO NOT break it. Even if you disagree, doing so may cause untold miseries for the other missionaries. Assume that since you are the newcomer, you do not know all the reasons behind the regulation and grant them the decency of honoring their rules and regulations. If you are uncomfortable with it, ask for an explanation and then look for alternative ways to give. One option is to give to the Salvation Army or other Christian-based local ministry working with the poor, since some money begged is used for drugs or alcohol and presumably those agencies will have a better filter than you will have. Contributing to a benevolence fund at the hospital or clinic (even if you have to fund the

---

[2] Much of what follows has been adapted with permission from an excellent article by Dr. William Ardill "Begging and Beggars: A Missionary's Dilemma," Evangelical Missions Quarterly, Vol 36 (3) July 2000, pp. 328–331.

beginning of such a fund), purchasing the drugs used in the pharmacy, paying for treatment not available at your location and other imaginative ways can all serve to fulfill your desire to help. Do this in a quiet self-effacing Christian manner and if you have doubt as the legitimacy of a request, use a concerned national to front for you. They often can tell immediately whether you are being misled by lies and can often suggest an amount that is reasonable and a method of giving that is more culturally apropos.

If there is no stated policy, make sure you and your family or your group does have an understanding of what philosophy and range of giving will be acceptable. Developing this with a caring national or expatriate may prevent some major errors in judgment. Some guidelines:

▶ Set a budget *after prayerful consideration and with a sensitive heart*. When it is gone, it is gone and you need not feel guilty.

▶ If you want to give personally to the beggars, make sure you are prepared. Carry low denomination bills or coins.

▶ If at all possible, offer legitimate work (carrying bags, washing cars, shoes shined) in exchange for money. An unwillingness to work often clarifies whether there is a real need.

▶ If you are concerned that the money will be used for nefarious purposes, give food (fruit, rice, beans) instead of money.

▶ Do not be disturbed by the many requests. In some cultures, the concept of sharing resources is very ingrained, and they do not feel that they are necessarily imposing since you obviously have so much. Requests are often greater than they would realistically expect and being turned down is not as hard for them to hear as it is for the Americans to say. At times, it is appropriate to think, "If they don't mind asking, I won't mind saying, 'No'."

▶ If you give school fees (a popular request), make it clear at the time of the gift what the limits of your generosity are, e.g. only this amount, only this semester, only this year, etc. They will often assume you have taken on the life long support of this person's education and indeed, sometimes that of all their relatives.

▶ If you decide that a loan is the best way to handle the problem, realize that repayment schedules are very difficult to arrange for most short-term missionaries. Consider giving it to a long-term missionary to handle and discuss with him the acceptable terms of payback. Accept the fact that many loans will never be repaid. Never loan what you cannot afford to lose.

▶ Err on side of being generous but be careful for your own safety. Do not distribute on the street; you can be mobbed.

▶ Be careful about giving out your address to nationals. You will very likely receive a request for money, perhaps not in the first letter but often in the second or third. It can get very uncomfortable for you in some instances.

▶ Remember that if you give to a professional beggar, the money may never go to his or her benefit but rather to their parents or other people who control them. This is true, but remember also that you will not invariably be able to tell "legitimate" beggars from the professional ones.

▶ If you have exceeded your budget, or don't feel led to help them, tell them (if it is true) that you depend on God for His provision and they can do so too. Pray with them. There is a danger of doing this as a trite response, so be wary.

▶ Always pray with the people and use the opportunity to witness. They will listen out of politeness and a sense of obligation if for no other reason, and you never know when the seeds of the Gospel will strike fertile soil.

▶ Prepare to be hurt—ingratitude is rampant. Some will lie, divert the money for other use, and take advantage of you. Some will feel that they are really doing you a favor in giving you opportunity to gain merit with your God. Keep Christ's attitude as your attitude.

The real question is whether you would rather explain to God that you were conned but you gave in Christ's name, spreading the good news of salvation at the same time, or that you were too worried about losing money than to give at all. Dr. Ardill's article in the suggested reading points out that a little guilt is a good thing. It is a sign of a heart still sensitive to the needs of others. It is when you can walk away without concern that you are in danger.

CHAPTER 13

OTHER THINGS ONE COULD DO

Missionaries themselves often feel like they need to do more.

Caring short-term missionaries themselves often feel that they need to do more. Spouses and families are often concerned that they don't have the talent to go on a specific mission trip. Let us correct that misconception now. The only talent needed to serve on the field is a willing heart! Every child of God has been given a gift of the Spirit and living has given you a long list of experiences and abilities, even if you think they are not special. Just because the Lord has called a missionary to be a teacher, translator, preacher, evangelist, pilot, or physician does not mean that he or she is automatically blessed with all the skills of life nor all the time necessary to do everything he or she must do. There are literally hundreds of ways that the spouse and children of visiting staff can make a major impact. Experience has shown that your time abroad will be most satisfactory if you can look back on any job well done.

Missionaries are just like most of us, reluctant to ask for help. They know you are suffering from jet lag and adjusting to a new culture. If it isn't too far in their past, they remember those feelings all too well! They also don't know you, your background, your abilities or your inclinations, but they are always grateful for the help. Getting involved is easy. Just go to the station hostess or to a missionary and explain your desire to help. It will be accepted

If you have special skills, they will be more than appreciative if you put them to use for their benefit or for the benefit of the mission outreach. Your efforts will continue to bear fruit long after you leave. Your mere presence there, demonstrating Christ's love, will have an effect.

A caveat: Keep your expectations on a reasonable level. Don't try to do too much, but rather try to show Christ's love and do a good job at what you do. Set time limitations, if appropriate, by telling how much time you will be able to give and still meet your other obligations. Also, ask to be included in daily activities that will give you a better understanding of missionary life, such as group meetings, grocery trips, or home visitation in the community. Realize that just taking care of your family and supporting your spouse is a legitmate and valid use of your time. Just living in the Third World takes longer, and that is okay!

As you can see from the list to follow, many of these tasks do not take special skills, but they are needed, appreciated, and demonstrate your servant heart. God will make it special.

CLERICAL
- Type
- File
- Transcribe
- Teach computer skills
- Process data
- Inventory and organize supplies

ACCOUNTING
- Book entries
- Balance the books
- Perform audits if you have the skill

HOUSEHOLD HELP
- Prepare food; invite missionaries to eat with you; entertain other guests
- Teach cooking to national women
- Grocery shop for missionaries
- Assist with laundry for guests

PATIENT CARE
- Hold, bathe babies in the nursery
- Walk patients
- Serve as an aide in the outpatient ward
- Clean equipment
- Visiting children's and women's ward; bring stuff from home to use

TEACHING
- Teach missionary kids subjects in which you have expertise
- Teach basic hygiene to patients, if language is not a barrier
- Teach handicrafts (bring necessary supplies from home)
- Teach VBS; help the missionary kids stage a play or musical, etc.
- Teach puppet creation (sock puppets), stage construction, and presentation techniques
- Teach music
- Teach arts
- Teach computer skills

SEWING
- Sew or repair clothes for missionaries
- Sew hospital items: gowns, surgical linens, caps, scrubs, baby caps, baby blankets, baby clothes, curtains, privacy partitions
- Teach a sewing class for women
- Sew holiday items for the compound's celebrations of holidays

ORGANIZATION
- Help organize pharmacy or central supply
- Organize records system or xray files
- Organize operating theater (operating room) or ward supplies
- Organize and label the medical reference library
- Create shelving, clean storage areas, etc.
- Start a lending library; organize a media library

BIBLE TEACHING
- Teach with a flannel graph
- Share in patients' chapel
- Lead in prayer meetings
- Preach in church
- Hold weekly Bible study
- Teach Sunday School
- Lead regular prayer meetings for spouses and single missionaries
- Lead Bible Studies, women's groups, etc.
- Do studies of popular books (bring copies and workbooks)
- Teach a method of Bible study

CLEANING / PAINTING
- Offer to do guest house spring cleaning
- Teach staff different and/or better cleaning methods
- Paint hospital items such as IV poles, beds, cupboards, etc.
- Paint wards, chapel, furniture
- Clean windows

BABYSITTING / CHILDCARE
- Offer to care for MKs
- Care for an orphan child
- Do activities with children on compound: hikes, games, etc.
- Teach the children to bake (one great idea—have a bake sale and contribute the profit to the indigent patietn fund or some other meaningful project)

OTHER MINISTRIES
- Provide special music
- Play the piano or other instrument
- Make balloon animals for kids in hospital
- Fly Parafoil kites with the children
- Visit staff in their homes

- Organize a party for the compound
- Listen, pray
- Cut and style hair

OTHER SKILLS
- Carpentry build a playground or do repair jobs
- Electronics—repair jobs
- Plumbing—repair jobs
- Assist with vehicle maintenance
- Plant or work in a garden—bring the seeds from home.
- Draw/paint pictures on hospital wards
- Take pictures to send back to the missionaries
- Organize a holiday party with favors, banners, etc. that you bring with you
- Arrange a movie night
- Show the Jesus film in the villages
- Organize sports events for misisonary kids and national children

Summary

As you can see, the list is almost endless, Whatever your interests or skills, they can be well used on the mission field. You are only limited by your imagination and willingness to help. You are encouraged to get involved and minister to missionaries and nationals alike. Sometimes, the most valuable thing you can do is to just be a friend. Many missionary wives and many missionaries themselves are hurting and need a confidant. Relationships on the mission field can be a strain. They are often forced to live and work in close proximity with people that, despite their missionary status, may not have qualified as close friends back home. One of the most valuable service you can do is listen and be non-judgmental. You are not responsible for giving an answer to their problem. Listen without offering advice and do so with prayer for them. When you return home, keep confidential what you have learned, continue to pray and continue to be a good friend to them through the distance. Some short-term missionary wives have complained that they have trouble bonding with the long-term missionaries. This is often true where there are frequent visitors on the missionary compound. This seems to be almost unqiuely a complaint among the women. This may be partly due to the God-given differences between men and women. Men are often very happy and satisfied with a 3 or 4 week relationship but women who give their hearts in friendship are often very hurt when the short-term missionary wife goes home and then never keeps up any form of communication. Make a point of staying in touch—through prayer, e-mail and letters.

CHAPTER 14

OH, FOR A REPEAT OF PENTECOST! SPOKEN COMMUNICATION WHEN YOU DON'T HAVE THE GIFT OF TONGES

Anyone who has been overseas for any length of time and struggled to understand and be understood has had ample reason to regret God's method of punishing mankind when they decided to build the tower of Babel. On more than one occasion, it may cause you to wish fervently for a personal involvement with a repeat performance of the experience at Pentecost.

How nice it would be to speak in an unfamiliar language and have your audience comprehend with equal ease! Sometimes this desire is true even if you are speaking the same language. It is painfully obvious to visitors to and from England, Australia, New Zealand, Canada, United States, and South Africa that they are English-speaking countries separated by a common language!

Communication is a two-part process and involves both the expression of ideas and comprehension of those ideas. At the start, you never can be certain how fluent someone is, no matter what claims they make of their familiarity with a language.

Always speak slowly, clearly, and distinctly in unambiguous English using a simple vocabulary. Contrary to popular belief, not everyone will understand English if spoken loudly and slowly enough. Non-native speakers process language at a slower rate. This is especially true if you are trying out your rusty language skills left over from high school or your newly acquired vocabulary from language school. The process for non-fluent people is in two stages. Our mind translates the sentence from the non-native language to the language in which we think, and it is only then that we begin assimilating the information in our native language. This means that you should enunciate carefully, speak slowly, use short sentences and phrases, and be willing to break up a long sentence into short ones. Some things to keep in mind:

▶ Carefully define any term that may be unfamiliar but cannot be avoided.

▶ Realize that words with similar sounds and dissimilar meanings can be misunderstood.

▶ Do not use contractions. Although we use them so much in common usage that we are not often aware that we are even doing it, most non-native speakers of a language will be more familiar with the more correct and classic textbook grammar.

▶ Do not drop words like "that" and "which." The phrase "Like the book I read" should be "like the book that I read" and "The products we sell" should be "products which we sell."

▶ Explain abbreviations, or preferably, avoid them altogether so there can be no confusion. An abbreviation that may be familiar to you may mean something entirely different in another country or culture.

▶ Avoid long strings of nouns. There is a tendency, especially in the computer industry, to express concepts by using strings of unrelated nouns, e.g., word search retrieval methods, office equipment maintenance seminar reimbursement. Individual words can be understood but the meaning in a noun string is likely to be unintelligible.

▶ Try to avoid two-word (phrasal) verbs, e.g. "coming around," "pulling off." These are often misunderstood.

▶ Do not use colloquialisms, jargon, slang, made-up words, acronyms and idioms. As examples, "bottleneck," "linchpin," "get up to speed," "take the red-eye," "Windows-literate" are examples of phrases and words that are hard to grasp. Don't use sports idioms, especially those from sports that are rarely played in the country where you are. "Don't wait until the two minute warning before making a decision," "It's a slam-dunk!" and "Get to first base" are all examples. If you don't believe us that this is a problem, just what exactly is a "sticky wicket," anyway?

If you still don't understand the problem, try translating this testimony "I had, like, hit rock bottom and was really bummed out, was really on the ropes, you know, until, you know, the Man Upstairs grabbed me when I was going down for the third time. I did a one-eighty and now He is the Big Cahuna in my life. I now have a totally extreme way of living, Bible-wise." Even some of the native speakers of American English want an interpreter for that one!

Supplement your conversation or presentation with visual aids if possible. Multilingual aids are a great help for rehearsed presentations and can be made up with some help from one of the nationals or the missionaries. Be sure to use the same words in the visual aids that you will use in your speech. The old saw that a picture is worth a thousand words is generally true, especially in this situation. A word of caution: the oldest visual aid is the use of your hands and some cultures and some people couldn't communicate if you tied their hands. Just be aware that not all gestures mean the same thing in each culture. In some cultures, a simple gesture which is innocuous in your culture can cause great offense to your audience. One of the most common examples is the use of the "okay" sign with the finger and thumb encircled and the other fingers extended. It can be interpreted in some cultures as an obscene gesture. If you are an "okay" person, practice the "thumbs up" sign instead, after checking that it is acceptable to use that sign where you are. Sometimes, it will get you into trouble as well!

Also affirm your listeners' understanding on a regular basis. Because of cultural differences, you may read their body language in one way and they intend it another. For example, non-verbal affirmation (nods, smiles) may indicate only courtesy, not true understanding, and their pleasant face will mask their real feeling—just what is this person talking about?! The best way to affirm that understanding is to ask for a paraphrase of what you are saying. Just asking if they understand will often not be enough, because you may get a polite nod in order not to offend you. If the meeting is of critical importance, it is perhaps wise to follow up the conversation with a written memorandum of what was discussed and make sure it is written in both languages.

"A funny thing happened on the way to. . . ." And, now, a touchy subject: humor. There is a perhaps apocryphal story of a speaker who told a humorous anecdote and was gratified by the wave of laughter from his audience. Only later did he find that the interpreter had said, "Our honored speaker has told a story that he considers funny. Please laugh in appreciation." At the risk of offending the author of every toastmaster and after-dinner speaker "How-to" manual, we have some advice: avoid humor in almost all instances. After all, many people can't tell a joke well in their own language! It is better to be thought humorless than to be thought offensive. There is always the risk of offending cultural and religious sensitivities that are unique to a country or region. There is no guarantee that you will be adequately sensitized to those areas in time to avoid creating a fiasco. Peter Weinberg wrote, "Humor is perhaps the least portable and most parochial element of a language or culture."[1] Comedians have tried to analyze humor for years and exactly what is funny is very elusive. Most humor is based on subtlety, nuance, and timing. Most humor is very culturally sensitive and rarely translates well. Even if you *are* the funniest person in your circle at home, there is no guarantee that your interpreter can pull it off on your behalf. So the best advice is still this: do not incorporate humor unless you are certain it will not be misunderstood and that it will be appreciated.

Speaking with interpreters

As an honored visitor to a country, you may often be asked to speak to a church or other gathering. Never mind that you are not a seminary graduate and are terrified to speak in front of others. You will be asked. That is when the use of interpreters[2] is a needed skill but, like everything else in this new experience, it is not always as easy as it seems. Virtually all of the concepts discussed previously in this chapter will apply, but there are some other hints that will make the team of speaker and interpreter more effective.

---

[1] Peter Weinberg. "Meeting the Challenge: A Guide to Protocol in the Global Village. Part 3: The Use of Language in Multi-Lingual Meetings" ASA Connections magazine, July/August 2000, page 11.

[2] Interpreter and translator are not synonymous terms. An interpreter is one who deals with the spoken word; a translator is one who deals with the written word.

▶ Conceptual interpretation (dynamic equivalency) is better than word-to-word interpretation. What that means is that you want the idea to get across and not necessarily the exact wording. Giving your interpreter the transcripts ahead of time may help familiarize the interpreter with what you mean to say, but do not let them be read it word for word. You may change what you want to say as the Lord leads you and secondly, it allows for a more dynamic delivery. It is important to give the interpreter the Biblical references ahead of time so he or she can find them easily at the right time, and so they have a chance to read them over before they have to read them aloud. Often reading skills of the interpreters are not on par with their speaking skills.

▶ Avoid spontaneous Biblical quotes when using interpreters. Biblical English, especially that of older versions, uses English words and forms that may be difficult for him to interpret on the fly and you cannot expect him to have memorized all the verses you might use. Avoiding such situations has two additional advantages. The first is that he doesn't drop dead from panic, leaving you in an awkward position of having something to say and no one to say it with. The second is that you will get a more accurate translation reflecting God's true meaning if he reads from a published translation than if you ask him to interpret as you go.

▶ Write out and practice your testimony, speech or sermon ahead of time with the above considerations in mind. Practice the delivery in front of someone who is willing to critique you honestly.

▶ Use short phrases. It is not without reason that many people who use interpreters regularly laughingly call them "interrupters." It is better to use short sentences than phrases for two reasons. A practical one is so the interpreter doesn't have to remember so much. Another is that many languages place the verbs at the beginning rather than the end of the sentence. English may place it in the middle or end. Without the verb the translator doesn't know what to say. In a rare instance, you may get someone who can interpret simultaneously (listening in one language and talking in the other), but you can never count on it. If you do, it is sometimes unnerving because you talk while he talks, a cultural no-no for most of us most of the time. It also makes listening very difficult.

► Be sure that any illustrations you use are culturally understandable.

► Keep the message short. Realize that only half of the allotted time is for you. Your interpreter gets the other half!

Before you panic and say you aren't going if you have to preach, remember that the most likely thing is that you will be asked to give your testimony. Evangelistic teams often ask people to give their testimony in some sort of rotation. That is not too much to handle but even here preparation helps. See Appendix C for a suggested method of writing out your testimony. Talk with your missionaries, team leaders, or chaplains about appropriate and inappropriate topics to mention. If you are part of a team, scheduling your evangelistic outreach in advance will prevent the inevitable panic that occurs when you ask someone to speak at the last minute. It also ensures that everyone will get to share. Remember, in addition to the things discussed above, "honest" and "short" are both good bywords to keep in mind!

The "Do's" of Giving Your Testimony

► Do share your name, where you live, your profession and why you came.

► Do share what being a Christian means to you, giving a brief description of your life before Christ and how it changed.

► Do share how and why you became a Christian.

► Do share how someone else listening can become a Christian and allow some way for the person to respond. An altar call is not necessary.

► Do express your thanks for being able to share your testimony with them.

The "Don'ts" of Giving Your Testimony

► Don't talk about things that are items of Christian liberty and may be misunderstood in the local culture. Among those are divorce, smoking, and social drinking.

► Don't talk about the money, how much the trip cost or how God provided. That He did is good. Just leave out specifics so that the listener hears the important things and not how comparatively wealthy you are.

► Don't be long winded.

▶ Don't use religious jargon.
▶ Don't use humor.

For those who want to speak more than just giving a simple testimony, look for opportunities. Ask to speak in chapel, prayer meetings, Sunday services, and on soapboxes. Tell your hosts that you would like to speak and have them help you find opportunities. Listen to their counsel on what to do and what not to do, what topics might be appropriate, and what is needed most. Most importantly, keep it theologically simple. One of the best things to talk about is your life and God's impact on it.

If speaking is just not your thing, but you have talents in music, art, magic, balloon sculpture, clowning, or anything else, use them as a springboard for sharing the good news of Jesus Christ. If nothing else, distribute tracts, Bibles, and books if appropriate. These ministries work almost anywhere: the hospital, the street and in prisons.

Talking to and sharing with others can be scary, but remember you are responsible only for the telling, not for the results. That is the work of the Holy Spirit. God has promised that His Word does not return without result (Ecclesiastes 11:1; Isaiah 55:10,11) and He has prepared for your good works before you do them (Ephesians 2:10).

CHAPTER 15

SHARING THE GOOD NEWS

Pretend for a moment that you are a healthcare provider. If you had a cure for your patient's disease and refused to tell him or her how to be cured, we would all consider it unethical and unprofessional.

As a healthcare provider, if you had a cure for HIV/AIDS and allowed 30 million to die this year without telling even a single person how to avoid death, it would be reprehensible and inhumane. Excuses about difficulty and expense would be irrelevant. Governments would spend their entire budgets to cure their people. The truth is that as Christians, we don't have to be medically trained to know the cure that would prevent eternal suffering and death for literally hundreds and millions of people. Furthermore, the efficacy is complete, there are no true deleterious side effects and the tremendous price has already been paid. The disease? Sin. The cure? The death of Jesus Christ in our place, and the resurrection that gives us eternal life.

Sadly, we are often not as good at sharing that good news, as we would like to be. 1 Peter 3:15b commands us that we should, *Always be prepared to give an answer to everyone who asks you to give the reason for the hope that you have.* There are many methods of doing personal evangelism available (Evangelism Explosion, FAITH, and others), and you may find taking such a course to be valuable. In order to give some help to those who have not taken such a course and who are not in the habit of sharing Christ regularly, we have presented three different ways below. We hope that you will find one that you are comfortable with (or make up your own) and use it regularly. The first two have materials that you can order so you can more fully understand the method.

Just remember, you must be sensitive to the Holy Spirit and to the person with whom you are talking. Some questions or comments, and their response to them, can give you a clue about whether the time is right to talk to this particular person about what Christ has done for you. There is an expression that you should "run it up the flagpole and see who salutes." One program (the Christian Medical and Dental Association "Saline Solution") calls these comments "faith flags." You can wave a faith flag to determine how ready the person is to receive the gospel. You are looking to see where God is already working. One way to do it is to mention some spiritual topic that is part of your life—church, an event, or a person—and then ask something like "What is *your* religious background? I have never heard you mention a church and I was wondering about that." Other such comments: "I am glad I don't have to go through something like that again alone," "I am sorry to hear about that. When something similar happened to me, I am not sure I would have made it if I hadn't had my faith to fall back on," and for the more direct "I just realized I have never told you about something very important to me, my relationship with Jesus Christ. Would you let me tell you about it?"

You can never tell what impact your words will have. Remember: You cannot (and should not try to) talk someone into accepting Christ. You are not responsible for their salvation. The Holy Spirit is in charge of that. You are only responsible to tell what you know and what Christ has done in your life (Daniel 4:2 *It is my pleasure to tell you about the miraculous signs and wonders that the Most High God has performed for me*). You are responsible to pray for someone to share the good news with and to pray that you might have the courage to share it. You do not have to be a Biblical scholar or have all the answers to all possible questions in order to share what Christ has done for you.

Consider the following verses:

▶ *"For it is by grace you have been saved, through faith—and this not from yourselves, it is the gift of God."* Ephesians 2:8

▶ *"I came to you in weakness and fear, and with much trembling. My message and my preaching were not with wise and persuasive words, but with a demonstration of the Spirit's power".* Corinthians 2:3–4

▶ *"No man can come to me unless the Father who sent him draws him."* John 6:44

▶ *"That is why I told you that no one can come to me unless the Father has enabled him."* John 6:65

▶ *"We are therefore Christ's ambassadors, as though God were making his appeal through us."* Corinthians 5:20

▶ *"So is my word that goes out from my mouth: It will not return to me empty."* Isaiah 55:11

There are two important principles that can guide you in sharing your faith by using verses from the Bible. It is important to have the person read the verse aloud so they can hear it. This principle comes from Romans 10:17: *Faith comes from hearing the message, and the message is heard through the word of Christ.* It is then also important to ask, "What does this say to you?" or "What does this mean to you?" when the person has finished reading the verse. This principle comes from Luke 10:25–26: *On one occasion an expert in the law stood up to test Jesus. "Teacher," he asked, "what must I do to inherit eternal life?" "What is written in the Law?" he replied. "How do you read it?"*

It is important that you let God do the work. You do not have to hold long theological discussions or give complex explanations of the text. Merely listen in a way that shows you are paying attention. Limit your comments to those that encourage the person to talk, such as "Umm," or "Uh huh."

Remember:

▶ The nonbeliever will be doing the reading out loud.

▶ The nonbeliever will be doing the talking. Listen in a way that he or she will want to talk.

▶ The Holy Spirit will be doing the convincing.

▶ God's Word will bring conviction.

Many people feel that they cannot witness if they have not memorized all the verses they are going to use or might have to use to answer any conceivable question. While you may certainly wish to memorize God's word for many good reasons, failure to have memorized the verses isn't a reason not to witness. Whatever verses or method you decide to use, mark your Bible before hand.[1] Highlight the passages and underline the important words. Write the next verse at the top of the page both right side up and upside down—that way you can know where to go next even if you are sitting across from the person and sharing the Bible from that vantage point. A small card kept in your Bible or your wallet as a crutch is not unacceptable. There is no evidence that people are more likely to be saved from a glib and polished presentation than from hearing the Gospel from someone who stumbles through it.

The three methods that follow have been tried and true for many people but may not be right for you. Feel free to adapt any of these as best fits your personality, your needs and your situation. It is not as important *how* you do it as it is that you just do it!

METHOD ONE: THE BRIDGE PRESENTATION[2]

One method that works well in informal settings is the "bridge presentation." Practicing this so you can do it smoothly is helpful but it is not designed to be a sophisticated, highly polished presentation. Because of the visual component and the small number of verses, this works particularly well in a cross-cultural situation.

▶ Wave the Flag. Ask the sort of questions mentioned above. If they express interest, then . . .

▶ Tell your story. It is a good place to start. Others are usually interested, they can relate to it and they will find it hard to dispute. The best

---

1 In marking your Bible, there is a caution. Be sure to know your target audience. There are some groups (in North America and abroad) who hold the Bible to be the HOLY Bible. Writing in it in any form is looked on as defacing that which is holy. To show them a marked Bible will successfully cutoff any opportunity for you to witness to them or to get them to believe that you really do honor God's holy word. For example, some old German groups hold this belief. Muslims put their holy book on a stand as a mark of reverence and usually do not even touch it with their left hand. Some people carry an unmarked Bible just to witness or minister to such people.
2 Modified from material presented at the Billy Graham Training Center at the Cove (www.thecove.org), which is based on the Becoming a Contagious Christian program developed by the Willow Creek Association (www.willowcreek.org)

evidence for your story is your changed life. They may doubt your particular set of beliefs, they can criticize your church or denomination but they cannot avoid the fact that *something* changed your life! You are not setting yourself up as a model Christian, only giving glory to God. The principles of giving your testimony (see Chapter 14 and Appendix C) are helpful in enabling you to learn the principles of how to tell your story in a brief, clear and concise way.

▶ You need to convey (without necessarily using these particular verses) the following truths about the four points of the gospel message

    Truths about God: God is loving and giving (1 John 4:10), holy (Leviticus 19:2; 1 Peter 1:15–16), just (2 Thessalonians 1:6–9).

    Truths about all people: We are sinners (Romans 3:23), the just result of sin is death (Romans 6:23a) and in God's eyes we are unclean (Isaiah 64:6).

    Truths about Jesus: He is God with all of His attributes (John 1:1, 14). He gave His life as our substitute (1 Peter 2:24). Salvation comes not because of our works, but because of grace, the gift of God (Ephesians 2:8–10).

    Truths about Us: We (you and I) must believe to receive Jesus and become children of God (John 1:12). We must ask Jesus to be our Savior and Lord (1 John 1:9)

▶ Use the "bridge presentation" to actually share these ideas. There are 7 steps. You can use a blank piece of paper, a whiteboard, or a dirty windshield.

THE BRIDGE PRESENTATION

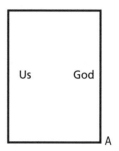

A

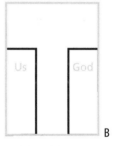

B

C

(cont'd on p. 254)

A. Write "Us" and "God." Point out that we matter to God and He wants a relationship with us. At this point, draw the box around the two words to suggest that God wants "us" included in a relationship with Him.

(cont'd from p. 253)

D

B. Draw the lines that show the separation between us and God. Explain that we have rebelled against God (either actively or passively) and that our sins have therefore separated us from Him

C. Describe the things that we do to try to please God to get His favor (e.g., attend church, read the Bible, give charity, good works). Point out that the Bible says it is never enough. Draw lines that try to bridge the gap but all fall short (Romans 3:23, *For all have sinned but fall short of the glory of God*).

E

D. Point out that the Bible says the sins we have done require punishment and that punishment is death (Romans 6:23a, *For the wages of sin is **death** . . .* Write that word on your diagram.

F

E. Explain that God did for us what we could not do for ourselves. He built a bridge between us and Him. That bridge is His Son, Jesus Christ. He took the penalty for us by dying on the cross (John 3:16 *For God so loved the world that he gave his one and only Son, that whoever believes in him shall not perish but have eternal life.*) As you talk about this, draw first the horizontal line over the gap and then the vertical line to finish the cross.

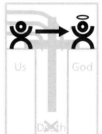

G

F. Place an "X" over the word "Death" and explain that when Jesus paid the penalty for our sin, death was cancelled out as a result of sin and He gave us eternal life (2 Corinthians 5:21 *God made him who had no sin to be sin for us, so that in him we might become the righteousness of God.*)

G. Explain that in order to receive this gift of peace with God and the eternal life that results, you have to cross over to the other side by personally choosing to accept Christ. (Romans 10:9 *That if you confess with your mouth, "Jesus is Lord," and believe in your heart that God raised him from the dead, you will be saved.*) As you explain this, draw the stick figure on the "Us" side and a line with an arrow to the other side. Draw a second stick figure on the other side.

When you are finished, check your friend's understanding of what you have shown him by asking:

▶ Does this make sense to you?

▶ If you use this illustration, where do you think you are now?

▶ Is there any reason you wouldn't want to cross over to the other side?

If the person agrees to accept Christ, then help that person pray a prayer of confession and acceptance. If he or she is not ready or not sure, don't press. Ask if you can clarify any points and answer any questions or concerns they have. Tell them to think about it and offer to talk again later about any questions they may have.

METHOD TWO: SHARE JESUS WITHOUT FEAR

The following notes are adapted from William Fay and Ralph Hodge, *Share Jesus without Fear* (Nashville: LifeWay Press, 1997). The following resources will enable you to learn more about this way of sharing about Jesus without fear. Order these by calling 1-800-458 2772.

• *Share Jesus without Fear* Workbook by William Fay and Ralph Hodge.

• *Share Jesus without Fear Leader Guide.*

• *Share Jesus without Fear Kit.*

Prepare your Bible by highlighting the following verses and writing the next verses at the top of the page (remembering to do it right side up and upside down).

▶ Romans 3:23
▶ Romans 6:23: Circle the words *sin, death,* and *in.*
▶ John 3:3: Draw a cross in the margin near John 3:3. Draw an X beside the cross. Alongside the cross you have drawn, write the question, "Why did Jesus come to die?" The X reminds you that this is the only exception in the process. You don't want to ask, "What does this verse say to you?" after the person reads this verse. Not many nonbelievers know the answer to this question. You would be applying undue pressure. He or she may feel unfairly placed on the spot.
▶ John 14:6
▶ Romans 10:911
▶ 2 Corinthians 5:15
▶ Revelation 3:20

Having marked your Bible or New Testament, you are ready to share Jesus without fear. To do so, you simply follow three steps.

Step One
Use questions like these that determine where God is working.
▶ Do you have any kind of spiritual belief?
▶ To you, who is Jesus?
▶ Do you believe there are a heaven and a hell?
▶ If you died right now, where would you go? If heaven, why?
▶ If what you believe were not true, would you want to know it?

If the answer to the last question is "Yes," then open your Bible and proceed to Step Two.
If the answer to the last question is "No," do nothing but thank the person for their time.

Step Two

Let the Bible speak. Ask the person to read the verse aloud, and then ask, "What does this say to you?" Listen to the person.

▶ Romans 3:23 "All have sinned."

▶ Romans 6:23 "The wages of sin is death."

▶ John 3:3 "You must be born again." (Remember, ask, "Why did Jesus come to die?")

▶ John 14:6 "I am the way."

▶ Romans 10:911 "If you confess...you will be saved."

▶ 2 Corinthians 5:15 "No longer live for themselves."

▶ Revelation 3:20 "I stand at the door, and knock."

Now you are ready to use the closing questions in Step Three.

Step Three

Close with key questions.

▶ Are you a sinner?

▶ Do you want forgiveness for your sins?

▶ Do you believe Jesus died on the cross for you and rose again?

▶ Are you willing to surrender your life to Christ?

▶ Are you ready to invite Jesus into your heart and into your life?

After you have asked these questions, just be silent . . . and pray. Do not push. If he answers affirmatively, offer to pray with him in a prayer for confession of sin and acceptance of Christ as Savior and Lord. If not, offer to answer any questions they have at the time and then offer to speak with them again if they wish.

METHOD THREE: THE ROMAN ROAD

There are many variations on the so-called "Roman Road," but every one leads to the throne of God. As you use this method to show Christ to unbelievers, you may find it helpful to underline these verses and then at the top of the page, write the next stop in the road. Write them the right-side up in case you are sharing a Bible and write them upside down, in case you are seated across from the person and sharing the Bible. Have them read the verses so there is no mistake what the Bible says. The suggested "conversation" is not a script but is an example of what might said to make a smooth continuation to the next point. Obviously, their questions and the leading of the Holy Spirit may change things considerably.

King David, the psalmist, wrote that that the fool has said in his heart that there is no God. For those who do not consider themselves to be fools, God says that His existence and His qualities are evident if we just look around us. If there is indeed a God, then we must either accept Him as God or deny that He is God—there is no meaningful middle ground. If there is a God, an eternal, totally good but totally just, all-wise, all-present, all-knowing God, then we must seek to know more about Him. If we do not, then what we become by following our own ideas is not a pretty picture.

Romans 1:20–21

"For since the creation of the world God's invisible qualities—his eternal power and divine nature—have been clearly seen, being understood from what has been made, so that men are without excuse. For although they knew God, they neither glorified him as God nor gave thanks to him, but their thinking became futile and their foolish hearts were darkened."

Romans 1:29–32

"They have become filled with every kind of wickedness, evil, greed and depravity. They are full of envy, murder, strife, deceit and malice. They are gossips, slanderers, God-haters, insolent, arrogant and boastful; they invent ways of doing evil; they disobey their parents; they are senseless, faithless, heartless, ruthless. Although they know God's righteous decree that those who do such things deserve death, they not only continue to do these very things but also approve of those who practice them."

"Many people think they will go to heaven because they have lived a good life. Perhaps they treat all of their neighbors fairly. Maybe they volunteer for charity work and have never broken the law. Maybe they were even baptized or go to church regularly. But the Bible, God's Word, says that no one can live up to God's standard of righteousness."

Romans 3:10–12

"As it is written: 'There is no one righteous, not even one; there is no one who understands, no one who seeks God. All have turned away, they have together become worthless; there is no one who does good, not even one.'"

Romans 3:23

"For all have sinned, and come short of the glory of God . . . ."

"If all of us have "missed the mark" and since God is totally without sin and cannot tolerate the presence of sin, what can we do that will ever make us good enough to be with him? The answer is "nothing." But fortunately, that is not the end of the story. God could, and did, do something. Not because we were good enough, not because we deserved it, and certainly not because we were on His side! If we got what we deserved, it would be death—eternal death. God gave us what dead people need—life. It was a gift, freely given, but like any gift, must be accepted."

Romans 5:8–10

"But God demonstrates his own love for us in this: While we were still sinners, Christ died for us. Since we have now been justified by his blood, how much more shall we be saved from God's wrath through him! For if, when we were God's enemies, we were reconciled to him through the death of his Son, how much more, having been reconciled, shall we be saved through his life! "

Romans 6:23

"For the wages of sin is death; but the gift of God is eternal life through Jesus Christ our Lord."

"Salvation cannot be earned. Everyone is a sinner and deserves death, but God gives eternal life. So how can we receive God's gift of eternal life?"

Romans 10:9–10

*"That if you confess with your mouth, 'Jesus is Lord,' and believe
in your heart that God raised him from the dead, you will be saved.
For it is with your heart that you believe and are justified, and it is with
your mouth that you confess and are saved."*

"Is just accepting Jesus as Savior and Lord of your life all you
have to do? Is confessing honestly that Jesus will be Lord of your life
and believing that Jesus lives again after being crucified all you have
to do? Yes. There is nothing else we *can* do; no works that will add to
the work that Jesus has already done on our behalf, nothing of value
that will add to the price he paid for our sins. Are you a sinner? Do
want forgiveness? Do you believe Christ died for you and rose again?
Do you want to accept Christ as your Savior?" (If they answer yes,
help them pray to accept Christ and go over the following verses to
give them God's promises to them. If they decline, offer to answer any
questions they may have. Do not press. Offer to talk with them in the
future if they wish).

If they accept Christ, then go on to the following verses (writing
them down may be helpful so they can reassure themselves in the
future):

Detour to Ephesians 2:8–9

*"For by grace are ye saved through faith; and that not of your-
selves: it is the gift of God: Not of works lest any man should boast."*

Back to Romans 8:1–2

*"Therefore, there is now no condemnation for those who are in
Christ Jesus, because through Christ Jesus the law of the Spirit of life
set me free from the law of sin and death."*

"There is no boasting in heaven because we will be there sole-
ly to the work of Jesus Christ. But now no one can condemn us either!
We are set free from the consequences of death because Christ has
brought life."

Detour to 2 Cor. 5:17

"Therefore, if anyone is in Christ, he is a new creation; the old has gone, the new has come!"

"But how do we know that we are now saved? God has promised it and He keeps his promises but the Holy Spirit deals directly with our spirit, testifying that we are now God's children and then He "seals" us, making sure we are always God's children. Once we are children of God, nothing can separate us from the God's love!"

Romans 8:16–17

"The Spirit himself testifies with our spirit that we are God's children. Now if we are children, then we are heirs—heirs of God and co-heirs with Christ, if indeed we share in his sufferings in order that we may also share in his glory."

Detour: Ephesians 1:13–14

"In whom ye also trusted, after that ye heard the word of truth, the gospel of your salvation: in whom also after that ye believed, ye were sealed with that holy Spirit of promise, which is the earnest of our inheritance until the redemption of the purchased possession, unto the praise of his glory."

Romans 8: 38–39

"For I am convinced that neither death nor life, neither angels nor demons, neither the present nor the future, nor any powers, neither height nor depth, nor anything else in all creation, will be able to separate us from the love of God that is in Christ Jesus our Lord."

"As a new Christian, we are to be "living sacrifices." In other words, we are no longer to follow our old desires, dreams and inclinations. Rather, we are to have a new way of thinking, a new set of priorities and a new center of our life. In doing so, which we can only do because Jesus Christ had paid the price of sin for us and because we are willing to accept His free gift, we can now have something we have never had before: joy and peace despite the trials and troubles that may come your way."

Romans 12:1–2

"Therefore, I urge you, brothers, in view of God's mercy, to offer your bodies as living sacrifices, holy and pleasing to God—this is your spiritual act of worship. Do not conform any longer to the pattern of this world, but be transformed by the renewing of your mind. Then you will be able to test and approve what God's will is—his good, pleasing and perfect will."

Romans 15:13

"May the God of hope fill you with all joy and peace as you trust in him, so that you may overflow with hope by the power of the Holy Spirit."

CHAPTER 16

HOME, SWEET HOME?

Why is there a whole chapter on reentry?
Aren't you just coming back home?
"Well, yes . . . and no. Mostly no."

Upon our first trip to Africa, we returned home almost bursting with excitement, eager to tell of our experiences and our new-found closeness to God and the knowledge of God's work in our lives. Our parents had met us during our layover at the first U.S. airport and we had dinner together. We could hardly enjoy it—we shrank from the noise, the hustle and bustle of life around us and the tremendous number of choices on the menu. We could barely decide what to order and we didn't enjoy the huge portions. Figuring things would be better once we were in our home church, we were crestfallen when a church member did not even realize we had been gone. In response to our comment that we had been in Africa, she responded, "Really? That's nice. We spent the summer in Myrtle Beach" and she proceeded to regale us with story after story of their summer adventures. We never got to say anything further. We have come to find out that this is not an uncommon experience.

"Reverse culture shock" or "cross-cultural reentry" is an inevitable part of your trip and can be for some the most stressful and long-lasting part of your trip. It is important that you have an understanding of what you might go through. No one can return from a short-term mission experience and remain unchanged. If you have not used the experience to build your spiritual strength and your relationship with God, it may have merely intensified your areas of weakness. Often, those weaknesses will be more glaring upon your return. You will also find that you will see these same dynamics in career missionaries who have returned from the field and a better understanding of what they are going through will help you minister to them more effectively.

Reentry shock has to do with change. Time does not stand still. There will be changes within your home environment during your absence and there were will be changes within you. Things that accentuate the magnitude of the changes and the length of the time that the changes exist will increase the severity of the reverse culture shock. If you have not worked and had time to understand and ameliorate the expected effects, the severity of the shock will be greater. For example, an involuntary or unexpected return is harder than a voluntary or expected return because there has not been sufficient time to process the change. The greater the difference in cultures between the mission field and the home culture (and the better you adapted to the other culture), the more difficult will be the re-entry. A lack of previous experience with such a transition will make it more difficult. Older persons, with a history of similar life transitions, may not be as bothered as much as younger people. Conversely, the more you stayed in touch with changes in your home culture and the more supportive and familiar your environment is upon your return, the easier it is.

Storti, in his book *The Art of Coming Home*, describes the concept of "home" as having three key elements: familiar places, familiar people and routines and predictable patterns of interaction.[1] Even a short mission trip will alter those elements. It is logical that the first two are affected by time. The longer you are away from your home, neighborhood and city, the more they will change. New businesses will open, familiar ones close, buildings and neighborhoods will change appearance, traffic flow patterns will change and so on. As

> "The whole object of travel is not to set foot on foreign land; it is at last to set foot on one's own country as a foreign land."
>
> —Gilbert K. Chesterton

---

[1] Storti, Craig. *The Art of Coming Home*. Yarmouth, ME: Intercultural Press, 2001, Page 8–9.

you spend more time overseas, the more likely it is that family members and friends will die or be born, marry or divorce, make new friends and develop other interests that may not include you. You may be forced to face grief or have personal reactions to those changes upon your return, changes that are out of step with others who have handled their reactions and already moved on.

Changes within you are an expected, and even desirable, part of your trip. You have had a unique and life-changing experience and in both a literal and figurative manner, you have traveled far beyond your family and friends. However, the consequences of having experienced those changes and your reactions to those changes are both often more frequent and greater than expected. You have developed a new viewpoint of your country, your religion and your beliefs and the contrast (and conflict) with those held by your friends and family can cause distress to both you and to them.

After the first blush of excitement about being home fades, there are common reactions to being home that tend to be almost universal. They include the following general areas but they are not listed in any particular order:

▶ American materialism and life-style is something you will face daily when you return home. It may not seem to be as attractive as it once was. After seeing poverty at its worst and having emotionally connected with people whose lives hold little hope, it is sometimes hard to face the conspicuous consumerism and wastefulness of life in North America. The site of a fully-stocked grocery superstore or a multi-page menu can paralyze the returnee. Since the pace of life in most developing nations is much slower and social interaction emphasizes interpersonal relationships, the impersonal and hectic pace of life in North America can overwhelm and seem undesirable. You may find yourself now angry with those around who do exactly the things you used to do. You then are angry with yourself when you fall back into the cultural norms and resume the same behavior that was so repulsive to you when you first arrived home. Remember to extend grace to others and to yourself. The real trick is to learn what Paul talked about in Phil 4:11–13, *"I am not saying this because I am in need, for I have learned to be content whatever the circumstances. I know what it is to be in need, and I know what it is to have plenty. I have learned the secret of being content in any and every situation, whether well fed or hungry, whether living in plenty or in want. I can do everything through him who gives me strength."*

▶ You may find a real dissonance between your values upon your return and those of other Americans. This is sometimes because the American culture has changed while you are away, but perhaps you have achieved a new sensitivity to the cultural mores, sexuality, depravity, racism, denominationalism and other characteristics of life in North America. This new perspective can give you a clear vision of the worth and legitimacy of some values held by others and of the isolationistic or self-serving viewpoint of many Americans. Politically, you may find yourself more patriotic because you better understand the good in the American lifestyle, but paradoxically, in some areas, you may be less jingoistic, better understanding the impact of American politics and business decisions. You may have a greater sympathy of the appeal of some other political systems to people who have nothing. You may understand why some consider the "Ugly American" stereotype to be valid. We can only suggest caution in your verbalization of these new ideas. It is very common to hear upon your return that "It must be good to back in America" and of course, it is. However, you will not be able to hear that question without thinking, "Yes, BUT. . . ."

▶ Perhaps the second most profound impact is the apparent apathy, disinterest and misunderstanding of those around you. You are far more interested in what you were doing overseas than anyone else is. When you have falsely high expectations of your return, your welcome back is often best described as underwhelming. Even if you admit that few welcomes could possibly live up to your expectations, it is so hard to come home and have no one who wants to listen. You want to tell your stories, not to show off or because you crave attention, but to explain to people you love how and why you are now different. How can you have a relationship with someone you love if they don't know what is important to you? Without telling your stories, especially about something this important to you, you must remain a stranger to those you love. Also, telling your stories helps to justify why you made such a dramatic decision in the first place. Even if you find an audience, there are two things that will affect how the audiences process your report of your experiences.

The first is how they view missionaries in general and how they view you specifically. Many people have difficulty in relating to missionaries. They may be suspicious of your motives and have a stereotype of missionaries as boring, ill-dressed, hyper-spiritual, and fun-avoiding people who are fixated on missions and unable to make it in the real world. For those who are Christians and who may have ignored God's call to missions, there may be feelings of guilt, ambivalence and internal tension. They may also be jealous of your trip and experiences. If you spend a lot of time telling how wonderful things were on the mission field, your listeners may feel rejected, devalued and unappreciated. The second difficulty that can arise is in how they handle the information. It may be that the presuppositions of your audience are so loaded with half-truths and imaginings that they tend to pay attention to only that which reinforces what they wish to believe. Alternatively, they may be suffering from information overload. Nightly, the television screen brings pictures of the war victims and the starving into their living rooms. Daily, radio, newspapers and magazines bring more information of similar distressing nature. All people develop some way to handle this overload of negative information and denial is the most common defense mechanism. Such a reaction may numb your families', friends' and colleagues' sensitivities to your experiences.

If you fail to recognize that this is largely *their* problem and not yours, you may feel rejected and lonely. Remember to take it slow and do not overwhelm your listeners. Tell them only as much as they want to hear or seem able to be able to digest at the time. It is important for you to realize that part of the problem with communication may lie with you. Much of what has become important to you is difficult to put into words. If you compound the problem of the listener's limited interest with your limited ability to verbalize ideas and concepts that may not solidify in your own mind for months or years, it can lead to poor communication. The disappointment created thereby can cause a tendency to quit trying or lock up these feelings and experiences without allowing them time to age and ferment sufficiently. You must often meditate for months on an experience before all of the significance is evident. Select the experiences to share that you can get hold of and leave the others until later. Just don't forget them.

▶ A related problem that is opposite to apathy is sometimes seen— unreasonable expectations of high productivity from you. These expectations can be internal or external. An unreasonable internal expectation is manifested by the short-term missionary who tries to over-achieve. This is often seen in short term medical mission trips that host clinics that emphasize number of patients seen, or numbers preached to or some similar yardstick. This puts the pressure of success upon you and your actions; the success is therefore not dependent upon God. This is faulty thinking. God may not (and probably does not) judge the success of your endeavors with that yardstick at all. Pressure from an external source comes when donors want success stories as a "payback" for their donations. Some trips can supply these stories, others cannot. In the context of an alien culture, it may be hard for a North American to judge what the real impact is of what you have done. This is especially true on shorter trips. Success should be measured by the degree you followed your understanding of what God's will is for your life, not by some artificial temporal metric. It does not matter whether that metric is internally or externally generated. Judging success by God's criteria requires an eternal perspective that, no matter how hard we try, we cannot completely obtain.

▶ Another common complaint by those returning home is a sense of personal disorientation. At first, you have a sense of not belonging in your own culture. The cultural change from one of abject poverty to wealth can aggravate this feeling as we described above. Serving and dealing with people who do not have the same world perspective and broad experience as you now have can make it worse. There is often a realization that you don't want to be like these people at home. Often you feel a lack of a defined support group. On the mission field, there was a sense of being a member of a dedicated, hard-working team that had unified goals. You may have had a sense of high self-motivation, fostered by the sense of community and a defined role. Now you may have entered a culture that favors independence and you have lost a sense of self-worth and no longer have a definite goal in your life. On the mission field, as an expatriate, you were someone "important" and

> *"Certainly, travel is more than the seeing of sights; it is a change that goes on, deep and permanent, in the ideas of living."*
>
> —Miriam Beard

may have had access to social circles that are now no longer available to you. You have gone from being someone important to someone who is like everyone else. The highly spiritual atmosphere of the mission field has given way to two or three services a week at most. Even outside the area of ministry, you may have to exchange a vacation on safari for one that involves a long car trip to Aunt Tilda's house. Now you have a standard of living that is relatively more modest than you could have afforded on the field.

▶ You may have a significant change in your personal relationships. It is sometimes hard to realize that people have been able to get along without you and moved on with their lives. You have been "out of sight, out of mind". You may have had changes in your physical appearance to which they react either favorably or unfavorably. Those changes are visible to you in the mirror and with some honest self-assessment, reactions can be predicted and dealt with beforehand. It is much more difficult to gauge the social, emotional and spiritual changes in your life. Your interests and concerns have diverged from those at home. When they realize that you are now marching to a new drummer, the emotional reaction from your loved ones can be profound. You may face jealousy and represent a threat because your new ideas, experiences and spiritual insights may challenge the status quo and the standards at home. You may now be more sensitive to racism, chauvinism, bigotry, and denominationalism—and may be more apt to react critically when you see those things in the people you love. You may be less ethnocentric and demonstrate more tolerance of other theological viewpoints. Dogmas and practices of your culture that are important to them may no longer be as central or as absolute to you.

"Travel is fatal to prejudice, bigotry and narrow-mindedness."
—Mark Twain

Your loss of interest in "things" and a better understanding of the Christ's role in your life can cause great turmoil in your relationships. You may find that finances and possessions are a point of contention. It is almost axiomatic that service on the mission field, even for the short term, requires some financial sacrifice. This sometimes includes making a deliberate choice between types of housing, cars, vacations and other possessions. Be prepared for the resentment that your sacrifice may cause in others (even if they don't support you financially) and be prepared for the twinge of jealousy within your heart when you see what others have. Sometimes, you will find yourself cloaking your true reaction in a mantle of spiritual superiority toward others.

How you handle this disruption in relationships is very important. The most important thing is that you do not hold yourself out to be consciously or unconsciously superior to others. Do not be expectant of special treatment because of your experience on the mission field. Serving on the mission field is not somehow more blessed by God than if one obeys in any other thing in life. You are not a special case and you have no right to judge others. Your identity should be secured by who you are in Christ.

Do not make the error of trying to apply the same high-power ministry methods in your own home environment that might have worked for you on the mission field. Such methods can be a major turn-off in your North American culture. It is good that you are willing to be bold for Christ, but it is important that you are willing to be sensitive to the Spirit's leading, realizing the cultural differences.

You do not want to lose the valuable knowledge, insight and experiences you have gained, but neither do you want to destroy your relationships. It is important that you realize that it is not "either-or" but rather "and". Keep alive your new horizons and deepened consciousness, but do so by using those same skills that have been newly honed overseas on those at home. Use respect, trust and integrity, just as you did overseas. Realizing that you may otherwise be as popular as a reformed smoker, do not try to impose your new insights on others—some will resent it, some will think your faith has been diluted, and still others that will be convinced that you have fallen into error or heresy. You must realize that that you and your family and friends have all changed—communicate as much as possible, try to understand and if that fails, extend grace to each other.

▶ Another common area of dissatisfaction upon return is your experience with your church and Christian friends. It is very common for returning missionaries to make complaints that fellow Christians in their local church have a lack of spiritual focus, that the worship services are not alive or meaningful enough, that they do not understand you, that the pastor won't accept your advice, that the people have their priorities wrong, that the church doesn't have an adequate emphasis on missions and so on. It may or may not all be true, but an inappropriate attitude and reaction will not change it. It must be realized that the function of the local church is not the same as the function of a mission organization. It cannot select its members by level of spiritual maturity, training or commitment. There is by definition a broad spectrum of emotional and spiritual maturity. The pastor must accept people where they are, not where he would like them to be. Lastly, the church has a much broader focus than just evangelism or just missions.

Pastors and the churches aren't always so pleased with returning missionaries either. They often are too "heavenly minded to be any earthly good", expect to be served than to serve, do not submit to the authority of the pastor and deacon board, are too reliant on the team concept to accomplish anything individually, have a sense that the mission field is superior to the church in method and purpose, are more critical than constructive in their comments and feel they have the answers to the problems of the church.

The solution to these problems lies largely in your own court. When you return to your church, make an appointment to make a concise report of your experience to your pastor, answering any questions he may have. Express your interest in sharing your experience. Ask how you can serve the purposes of the pastor and the church as teacher, speaker, committee member and so on. Make it clear that you are under his authority. Thank him for his support and prayers and those of the church.

Don't be critical. Be a servant. Be accountable to others—choose people who will help you maintain the level of spirituality you want to maintain and who will help you retain the new insights you have gathered, but who will keep you honest. If people are not reaching out to you, make sure that you reach out to them. If you are not demonstrating an interest in their lives, they are unlikely to demonstrate more than a polite interest in what you did. Make sure you get your prayer team and supporters together to give them a thorough report and express your heartfelt appreciation. Look for opportunities to tell your story and show your pictures, slides or PowerPoint presentation to civic organizations, youth groups, Sunday School classes, school groups, school classes, missionary support groups and so on. Write letters to supporters and friends when you return. Invite people to your home. Write an article for the church newsletter. Be interviewed for the local newspaper or on local radio show. Keeping these potential opportunities in mind, prepare while you are overseas to share when you return with the idea of challenging others. Record or purchase music of the country. Purchase curios that illustrate your story. Share parts of your journal to tell the story. Send e-mail updates from the field to friends and supporters. Tell the story of your ministry, how it is affecting you and share prayer requests. Take pictures of a day in your life overseas. If you are a healthcare provider, take pictures and notes on interesting medical cases and present them at Grand Rounds, local medical societies or other medical gatherings.

▶ It is important to honestly evaluate and gauge your thoughts and emotions as you adapt to life back at home. It may take months or even years to completely reacclimatize. Not all parts of your life will adjust at the same rate. You may find your professional life is affected more than your personal life or that those may not be in synch with your spiritual life. Remember that the longer the time away, the longer the recovery time often is. It often like climbing a sand dune—very slow, with two steps forward and one step backward. In one sense, reentry will never end. The effect of your experience and the changes it wrought will (God willing) be lifelong.

Loneliness, rejection, disorientation, disruption of personal relationships, and disruption of your relationship with God are common. You may feel alone, misunderstood and alienated. Escape and withdrawal are common reactions. Expect that you might be overly judgmental. Expect you will lose your patience at minor things. Expect that you might have an unreasonable criticalness about the trivial and the unimportant. These are irrational and strong feelings, but normal ones. You may monitor your own actions, feelings and conversation for fear of saying something wrong or inappropriate. It is helpful to remember that acceptance of your home culture does not have to undermine or invalidate your new insights and experiences. Readjustment is not an either/or experience—it is an integration of new experiences with old ones and of new thoughts with old ones. Extend your tolerance and open-mindedness to your own culture.

Look for someone with whom you can share your turmoil. You have left the support structure you had on the field and now you must once again establish a new support structure. These may be with new people rather than with your old friends. Often what you need to share has more to do with squaring your feelings about your home culture than with those you have about the economic depression, poor health conditions, malnutrition, pollution, illiteracy, and social inequity where you served. It is difficult for someone to understand who has not experienced those feelings. You must keep channels of communication open with others who were with you on your trip or who have had similar experiences. The keeping of a journal of your thoughts on the trip and after your return home helps as well. Try writing out your prayers and recording the insights you gain from them. Some returnees gain from the re-entry strategy of presenting to groups interested in learning about their travel experiences. This way, they can channel their excitement for missions abroad to those who share common interests. Withdrawal from God is a common mistake—there is nothing "wrong" with you or less spiritual about you because you experience these feelings. If you struggle to handle this in your own power rather than with God's help, you will suffer needlessly.

How Can You Avoid These Problems?

Here is a list of things you can do that might help:

▶ Prepare your own homecoming by preparing for your departure

▶ Take care of your physical health

▶ Plan proper good-byes and closure of your experience

▶ Schedule sufficient time to return and adapt, recognizing that it is a long and piecemeal process

▶ Get debriefed—either by others or by yourself

▶ Seek counseling help from your pastor or mental health professional if you need it.

▶ Realize that your family has to go through it as well

▶ Maintain effectiveness

Preparing your homecoming starts with making sure people know you are gone and by keeping them informed while you are gone. As mentioned in a previous chapter, you should strive to be sent with the blessing of your church. A public commissioning or prayer service will help. See if you can have articles placed in your church newsletter or bulletin in your absence. Perhaps a bulletin board about your activities can be maintained while you are gone. You can talk to various men's and women's groups, youth groups, Sunday school classes before you go and do the same on your return. Establishing a support group before you go and keeping them informed is the best way of generating a group of people interested in your return and your ministry while you were gone.

Coming home ill takes all the fun out of it! While you are the field, take good care of your health and if you think you have something that needs to be treated, do so before you leave. Everyone likes souvenirs of their trips, but sometimes parasites, intestinal worms and lice were not what you had planned to bring home. Treatment on the field is often more convenient and cheaper than at home. If you have some problem that cannot be properly treated on the mission field, make plans to see your physician as soon as you return home.

It is important to get good closure of this mission experience. Wonderful memories of the experience are fine, but continuing to try to live on the mountaintop is impossible. All directions are down from the top. Accept the bittersweet nature of this time. Expect the ambivalence you may experience about going home. You must recognize and come to terms with the reasons why you are leaving the mission field to come home—your project has been completed., new area of service, your commitment has come to an end, etc. Although it is difficult to leave the place where you experienced such spiritual highs and such growth, you need to recognize that your return home is also God's will for you. It should be viewed as the way God leads you to yet another passage in your life.

It is very tempting to feel guilty about how much work remains. Don't allow guilt about remaining work to persist. No missionary can complete God's work. The question is whether you completed His task for you as you understood it. If so, rest.

It is also important that you leave the field with a clean slate. If your ideals, actions or words have caused a clash with anyone, do your best to make sure you have done all you can to close those rifts. Don't let your frustrations over your ideals about how relationships should be, how the church, mission or hospital should deal with nationals or other similar points of contention spoil what was otherwise a great experience. Even if you have no such areas to correct, it is very important to say good-bye properly to all those folks with whom you need to take your leave. Don't work up to the last minute—you won't get all there is to be done finished anyway and you will miss out on a great blessing.

Another major error that can ruin your homecoming is the failure to schedule sufficient time to return, to experience these feelings and to adapt. All the problems of re-entry tend to hit at once and you may not find much patience in your family and friends. It is not uncommon for them to think (and sometimes say), something like "You have been home three days. Get over it." It took you a while to get used to the

new culture and getting used to your home culture also takes time.
Schedule yourself sufficient time, warn your family about your possible reactions, and also remind yourself.

Reentry with a family is a special situation. Before you leave the
field, encourage your children to take special things and lots of pictures home to North America. Be aware that your family members may
be feeling the same sort of grief
over a change in or loss of close-
knit relationships. They too may
feel the loss of personal significance. This grief and concerns
about peer-group acceptance at
home can be more severe than
you expect, especially if you have
been gone a long period of time.
This is often a time that may precipitate a crisis of faith, especially in teenagers. One home, parents may grieve at the loss of the
close family relationships they
had on the mission field as the
children's' desire to make up on

> *"Remember, when you see a
> missionary coming home
> broken in body and weary
> in soul, it isn't the privations
> or dangers or things he's
> done that leave a deep
> hurt; it's the things he
> couldn't do that break
> his heart."*
>
> —Anonymous

missed extracurricular activities and see missed TV and movies cause
the family to fragment. The best solution is prayer and non-threaten-
ing, accepting open communication. It is important to realize that
there are often marked individual variances in re-entry. The members
of your family are probably feeling the same sorts of things that you
are feeling but they may not be feeling them (or resolving them) at the
same rate that you are. Be patient with each other. If there seems to be
a major problem, do not hesitate to seek counseling help from your
pastor or mental health professional if you need it. It is not a sign of
weakness or a sign of a loss of faith. At the end of this chapter, there
is a list of organizations and resources that may help in this sort of
problem. Seek help if you need it.

Even if you are not having problems beyond the ordinary, it is very important to get debriefed. If you went with a group, some of them have a formal process that they will want you to go through. If you went alone or the group does not offer that service, it is important to do it with your family or for yourself. Philippians 4:8, 9 *"Finally, brothers, whatever is true, whatever is noble, whatever is right, whatever is pure, whatever is lovely, whatever is admirable—if anything is excellent or praiseworthy—think about such things. Whatever you have learned or received or heard from me, or seen in me—put it into practice. And the God of peace will be with you"* Storti writes "Moreover, simply because reentry can be frustrating, lonely and generally unpleasant at times is not to say that is either a harmful experience or even a negative one. After all, frustration, loneliness and unpleasantness are very often the precursors of insight and personal growth. Maybe reentry doesn't always feel good, but then feeling good isn't much of a standard for measuring experience".

Debriefing is a way to measure the experience. It is the process of thinking about what you have learned about yourself, about God, about others and then putting it into practice. It is sometimes easiest to do it with someone else but a few hours of quiet time putting down the answers to the questions below can be very productive. After you have answered them, pray about what has been revealed to you. Then put them aside and review them in a couple of days, a couple of weeks and a couple of months to see if you have any further insights. You may find that you have forgotten much of the lessons you were taught. That loss of clarity is a very rapid process, so it is important to do this as soon as possible after you return.

▶ Was I effective on this trip? What did I do right? What did I do wrong? What would I like to work on expanding or improving next time? What would I like to make sure I don't do again?

▶ What have I learned from God about myself on this trip? What have I learned about others? What have I learned about God? Which of these surprised me the most? What disappointed me the most? What as God taught me about how to deal with these?

▶ What have I learned from fellow workers that I would like to incorporate into my life? What have I seen God do in the lives of others?

How can I seek those experiences for myself? What barriers do I have in my own life that might prevent God from working?

▶ What insights do I have that might help fellow workers? What suggestions do I have that might improve the next trip, either for the group or for myself?

▶ How do I incorporate these new insights into my life? What will I change about my day-to-day life? How will this trip change my outlook on my family, my job, my church, my Christian witness, and my involvement with missions at home and abroad? What are the obstacles in my life that will preclude me from incorporating these changes into my life?

It must be recognized that sometimes it seems obvious that your trip was not "successful". It was not the glowing, mountain-top type of experience you had hoped to have. That is even more reason to go through debriefing. In going through this process, it may become apparent to you that your trip wasn't "successful" but that does not mean that it was a waste of time and money or that God didn't show you exactly what He wanted to show you. You may just have missed it at the time. It may be that the trip was not a good experience precisely because there is a major disconnect between how you see yourself and your life and how God sees you. Such "bad" experiences can be some of the most enlightening of your life if you let them be.

> *I haven't been everywhere, but it's on my list."*
> —Susan Sontag

Once you are home, one of the biggest problems is how to maintain a sustained effectiveness. By that, we mean how do you make sure your experience is not "wasted" and that it continues to bear some sort of fruit. There are many things you can do. One of the first is to realize that you are now a tangible link between your church and the place and culture you left. In the short run, make sure you have brought suitable gifts or reminders for your support team and make arrangements to give them a full report using whatever tape recordings, video, pictures and souvenirs you had prepared to bring back to them. Speak to whatever groups you can get permission to address. In the long run, support the ministry you visited. Pray regularly and get updated prayer requests. Stay informed about the mission field. Keep lively correspondences going by e-mail or snail mail. Be supportive of your new friends and missionary friends. To whatever extent you can, support the work financially. Think about what projects you can develop that will help advance the work of the mission where you were. Be a recruiter for other people to go as short-term help. Return yourself for the short-term. Consider being part of a mission board or agency. Be part of your church's mission committee and be an advocate for that mission field whenever possible. Last of all, prayerfully and seriously consider the option of career missions for yourself.

WEB RESOURCES

www.missionarycare.com
www.crossculturalworkers.com

ORGANIZATIONS

Alongside, Inc.
PO Box 587
Richland, MI 49083-0587
Phone: (269) 671.4809
URL: www.alongsidecares.net
Restoration and growth
programs for missionaries

Barnabas International
PO Box 11211
Rockford, IL 61126-1211
Phone: (815) 395-1335
E-mail: barnabas@barnabas.org
URL: www.barnabas.org
The mission of Barnabas
International is to edify, encourage and strength servants in
ministry

Consultation on Debriefing & Renewal
Mission Training International
PO Box 1220
Palmer Lake, CO 80133
Phone: (800) 896-3710 or
(719) 487-0111
E-mail: info@mti.org
URL: www.MTI.org
Seminars and workshops to assist mission leaders and missionaries in reentry. Also, they host the Mental Health and Missions Conference, an annual conference for those committed to serving and supporting a healthy missions community (Contact Dr. John Powell)

Fairhaven Ministries
#1-8191 Rogers Road
Vernon, BC V1B 3M8
Canada
Phone: (250) 260-1616
E-mail: info@fairhaven
ministries.org
URL: www.fairhaven
ministries.org
Retreat center and/or counseling for returning missionaries

Heartstream Resources
101 Herman Lee Circle
Liverpool, PA 17045
Phone: (717) 444-2374
E-mail: HeartstreamResources
@hotmail.com
URL: www.heartstream
resources.org
Residential programs with professional services. Programs of restoration and renewal for cross-cultural workers wounded or depleted in service.

Link Care Foundation
1734 West Shaw Street
Fresno, CA 93711
Phone: (559) 439-5920
E-mail: info@linkcare.org
URL: www.linkcare.org
Residential programs to help families or individuals focus on leaving and grieving, transition, adaptation, closure and action planning.

Mission Family Counseling
Stratford Oaks Building
Suite 306
514 S Stratford Rd # 306,
Winston-Salem, NC 27103
Phone: (877) 623-5559
E-mail: care@mfcs.org
URL: www.mfcs.org
A mission of providing pastoral counseling and support to missionaries, ministers and their families.

Emmaus Road International
7150 Tanner Court
San Diego, CA 92111
Phone/Fax: (858) 292-7020
E-mail: Emmaus_Road@eri.org
URL: www.eri.org
Publications, seminars, training courses, ministry trips and speakers bureau to help equip individuals, churches, and agencies to develop cross-cultural ministry and support of missionaries

CHAPTER 17

"IF ONLY "

As Frank Sinatra sang, "Regrets, I've had a few." We all wish we had the wisdom to avoid a mistake or live a certain time or event over. Here, presented without comment, are some remarks made by ourselves and other short-term missionaries we have talked to over the years. The first several were made by men and women doing short-term medical missions but the truths within them apply to all short-term missionaries. They were all made in reference to previous short-term mission trips.

"I wish I had not set personal achievement and "numbers" above experiences and relationships. I should have made a point to do more local sightseeing, had more new experiences, visited their (the nationals') homes when invited, gone to more national churches, and invited more nationals into my home. Instead, I was more concerned about how many patients I could see and how many procedures I could or should do."

"I wish I had achieved a better balance in the number of patients I saw and with the surgical cases I did. I overworked myself and the staff and I lost out on a lot of the blessing."

"I wish I had not been so reluctant to ask for and accept support from others who wanted to help. I thought I needed to do it all and people wouldn't want to give financial support to a physician."

"I regret that I did not spend more time telling of Jesus' love to my patients. I let the language barrier intimidate me."

"I regret having isolated my children as much as I did from the nationals and from the hospital. I was too concerned about health issues (what diseases they might pick up), and they lost out on a great deal of cross-cultural growth and experience because of it."

"I wished I had encouraged my children to spend more time with my spouse in the hospital. It was the greatest experience along that line that they would ever receive. They can't do that here in the States. I think it would have made a difference in how they accept the downside of being physician's children."

"I should have spent more time in spiritual preparation before the trip."

"I should have asked more people to pray for me. I never realized how important that would become on a day-to-day basis.

"If I had it to do over, I would work at a deeper relationship with one or two nationals with whom I 'clicked.'"

"Next time, I will start sooner to develop relationships with the nationals. I focused on relationships with other expatriates to my detriment in the area of my relationships with the nationals."

"I wish I had kept my big mouth shut and kept my criticisms to myself until I better understood the dynamics of what was really going on. My well-meaning comments actually fed the flames."

"I am sorry I let so many chances to encourage both the national staff and missionaries get away from me."

"I wish I had kept a journal in much more detail. So many of the vivid experiences and details I thought I would never forget are already fading."

"I wish I had gotten national help with my household sooner than I did. I was afraid that I was somehow taking advantage of her but she was grateful for the income and I was grateful for the help while my husband worked at the clinic."

"I really regret having criticized the career missionary when I got there for having household help. I soon realized how much time it takes to take care of my family there and if the missionary wives were going to have any ministry, they had to make that choice."

"I wish I had brought my spouse with me."

"I wish I had brought my family."

"I wish I had brought my pastor with me."

"I wish I had stayed longer."

"Next time, I will try much harder to find out what I could bring for them (the missionaries) when I come."

"I should have not been so much concerned about the extra luggage cost and brought some more things that would have made a difference to the missionaries and to the work."

"Next time, I will take more advantage of the opportunities to speak to the staff, various national groups and churches."

"I am sorry I did not give and show more grace in my relationships with our team, the missionaries and the nationals."

"If only I had taken more pictures."

"I am sorry I ran out of film [memory] for my camera."

"I wish I had done a better job of taking pictures so I could present the work more effectively on my return home."

"I regret that I did not give more thought before I went to some of the issues the missionaries on the field face so I would not have been so taken aback and been so disturbed by some of the things I had to work through."

"I needed to keep in better touch with the missionaries once I returned home. No wonder they feel sometimes like they are forgotten."

"I tended to forget too quickly what the experience was like when I returned to my hectic lifestyle."

"I am only sorry that I didn't do this sooner."

"I regret that I had not woken up much sooner to the fact that I spent my life not striving for what was really important in the last analysis. It is too late now for a career in missions; I wish it wasn't."

CHAPTER 18

WHAT NOW?

Is it? Is it too late for you to rearrange your life to honor Christ's call on your life?

What did you learn on this short-term mission experience about how to serve the Kingdom of God better? We read in Romans 10:9–15 (NIV) *"That if you confess with your mouth, 'Jesus is Lord,' and believe in your heart that God raised him from the dead, you will be saved. For it is with your heart that you believe and are justified, and it is with your mouth that you confess and are saved. As the Scripture says, 'Anyone who trusts in him will never be put to shame.' For there is no difference between Jew and Gentile—the same Lord is Lord of all and richly blesses all who call on him, for, 'Everyone who calls on the name of the Lord will be saved.' How, then, can they call on the one they have not believed in? And how can they believe in the one of whom they have not heard? And how can they hear without someone preaching to them? And how can they preach unless they are sent? As it is written, 'How beautiful are the feet of those who bring good news!'"*

Not all are called to go and be career missionaries. Those who preach must be sent. As you have now seen and perhaps experienced, being sent requires an intensive program of prayer, support, and encouragement. Who is more qualified after this trip to do that for others than you are? You will have been there and you will have a better understanding than most of your friends and fellow church members. You will have seen the difference that prayer and even small bits of financial aid can make. You will be able to empathize better with career missionaries that have a difficult row to hoe and you will be a more effective cheerleader and prayer warrior.

Missions is not about how much we love people or even about how much we love God; it is about how much God loved us. Can we truly say that we are compelled to tell others because of Christ's love?

Was His death in vain or should we truly no longer live for ourselves but rather live for Him?

For Christ's love compels us, because we are convinced that one died for all, and therefore all died. And he died for all, that those who live should no longer live for themselves but for him who died for them and was raised again. (2 Cor 5:14–15, NIV)

What is Christ's love compelling you to do?

We close this book with some wise words from a veteran medical missionary[1]:

"You have seen the reality of missions. Their faces are imprinted on your mind; their sweat was so recently washed from your hands. You have heard the cries and you have wiped the tears—from their eyes and from your own. For a brief time, you became part of their lives, and they became part of yours. Missions took on a shape, but even more than a shape, the great need became a name and a face. What will you do next?

The Lord said (to Moses):

*'**I have indeed seen** the misery of my people . . .*

***I have heard** them crying out . . .*

***I am concerned** about their suffering . . .*

*So **I have come down** to rescue them!'* (Exodus 3:7–8)

God never gets on an airplane and flies back to suburbia. The eyes and the ears and the concern of God are forever directed toward the misery and the cries and the suffering of his people. Before you volunteered, before you gave a second thought about the needs of the people served by missionaries, God's heart was breaking over their suffering. It has always been so, and will be so until the end of time.

*'So now, go. **I am sending you!**'* (Exodus 3:10)

Moses had already tried to rescue the people in his own strength, and failed miserably. That is why God finds him on

[1] We acknowledge our debt to Dr. Bill McCoy, career missionary in Swaziland and now Papua New Guinea, for stating so well what we could not.

the far side of the desert tending sheep. Moses is trying to hide from the misery and cries of the people and, in doing so, is running from God's call on his life. But God invites Moses to participate in His own amazing redemptive purpose, and Moses' life will never be the same!

A missionary effort is not something we do, it is something God is doing, and we have the great privilege of participating in it. God is healing, God is redeeming, and God is changing lives! "Through God's mercy, we have this ministry" (2 Corinthians 4:1). It is only by the mercy and the grace of God that He invites us to participate in ministry. It is a profound mystery but it is clear that we are the instruments God has chosen to rescue his people, to redeem his creation. 'He has committed to us the message of reconciliation' (2 Corinthians 5:19).

What are we doing with the invitation of God and the message committed to us? Therein lays our only hope for fullness of joy, deep meaning, and freedom from all that would entangle us. Trouble free? Absolutely not! You have tasted some of the many difficulties encountered in medical missions. Cultural differences, limited resources, lifestyle changes, ingratitude, personality clashes, persecution, danger, sleepless nights, excessive demands—the mission field has all of these and more. But these are "achieving for us an eternal glory that far outweighs them all" (2 Corinthians 4:17). If the call of God for your life involves missions, then you are among the most privileged. For God has "come down to rescue them" and He is calling you to witness and participate in His miraculous work!

Seek the will of God, listen to His voice, and stay involved in missions! It may mean a career change. It may mean a new structure to your career or new priorities in the way you make and spend money. Maybe you are called to regular volunteer service or recruiting others or identifying resources to strengthen a specific ministry.

The life of Jesus Christ gives us a clear model for Kingdom ministry. Matthew chapters 8 and 9 vividly portray Christ teaching, preaching, and healing. "When he saw the crowds, he had compassion on them, because they were harassed and helpless." If your experience in missions has opened your eyes to the suffering of the crowds, then listen closely for the calling voice of the Lord of the harvest. That voice bears your name."

Get Ready! Get Set! GO!

APPENDIX A

SUGGESTED BIBLIOGRAPHY

*We have marked books of special value to us with an asterisk. A more extensive bibliography can be downloaded from www.S3Ministries.com

Missions & Mission Philosophy

Blackaby, Henry T. and Claude V. King
Experiencing God: Knowing and Doing the Will of God
Nashville: Lifeway Press, 1990.
ISBN 0-8054-9954-7

Bonk, Jonathan
Missions and Money
Maryknoll: Orbis Books, 2006, ISBN 978-1-57075-650-4

*Johnstone, Patrick
Operation World, 21st Century Edition: When We pray, God works
Paternoster Publishing, 2001.
ISBN 1850783578

Miller, Darrow
Discipling Nations: The Power of Truth to Transform Cultures
Seattle: YWAM Publishing.
ISBN 1-57658-015-6

Olson, C. Gordon
What in the World is God Doing: The Essentials of Global Missions—An Introductory Guide, 5th ed.
Cedar Knolls, NJ: Global Gospel Publishers.
ISBN 096248505-5

Pippert, Rebecca
Out of the Salt Shaker and into the World
Downer's Grove, IL: InterVarsity Press, 1999.
ISBN 0-8308-2220-8

Piper, John
Let the Nations be Glad! The Supremacy of God in Missions.
Grand Rapids: Baker, 1993.
ISBN 0-8010-7124-0

Rowell, John
*To Give or Not to Give?
Rethinking Dependency,
Restoring Generosity and
Redefining Sustainability*
Tyrone, GA: Authentic, 2006.
ISBN 978-1-932805-86-4

Saint, Steve
*The Great Omission:
Fulfilling Christ's
Commission Completely*
Seattle: YWAM Publishing,
2001.
ISBN 1-57658-216-7

**Short-term Missions
in General**

Backholder, Mathew
*Mission Preparation Training
—How to Prepare for Your
Short-Term Mission Trip*
Exposure Publishing, 2006.
ISBN-13 978-1846851650

Borthwick, Paul
*Missions—God's Heart for
the World*
Downers Grove, IL:
Intervarsity Press, 2000.
ISBN 0-8308-3090-1
Nine studies for individuals
or groups.

Christian Medical and Dental
Associations
Mission Survival Kit
Audiotapes and outline.
1-888-231-2637

Dearborn, Timothy
*Short-Term Missions
Workbook: From Mission
Tourists to Global Citizens*
Downer's Grove, IL:
Inter-Varsity Press, 2003.
ISBN 0830832335

Dunn, Norma K.
*Go Ye...Short-term Missions
Made Practical*
Authorhouse, 2004.
ISBN-13 978-1418419585

Eaton, Chris, and K. Hurst
*Vacations with a Purpose:
A Handbook for Your Short-
Term Missions Experience*
Colorado Springs: Cook
Communications Ministries,
1994.
Team Member's Manual:
ISBN 0-71814-5041-1
Leader's Manual (1993):
ISBN 0-7814-5042-X

Fann, Anner-Geri', and G.
Taylor
*How to Get Ready for Short-
term Missions: The Ultimate
Guide for Sponsors, Parents
and Those Who Go!*
Nashville: Thomas Nelson
Publishers, 2006.
ISBN 1-4185-0977-9

Greene, Leon
A Guide to Short Term Missions: A Comprehensive Manual for Planning an Effective Mission Trip
Waynesboro, GA: Gabriel Publishing, 2003.
ISBN 1-884543-73-1

Ives, Jane
Transforming Ventures: A Spiritual Guide for Volunteers in Mission
Nashville: Upper Room Books, 2000.
ISBN 0-8358-0910-2

Johnson, Kevin
Mission Trip Prep Student Journal
Grand Rapids: Zondervan/ Youth Specialties, 2003.
ISBN-13 978-0310240211

Johnson, Kevin
Mission Trip Prep Kit Leader's Guide
Grand Rapids: Zondervan/ Youth Specialties, 2003.
ISBN-13 978-0310244882

Kiekhaefer, Phil (ed.)
Short-Term Missions Leadership Handbook: Preparation and Field Guide
Palo Alto: Footsteps Missions.
SBN 0-9777583-0-3

Kirby, Scott
Equipped for Adventure: A Practical Guide to Short-Term Mission Trips
New Hope Publishers— Impact, 2006.
ISBN-13 978-1596690110

Kuhn, W., S. Kuhn, H. Gross and S. Benesh
Global Medical Missions: Preparation, Procedure and Practice
Published by W. Ted Kuhn, 2004.
ISBN 0-9763296-0-3

Lisech, Howard and Bonnie Lisech
Abide in the Vine (14 day Devotional Bible Studies)
Orlando: Deeper Roots Publications, 1995.
ISBN 1-930547-16-1
Also available in 21 and 50 day editions.[1] Other studies available.

Livermore, David A
Serving with Eyes Wide Open: Doing Short-Term Missions with Cultural Intelligence
Grand Rapids: Baker Books, 2006.
ISBN 978-0-8010-6616-0

---

[1] Deeper Roots Publication, www.DeeperRoots.com

Petersen, Roger, G. Aeschliman, and R.W. Sneed
Maximum Impact Short-Term Mission: The God-Commanded Repetitive Deployment of Swift, Temporary, Non-Professional Missionaries
Minneapolis: STEMPress, 2003.
ISBN 0-9711258-1-3

Priest, Robert (ed.)
Effective Engagement in Short-Term Missions: Doing It Right
Pasadena: William Carey Library Publishers, 2008.
ISBN-13 978-0878080052

Richter, Don
Mission Trips That Matter: Embodied Faith for the Sake of the World
Upper Room Books, 2008.
ISBN 13 978-0835899475

Robinson, George.
Striking the Match
e3 Resources, 2008

Wood, Lena. Challenged:
Mission Trip Devotions and Journal
Standard Publishing Company, 2008.
ISBN-13 978-0784722855

Culture Shock, Living Abroad and Coming Home, Cross-Cultural Experiences

Chinn, Lisa E
Reentry Guide for Short-term Mission Leaders
Orlando: Deeper Roots Publications, 2000.

Elmer, Duane
Cross Cultural Connections: Stepping Out and Fitting In Around the World
Downers Grove, IL: InterVarsity Press, 2002.
ISBN 0-8308-2309-3

*Jordan, Peter
Re-Entry: Making the Transition from Missions to Life at Home
Seattle: YWAM Publishing, 1992.
ISBN 0-927545-40-3

Knell, Marion
Families on the Move: Growing Up Overseas and Loving It
Grand Rapids: Monarch Books, 2001.
ISBN 0-8254-6018-2

Lanier, Sarah
Foreign to Familiar: A Guide to Understanding Hot- and Cold-Climate Cultures
Hagerstown, MD: McDougal Publishing, 2000.
ISBN 1-58158-022-3

Lisech, Howard and Bonnie
Lisech
*Fishers of Men: Reentry
Guide (14 day Bible Study
Guide)*
Orlando; Deeper Roots
Publications, 1997.
ISBN 1-930547-12-9 [1]

Maranz, David
*African Friends and Money
Matters: Observations from
Africa*
Dallas: SIL International,
2001.
ISBN 1-55671-117-4 [2]

Piet-Pelon, Nancy J, and
Barbara Hornby
*Women's Guide to Overseas
Living 2nd Ed.*
Yarmouth, ME: Intercultural
Press, Inc., 1992.
ISBN 1-877864-05-6

*Pirolo, Neal
*The Reentry Team: Caring for
Your Returning Missionaries*
San Diego, CA: Emmaus
Road International, 2000.
ISBN 1-880185-07-5

Rapaille, Clotaire
The Culture Code.
New York: Broadway Books,
2006.
ISBN-13 978-0-7679-2056-8

Storti, Craig
The Art of Coming Home
Yarmouth, ME: Intercultural
Press, 2001.
ISBN 1-85788-297-0

Raising Support

Barnett, Betty
*Friend Raising: Building a
Missionary Support Team
That Lasts, Revised ed.*
Seattle: YWAM Publishing,
2003.
ISBN 1576582833

Bromley, Dana and J. Allum
"Fund Raising Idea Packet:
Personal and Group Short-
Term Mission Fund Raising".
Available from STEM
Ministries (2005),
Minneapolis.
www.stemintl.org/publications/
order

Dillon, William P.
*People Raising: A Practical
Guide to Raising Support*
Chicago: Moody Press, 1993.
ISBN 0-8024-6447-5

---

[1] Deeper Roots Publication, www.DeeperRoots.com
[2] Obtainable from International Academic Bookstore, SIL International, URL
www.sil.org E-mail: academic_books@sil.org

Morton, Scott
Funding Your Ministry:
Whether You're Gifted or Not
Colorado Springs:
Dawsonmedia, 1999.
ISBN 0-9672480-0-0
See www.dawsonmedia.com.
4 video series "Raising
Personal Support" with an
85-page workbook, a 3 video
series "Fund Your Ministry!"
and the paperback Funding
Your Ministry

Nouwen, Henri J. M.
"The Spirituality of Fund-
Raising"
Booklet available from Henri
Nouwen Society via the web-
site www.henriNouwen.org,
2004.
ISBN 0-8358-9823-7

Sommer, Pete
Getting Sent: A Relational
Approach to Support Raising
Downers Grove, IL: Inter-
Varsity, 1999 ISBN
0830822186

Medical Books for
the Non-physician

Burns, A. August, Ronnie
Lovich, et al.
Where Women Have No
Doctor: A Health Guide for
Women
Berkeley: Hesperian
Foundation, 1997.
ISBN 0-942364-25-2 [3]

Dickson, Murray
Where There is No Dentist
Berkeley: Hesperian
Foundation, 1983.
ISBN 0-942364-05-820 [4]

Fountain, Daniel
Primary Diagnosis &
Treatment: A Manual for
Clinical and Health Centre
Staff in Developing Countries
Brunswick, GA: MAP
International Publication and
London: MacMillan Press,
Ltd., 1992.
ISBN 0-333-57605-5

Vanderkooi, Mary
Village Medical Manual, Vols.
I and II, 5th edition
Pasadena: William Carey
Library, 2000.
ISBN 0-87808-778-8 (Vol 1)
and ISBN 0-87808-779-6
(Vol 2)

[3] Many books from the Hesperian Foundation are now free for downloading at http://www.hesperian.org/publications_download.php

Werner, David
*Disabled Village Children: A
Guide for Community Health
Workers, Rehabilitation
Workers, and Families*
Berkeley: Hesperian
Foundation, 1987.
ISBN 0-942364-06-620 [4]

Werner, David
*Where There is No Doctor:
A Village Health Care
Handbook*
Berkeley: Hesperian
Foundation, 1992.
ISBN 0-942364-15-5 20 [4]

**Missionaries and
Missionary Kids**

*Hale, Thomas
On Being a Missionary.
Pasadena: William Carey
Library, 1995.
ISBN 0-87808-255-7

*Pirolo, Neal
Serving as Senders
San Diego: Emmaus Road
International, 1991.
ISBN 1-880185-00-8

Pollock, David, R.E. VanReken
*The Third Culture Kid
Experience: Growing Up
among Worlds.*
Yarmouth, ME: InterCultural
Press, 1999.
ISBN 1-877864-72-2

Taylor, William (ed.)
*Too Valuable to Lose:
Exploring the Causes and
Cures of Missionary Attrition*
Pasadena: William Carey
Library, 1997.
ISBN 0-87808-277-8

---

[4] Available in multiple languages: Spanish, French, Arabic, Hindi, Indonesian, Spanish, Portuguese, Swahili, Vietnamese, Italian, Aymara, Bengali, Chinese, Creole, Dari, German, Kannada, Korean, Lao, Marathi, Nephali, Pushtu, Quechua, Shuar, Sindhi, Sinhali, Tamil, Thai, Tigre, Tigrina, Tswana, Urdu and English editions adapted for specific countries.

SAMPLE SUPPORT LETTER

Dear _____,

    I recently heard about an opportunity to go on a mission trip with the (organization) to a (location) in (country) that needs my help. As I heard about it, I really sensed God calling me to be a part of this mission.

    The experience will be working with (description). I will be working with a team that will be involved with a health clinic and the team will be also working with orphanages, in schools and with the local congregation as they try to have an outreach to their town. (Or if a hospital, describe your work there) If God speaks to your heart, as He has to mine, I would love for you to go with me. For more information, just give me a call at or you can call the office of (organization) at (phone number).

    But if God is not calling you to go overseas with us, you can still take part in reaching the people there with the message of Jesus Christ by sending me to share that message. I would like to ask you to prayerfully consider helping me to go by providing a financial gift. The total cost of the mission trip will be

    Depending upon whether or not you are able to contribute any personal funds to the mission yourself choose from the following two paragraphs.

    OPTION 1: As I have looked at my own finances, I have determined I will personally be able to pay for $_____ of the trip price, leaving a balance of $_____. Would you be willing to invest $25, $50, $100, $200 or another amount to help me be a part of this vital outreach to the people of (country name)?

Continued on next page

OPTION 2: To help with this total need, would you be willing to invest $25, $50, $100, $200 or another amount to help me be a part of this vital outreach to the people of (country name)?

So that all gifts will be tax-deductible, I have arranged for my church (or the organization with which you are traveling) to accept contributions for my mission trip. They, in turn, will send a check covering my cost to the travel agency. Checks should be made payable to (name of church or organization) and enclose with it the separate piece of paper that I have enclosed with this letter. Please fill in your name and mailing address and it will show that the check is to be designated for (your name/name of mission trip or account number).

For your convenience, I am enclosing a self-addressed envelope. I am also planning to give you a phone call within the next week to answer any questions you might have and to see if you would be able to help. My deadline to have all my funds in is (date).

Please know that it is not my desire to pressure you in any way. If now is not a good time for you to be able to help, I certainly understand. In any case, please pray for me as I seek to raise the funds to go and while I am ministering overseas. Your prayers will be a great encouragement. If you would like to receive updates on what is happening and be a part of my prayer support team, I would certainly appreciate it. Please call me at (your phone number), write me at (your address) or e-mail me at (your address). Please remember to include your own e-mail address.

I promise to give you a full report of what the Lord is doing in (country name) when I return.

Sincerely,

TESTIMONY WORKSHEET

Introduction:
    Name: _____
    Profession: _____
    Hometown: _____

Why I came on this trip:

_____

_____

_____

_____

What my life was like before becoming a Christian:

_____

_____

_____

_____

How I became a Christian:

_____

_____

_____

_____

What it means to be a Christian—impact on my life:

_____

_____

_____

How others can have a similar experience—the plan of salvation:

_____

_____

_____

_____

Give the opportunity for others to make a decision for Christ:

_____

_____

_____

_____

My summary statement and thank-you:

_____

_____

_____

_____

_____

_____

_____

_____

_____

_____

_____

_____

PACKING CHECKLIST

Instruction

This list was made with the idea that it is better to travel light because you have consciously made the decision you don't need it—not because you forgot to think about needing it in the first place! *You certainly do NOT need everything—or even most of the things—on this list!* Primitive conditions will certainly require different supplies than a well-established mission compound. Six days is different than six months. Photocopy these pages, add the things you know you will need, and cross out the unneeded. When you pack, use the modified check list to make sure you are not forgetting something important. Don't forget to use TSA-approved padlocks on your luggage.

On Your Person

On you (carry the critical things in a money belt, or in a passport pouch or belt).

❏ Itinerary
❏ Airline tickets
❏ Passport
❏ Visas if separate
❏ International certificate of health
❏ Credit card/ATM/debit card
❏ Calling cards for use in North America
❏ Driver's license
❏ Cash
❏ Traveler's checks
❏ Regular bank checks
❏ SCUBA certification
❏ Overseas access numbers for AT&T, MCI, Sprint, etc.
❏ Keys to luggage
❏ Health insurance card, contact numbers
❏ _____

In Your Carry-On Luggage or Purse

❏ Inflatable pillow
❏ Ear plugs
❏ Sleep mask
❏ Sock-slippers
❏ Written inventory of your luggage contents
❏ Letter of invitation from the place you are going

❏ Letter of official standing from your sending agency
❏ Phrase books and/or electronic translators
❏ International driver's license (from AAA) if you plan to drive after arrival
❏ Keys (second set) to other luggage
❏ At least one week's worth of your vital prescription medications (including antimalarials)
❏ At least one change of clothing
❏ Toothbrush, toothpaste, washcloth, soap, deodorant, comb, brush, toilet paper, waterless hand cleaner
❏ Water filter bottle
❏ Reading glasses
❏ Bible and other reading material
❏ Laptop and critical or expensive electronics
❏ Small roll of duct tape (to reseal luggage after customs)
❏ Saline nose drops (to keep airways moist)
❏ _____
❏ _____

Clothing

❏ Visor or hat
❏ Shower shoes (flip-flops, thongs)
❏ Money belt
❏ Athletic shoes
❏ Walking shoes
❏ Sandals
❏ House slippers (folding)
❏ Foldable rubber overshoes
❏ Belt
❏ Lightweight jacket or sweater

Men

❏ Underwear (6 sets)
❏ Socks (8 pairs)
❏ Slacks (3)
❏ Jeans (1)
❏ Shorts (1)
❏ Shirts (6)
❏ Swimsuit
❏ Pajamas
❏ Sport coat
❏ Tie

Women

❏ Underclothing (6 sets)
❏ Tops (6)
❏ Skirts–or slacks if okay (3)
❏ Jeans–if okay (1)
❏ "Sunday dress" (1)
❏ Swimsuit and coverup (1)

Medication

- ❏ Your prescription medications (carry at least a week's worth in your carry-on)
- ❏ Contraceptives
- ❏ Analgesics
  - ❏ Over the counter (OTC) Acetaminophen, NSAIDs (e.g., ibuprofen, naprosyn, aspirin)
  - ❏ Prescription (N.B. Codeine can serve triple-duty for cough, diarrhea, and pain)
- ❏ Antimalarial (e.g., mefloquine, doxycycline, chloroquine, Malarone®)
- ❏ Antidiarrheals
  - ❏ OTC: Pepto-Bismol®
  - ❏ OTC: Loperamide (Immodium®)
- ❏ Altitude sickness (e.g., acetazolamide)
- ❏ Motion sickness
- ❏ Antibiotics
  - ❏ For traveler's diarrhea, (e.g., doxycycline, fluroquinolone)
  - ❏ Broad-spectrum antibiotic, (e.g., cephalexin, amoxicillin, Augmentin®)
- ❏ Cold and flu medication
  - ❏ Oral decongestants
  - ❏ Spray decongestants
  - ❏ Antihistamines
  - ❏ Cough drops/throat lozenges
  - ❏ Cough suppressants
- ❏ Antacids, antiulcer medication
- ❏ Sleeping pills
- ❏ Medication for nausea

- ❏ Antifungal
  - ❏ Topical powders or creams
  - ❏ Treatment for vaginitis
- ❏ Melatonin
- ❏ Sun block
- ❏ Lip balm (with high SPF)
- ❏ Lubricant jelly
- ❏ _____
- ❏ _____
- ❏ _____

Hygiene

- ❏ Toothpaste
- ❏ Toothbrush
- ❏ Dental floss
- ❏ Deodorant
- ❏ Cologne
- ❏ Comb(s)
- ❏ Brush
- ❏ Mirror (plastic is best)
- ❏ Razor(s)
- ❏ Shaving cream/depilatory
- ❏ Washcloth (in sealable plastic bag)
- ❏ Towels (absorbable synthetic)
- ❏ Toilet paper
- ❏ Tampons
- ❏ Menstrual pads
- ❏ Denture adhesive
- ❏ Contact adhesive for denture repair
- ❏ _____
- ❏ Hair dryer and/or curling iron (110/220 interchangeable voltage)
- ❏ Hair rollers
- ❏ Hair spray
- ❏ Hair scissors or clippers (110/220 interchangeable voltage)

Cosmetics

- ❏ Moisturizer
- ❏ Lipstick
- ❏ Blush
- ❏ Base
- ❏ _____
- ❏ _____

Cleanliness

- ❏ Bar soap or bath gel
- ❏ Shampoo/conditioner
- ❏ Pre-moistened (antibacterial) wipes
- ❏ Water-free hand cleaner
- ❏ Alcohol wipes
- ❏ Camp detergent (for dishes, clothing)

Contact Lenses and Eyeglasses

- ❏ Contacts (including spares)
- ❏ Contact cleaner
- ❏ Contact saline
- ❏ Contact disinfectant solution
- ❏ Spare eyeglasses
- ❏ Prescription for eyeglasses
- ❏ Prescription for contact lenses
- ❏ Eyeglass repair kit
- ❏ Sunglasses
- ❏ Reading glasses
- ❏ Eyeglass restraining strap

First-Aid Kit

- ❏ Tape
- ❏ Gauze pads
- ❏ Roll gauze
- ❏ Elastic support bandage
- ❏ Moleskin
- ❏ Alcohol wipes
- ❏ Burn/insect bite treatment
- ❏ Antibiotic ointment
- ❏ 1% hydrocortisone cream
- ❏ Petroleum jelly
- ❏ Band-Aids®, assorted sizes
- ❏ Tweezers
- ❏ Thermometer (contact strip type)
- ❏ Chemical cold pack
- ❏ Chemical heat pack
- ❏ Suture kit with
  - ❏ Syringes/needles
  - ❏ Anesthetic
  - ❏ Sterile gloves
  - ❏ Suture
  - ❏ Providine-iodophor (Betadine®)solution
  - ❏ _____
- ❏ Manicure set, nail clipper
- ❏ Insect repellent (20–30% DEET)
- ❏ Insecticide for room
- ❏ _____
- ❏ _____

Professional (Medical) Needs for Medical Missions Trips

- ❑ Scrub suits
- ❑ White coat
- ❑ Masks
- ❑ Wintergreen oil (for masks)
- ❑ Caps
- ❑ Examination gloves
- ❑ Sterile gloves
- ❑ OR shoes
- ❑ Oto-ophthalmoscope
  - ❑ Extra batteries
  - ❑ Disposable speculums
- ❑ Black bag
- ❑ Penlight
- ❑ Reflex hammer
- ❑ Measuring tape (inches and centimeters)
- ❑ Loupes
- ❑ _____
- ❑ Textbooks and CD-ROMs
  - ❑ *Handbook of Clinical Medicine in Developing Countries*
  - ❑ _____

Paperwork

You might be wise to send this to your own e-mail site for future access, but also, in separate waterproof bag or pouch, carry:

- ❑ 2 (or more) passport photos
- ❑ Photocopy of passport
- ❑ Photocopy of immunization certificate
- ❑ Copy of travel itinerary
- ❑ Photocopy of professional licenses, certificates, etc.
- ❑ _____

In Your Luggage

- ❑ International driver's license if you do not plan to drive until later in your trip
- ❑ Foreign language dictionaries
- ❑ Travel books
- ❑ Address book
- ❑ Envelopes
- ❑ U.S. stamps (for missionaries' and your use)
- ❑ Bible
- ❑ Notebook
- ❑ Diary
- ❑ Pictures of your family
- ❑ Wallet-size pictures of yourself, your family for distribution
- ❑ Materials about your city, state, and church
- ❑ Prayer cards
- ❑ _____

Miscellaneous

- ❑ Plastic travel luggage scale
- ❑ Fanny pack or backpack
- ❑ Collapsible (net) shopping bag
- ❑ Collapsible suitcase (e.g., Totes®)
- ❑ Sheets, pillowcase
- ❑ Sleep bag
- ❑ Ziploc bags (sandwich, 1 qt., and 1 gal. size)
- ❑ Extra-large garbage bags (big enough for suitcase)
- ❑ Cellophane tape
- ❑ Duct tape or reinforced tape
- ❑ Pens (extra ones for gifts)

❏ Gifts for hosts
   ❏ _____
   ❏ _____
   ❏ _____
❏ Gifts for nationals
   ❏ _____
   ❏ _____
   ❏ _____
❏ Travel can "safe" (with hidden compartment)
❏ Swiss Army knife or multipurpose tool (e.g., Leatherman®)
❏ Scissors
❏ Small outdoor thermometer
❏ Compass
❏ Nightlight (proper voltage)
❏ Whistle with lanyard
❏ Emergency blanket (foil)
❏ Pocket kit with fish lines, hooks
❏ Flashlight
   ❏ Extra batteries
❏ Chemical light sticks
❏ Disposable lighter(s)
❏ Candle
❏ Hand-operated can opener
❏ Mess kit
❏ Collapsible cups
❏ Silverware kit
❏ Snacks, gum, candy
❏ Flavored teas, coffees
❏ Cookbook
❏ Spice and sauce mixes, spices
❏ Sugar substitutes
❏ Powdered drinks (cocoa, Kool-Aid®, cider)

❏ Super glue (1 tube)
❏ Padlock (with 2 sets of keys or combination)
❏ Permanent marker
❏ Mosquito net (permethrin treated)
❏ Net hammock
❏ Water purifier (pump type)
❏ Water purifier (sport bottle type)
❏ Iodine drops for water puri-fication
❏ Umbrella
❏ Poncho (folded)
❏ Cable ties
❏ Clothes brush
❏ Shoe polish wipes
❏ Shoe polish kit/liquid
❏ _____
❏ _____

Laundry and Clothing Repair

❏ Laundry detergent
❏ Clothesline
❏ Clothespins
❏ Lingerie hanger (inflatable)
❏ Lightweight plastic hangers
❏ Sink stopper (flat, unisize)
❏ Sewing kit with patches, buttons, safety pins
❏ Folding scissors
❏ Replacement shoelaces
❏ _____

Electronic

❑ Laptop computer
   ❑ Extra storage media (CD, DVD, flash drives)
   ❑ Transformer/power source and cords
   ❑ Surge protector
   ❑ Modem
   ❑ Telephone extension cord
❑ Coupler for telephone cord
❑ Outlet splitter for telephone jack
❑ Adapters for telephone jacks
❑ Accessory drives (including back-up drive)
❑ Flash Drivers
❑ Back-up CD copies of critical programs
❑ _____
❑ Printer
   ❑ Cable connecting to computer
   ❑ Power cord
   ❑ Extra ink cartridges
   ❑ Paper
❑ Personal Digital Assistant
   ❑ Extra batteries
   ❑ Synchronization cable/cradle
❑ Transformer (220 V to 110 V —sufficient wattage)
❑ Multi-outlet extension cord
❑ Outlet adapters (kit)
❑ Surge protector

❑ Travel iron (110/220 V)
❑ Travel steamer (110/220 V)
❑ Solar-powered pocket calculator
❑ Portable shortwave radio
   ❑ Extra batteries
   ❑ Earphones
❑ Portable radio
   ❑ Extra batteries
   ❑ Earphones
❑ Portable CD/mp3 player
   ❑ Extra batteries
   ❑ Earphones
❑ Portable cassette player/recorder or digital recorder
   ❑ Blank tapes
   ❑ Extra batteries
   ❑ Earphones
   ❑ Connecting cords
❑ Travel coffee pot (110/220 V)
❑ Heating coil for single cup
❑ Travel alarm clock
   ❑ Extra batteries
❑ _____
❑ _____

Camera Equipment
- ❏ Video camera
  - ❏ Case
  - ❏ Transformer
  - ❏ Connecting cables
  - ❏ Instruction booklet
  - ❏ Video film
  - ❏ Memory Cards
  - ❏ Extra battery
  - ❏ Filters
  - ❏ _____
- ❏ Binoculars
- ❏ Tripod
- ❏ Still camera (with fresh battery)
  - ❏ 35 mm film ASA 100/200/400/800
  - ❏ Telephoto lens
  - ❏ Wide angle lens
  - ❏ Macro lens
  - ❏ Filters
  - ❏ Flash unit with spare batteries
  - ❏ Cords and battery charger
  - ❏ Replacement battery for camera
  - ❏ Cable release
  - ❏ Lens brush
  - ❏ Lens paper
  - ❏ _____

Entertainment
- ❏ Foldable "Frisbee" or throwing ring
- ❏ Pocket kite with string
- ❏ Musical instrument (e.g., ocarina, harmonica, jaw harp, etc.)
- ❏ DVDs
- ❏ Audio CDs
- ❏ Novels/Electronic books (e.g., Kindle®)
  - ❏ Connecting cords
  - ❏ Recharging cords/unit

MEASUREMENT CONVERSION TABLES

ALTITUDE

Meters	Feet
500	1,640
1,000	3,280
1,500	4,920
2,000	6,560
2,500	8,200
3,000	9,840
3,500	11,480
4,000	13,120
4,500	14,760
5,000	16,400
5,500	18,040
6,000	19,680
6,500	21,320
7,000	22,960
7,500	24,600
8,000	26,240

COOKING MEASURES

Cooking measures (approximate)
     Also many recipes that call for grams of something are not
asking for weight but rather for volume, on the assumption that
1 milliliter (cubic centimeter) equals 1 gram.

U.S. Cups	t = teaspoon T= Tablespoon	Milliliters (cubic centimeters)	Ounces
	1/8 t = "pinch"	0.6	1/50
	1/4 t	1.25	1/24
	1/2 t	2.5	1/12
	1 t	5	1/6
	1.5 t = 1/2 T	7.5	1/4
	3 t = 1 T	15	0.5
	2 T	30	1
	3 T	45	1.5
1/4 cup	4 T	60	2
1/3 cup	5 T	75	2.5
3/8 cup	6 T	90	3
	7 T	105	3.5
1/2 cup	8 T	120	4
	9 T	135	4.5
5/8 cup	10 T	150	5
2/3 cup	11 T	165	5.5
3/4 cup	12 T	180	6
	13 T	195	6.5
7/8 cup	14 T	210	7
	15 T	225	7.5
1 cup	16 T	240	8
1.25 cups	20 T	300	10
1.5 cups	24 T	360	12
2 cups	1 lb/ 1pt	480	16
3 cups	1.5 lb/ 1.5 pt	720	24
4 cups	2 lb/ 2 pt	960	32
16 cups	8 lb/ 8 pt	3,840 ml = 3.84 liters	128

Knowing the country of origin for your recipe can make a big difference!

Volume	United States	Australia	Great Britain
1 cup	8 oz	8 oz	10 oz
1 pint	16 oz	20 oz	20 oz
1 pint	2 cups	2 cups	2 cups
1 teaspoon	5 cc (4.8 g)	5 cc	5 cc
1 tablespoon	15 cc (14.8 g)	20 cc	20 cc
1 fluid ounce	30 cc (28.5 g)	30 cc (28.5 g)	30 cc (28.5 g)
1 gill	5 oz	5 oz	5 oz

CALORIES

	Multiply by
Kilojoules to Calories (kilocalories)	0.24
Calories to Kilojoules (kJ)	4.19

LENGTH, DISTANCE, AND AREA

	Multiply by
Inches to centimeters	2.54
Centimeters to inches	0.3937
Feet to meters	0.30
Meters to feet	3.28
Yard to meters	0.91
Meters to yards	1.09
Miles to kilometers	1.61
Kilometers to miles	0.62
Acres to hectares	0.40
Hectares to acres	2.47
Square miles to square kilometers	2.59
Square kilometers to square miles	0.39

PRESSURE

	Multiply by
Atmospheres to mm of mercury (mm Hg)	760.0
Kilopascals to mm of mercury	7.5

SPEED

1 mph = 1.61 km/h
1 km/h = 0.621 mph

TEMPERATURE

To convert °C to °F, multiply by 1.8 (or 9/5) and add 32.
To convert °F to °C, subtract 32 and multiply by 5/9 (.555).

	FAHRENHEIT	CELSIUS
Weather	0	–18
	32	0
	40	4
	45	7
	50	10
	55	13
	60	16
	65	18
	70	21
	75	24
	80	27
	85	29
	90	32
	95	35
	105	41
	110	43
Body temperatures	98.6	37
	99	37.2
	100	37.8
	101	38.3
	102	38.9
	103	39.4
	104	40
	105	41
Cooking	212	100
	250	121
	275	135
	300	149
	325	163
	350	177
	375	190
	400	204
	425	218
	450	232

Cooking at altitude: At sea level, water boils at 212°F. For every 550 feet above sea level, the boiling point of water is lower by about 10°F. For example, at 5,500 feet above sea level, water boils at 202°F, and therefore takes a corresponding longer time to cook food properly.

WEIGHT

	Multiply by
Ounces to grams	28.35
Grams to ounces	0.035
Pounds to kilograms	0.45
Kilograms to pounds	2.21
British tons to kilograms	1,016
U.S. tons to kilograms	907
Stones to pounds	14
British ton	2,240 lbs.
U.S. ton	2,000 lbs.

VOLUME

	Multiply by
Imperial gallon to liters	4.55
Liters to imperial gallon	0.22
U.S. gallons to liters	3.79
U.S. quart to liters	0.96
Liters to U.S. gallons	0.26
Liters to U.S. quart	1.04
Liters to U.S. cups	4.17 *(approximately 4 cups, 1 ounce, 2 teaspoons)*
5 imperial gallons equal just over	6 U.S. gallons

CLOTHING EQUIVALENTS

Men's Suits and Overcoats						
U.S.	36	38	40	42	44	46
U.K.	36	38	40	42	44	46
Europe	46	48	50	52	54	56
Men's Shoes						
U.S.	$7\frac{1}{2}$	8	$8\frac{1}{2}$	9	$9\frac{1}{2}$	10
U.K.	7	$7\frac{1}{2}$	8	$8\frac{1}{2}$	9	$9\frac{1}{2}$
Europe	$40\frac{1}{2}$	41	42	43	$44\frac{1}{2}$	46
Men's Shirts						
U.S.	14	$14\frac{1}{2}$	15	$15\frac{1}{2}$	16	17
U.K.	14	$14\frac{1}{2}$	15	$15\frac{1}{2}$	16	17
Europe	36	37	38	39	41	43
Women's Suits and Dresses						
U.S.	6	8	10	12	14	16
U.K.	8	10	12	14	16	18
Europe	36	38	40	42	44	46
Women's Shoes						
U.S.	6	$6\frac{1}{2}$	7	$7\frac{1}{2}$	8	$8\frac{1}{2}$
U.K.	$4\frac{1}{2}$	5	$5\frac{1}{2}$	6	$6\frac{1}{2}$	7
Europe	$36\frac{1}{2}$	37	$37\frac{1}{2}$	38	$38\frac{1}{2}$	39
Children's Clothes						
U.S.	4	6	8	10	12	14
U.K.—						
Height (in.)	43	48	55	58	60	62
Age	4–5	6–7	9–10	11	12	13
Europe—						
Height (cm)	125	135	150	155	160	165
Age	7	9	12	13	14	15

APPENDIX F

PHOTOGRAPHY HINTS

Choice of Cameras

▶ Point and shoot cameras have the advantage of being quick to use, cheap and small

▶ SLR-type cameras with interchangeable lens have the advantage of using various lenses to capture your picture

• Telephoto lens allows you to get faraway pictures and better portraits.

• Wide-angle lens may help, especially in urban settings.

• Macro lens allow close-ups of the some of the amazing flowers and insects you will see.

▶ SLR cameras with the entire set of lens can be expensive and difficult to carry around with you.

▶ Bring a cheap point-and-shoot underwater camera— these are valuable to capture high humidity and wet scenes.

▶ Digital cameras give you the benefit of being able to see right away if you got the picture and also they are a great ice-breaker when you show the pictures to your subject and his or her family and friends.

▶ The advantages of camcorders are obvious, but they make you stand out as "wealthy tourist". They are desirable items easily stolen. Self-consciousness arising from being videotaped can help create a barrier between you and the local people. The newer models that are small and combine high-quality digital still pictures and video are often a good compromise and have the advantage of a digital camera with an excellent zoom lens.

• Follow the same rules as for still photography.

• Take enough recording cassettes or memory cards. They are very expensive and hard to find overseas.

• Too bad there is nothing that can quite capture the aroma of the developing country!

General Hints

▶ Use the flash or reflectors as a fill-flash for dark-skinned people. Be careful in situations of back-lighting. It will fool the camera and underexpose their faces.

▶ Close-ups rather than panoramas.

316

▶ Architectural detail rather than the whole edifice.

▶ Include people in your scenery shots.

▶ Take many pictures of your group or family and let the pictures tell the story.

▶ Be sure to include yourself in the pictures! Let someone else take some pictures.

▶ Take more pictures of people and fewer of scenery.

▶ You can't take the picture if you don't carry your camera.

▶ Use a telephoto lens without a flash in order not to be obtrusive.

▶ Take lots of pictures! Delete or throw most of them away and show only the good ones.

Appropriate Subjects

▶ Ask what you will get into trouble for taking a picture of — government buildings, prisons, airports, bridges, police/armed forces personnel, government officials, security checkpoints and military camps are often off-limits. Be careful of sites of special spiritual significance.

▶ In those places, don't even pretend you are taking a picture by looking through the viewfinder!

▶ In some countries, it is not only rude but illegal to take pictures of the nationals without their permission.

▶ Some people groups will get very upset if their picture is taken because of culture, religious or monetary reasons. They may demand money and it may be an offer you can't resist.

▶ Be respectful of individual dignity. Always err on the side of asking permission first. If you don't want your picture taken while taking a bath in a stream, they won't either.

Travel with a Camera

▶ Airport X-rays usually aren't a problem unless you are carrying very high-speed film. A lead foil package can protect film.

▶ Register your new camera with customs when you leave N. America if there is any concern that you might be assessed duties on return.

▶ Dust can be a killer—take a lens brush and lens paper.

▶ Use a well-padded bag.

▶ Take enough memory if you have a digital camera—and then take some more.

▶ Take extra batteries for camera and flash—special sizes are very difficult to get overseas.

▶ If you use rechargeable batteries, make sure the recharger is compatible with available voltage.

▶ Make sure you have an adapter for your recharger plug.

▶ Don't leave your camera in a hot vehicle.

Film (for the two of you who still do)

▶ Take lots of film.

▶ High-speed film and color transparency film (slides) are very difficult to get in the U.S. and almost impossible overseas. Be sure to take enough.

Memory

▶ Take large-capacity memory cards or multiple cards. They are often difficult to find or expensive if you do find them.

▶ Consider taking a card reader to download the contents to your computer on a regular basis so that you have it backed up in the case of loss of the card or the camera.

▶ Set your pictures so that you have a reasonable level of resolution. It is rare that you need an 8 megabyte or larger picture unless you are trying to enlarge the picture to fit an entire wall. For most things, a 1 megabyte sized picture is more than enough detail and allows you to fit 8 times more pictures on the memory card.

▶ If you have enough memory, take pictures of everything. It costs you nothing to delete the ones you don't like.

TRAVELING WITH YOUR COMPUTER TO THE MISSION FIELD

You are going to a foreign place for the "Experience" with a capital "E". Why would you want to drag along a computer? You just might! Do you need to be a computer expert to go on short-term mission trips? Of course not. Do you need all of the things mentioned below? Even if you're a computer nerd, should you discouraged by this chapter and leave your laptop home? Of course not—but in our travels, we have run across each and every one of these problems and wished we had thought about it more. However, rest assured that no matter how much you plan, something will happen that is unexpected. The worst computer crash was actually of a type we didn't think about ahead of time. It was literally a computer crash. Walking down a dusty Ugandan road, there was a slip on the loose soil and a fall. No one was really hurt—the computer that was being carried cushioned the fall nicely but ended up much the worse for the wear. All of our work from the past four months was on the hard drive. *That* tested our Christian equanimity! At yet another time, our child pulled the laptop onto the concrete floor. A true crash of the hard drive—and everything else. That tested our compliance to the sixth commandment. Fortunately, God is always in control and even those events didn't surprise Him.

The Advantages of Taking Your Computer with You to the Mission Field

▶ It avoids the separation anxiety if you are one of those who sleep with your laptop or check your e-mail on your nocturnal trip to the bathroom.

▶ You can e-mail your family, church and support team if Internet is available where you are going—even if you cannot connect to your usual server, you can type your e-mails at your leisure on your computer. You can save them as e-mail files and/or "cut and paste" the text messages from your flash drive to your host's computer.

This avoids tying up your host's computer when everyone else may want to use it.

▶ If you are a typist, even of the "hunt and peck" variety, you can keep your journal on the computer and even share daily entries via e-mail with close friends and family members who want all the "excruciating detail".

▶ You can keep up on your blog or other social media—if you can get internet access.

▶ If you have brought along a digital camera, pictures can be downloaded, manipulated, stored and even reduced in size for cost-effective and time-effective e-mailing with your newsletters.

▶ Use your laptop as an entertainment center—games, audio CDs, DVDs. It can also be a worthwhile resource center if you take CDs that contain books, Bible software, encyclopedias, cookbooks, etc.

▶ With access to a missionary's printer or carrying a portable printer with you, many projects can be accomplished more effectively and professionally for the good of the place you are visiting. Also, you can print cards, invitations, banners, pictures and other special things that will be appreciated. If you have in mind a project that requires special paper, business cards or labels, you probably should plan on bringing those with you. They are often hard to find overseas when you want them.

▶ If you have access to the Internet and you will be gone a while, you can use it to do banking if you have electronic banking set up (e.g. Intuit's Quicken®, Microsoft's Money® or web-banking through your own bank). Also, websites like www.skype.com can allow voice communication if both computers are set up for it. Be forewarned—good voice communication will require a baud rate near 56K and many mission settings do not have that fast a baud rate on their dial-up service. You will have to remember to make sure your computer has a microphone and earphones or take a supplementary set. It is only a rare mission setting which has the bandwidth that will allow you to use the video component of Skype and similar programs and even if it is possible, you may be hogging the bandwidth to the point that no one else on the mission compound can effectively use it. Be very careful about downloading video files at any time and also about ordering any download for your mp3 player for the same reason. Check with the missionaries first.

If you have convinced yourself to take your computer, there are some things you should do before you leave home:

▶ Back up any critical files (including databases, address books, e-mail files, etc.) and programs.

▶ Back up any critical files and programs. Buy a portable hard-drive big enough to back up your entire computer but small enough to carry. Take it with you. Use it. Regularly. Consider remote back-up (Internet-based) of your computer.

▶ Back up any critical files and programs (Get the idea?)

▶ Especially if you will be gone for more than a few months, download up-to-date virus definition files and engines for your anti-viral software.

▶ Also make sure you know how to use the zip utility which is part of Windows XP and Vista. It will allow you to shrink some attachments considerably (some files won't shrink at all). E-mail may be expensive to send due to long distance calls to the server. Not all countries have Internet access and it may be very expensive, especially if sent over satellite telephone, which have low baud transfer rates.

▶ Know how to compress the pictures you put in your Word documents and in PowerPoint. It can dramatically shrink the size of the e-mails you are sending out with those attachments.

▶ Remember to take emergency boot disks with you and copies (not the originals) of any software CD-ROMs (including registration numbers, software identification numbers, etc., that it may take to reinstall it). Do this for all of your vital software including your operating software. It is not illegal to make copies of CD-ROMs if it is for your own use and it is perhaps wiser to risk losing a copy than the original software. If you have dial-up service at home, see if your e-mail and Internet company has a server in the country where you will serve. It is often rather expensive if you include the additional fee for the use of that server plus the cost of long-distant connections, but the convenience may be worth the costs. Get the access numbers into your computer before you leave the US because it may be impossible later. If your North American company does not allow you to access your e-mail account via the Internet (and you have found out that it is possible to use the Internet via your host's computer), you may wish to set up an account with a free or low-cost e-mail company that allows access via the

322   Your Mission: Get Ready! Get Set! GO!

Internet (e.g. Google's e-mail, Yahoo and others). You will then just reimburse your host for the access time. Other options include the possibility that you might be able to send e-mails on the hospital or missionary account without needing a separate personal account. This can be inconvenient for you and your host, so ask for permission first. Sometimes, if you are a heavy e-mail user, it is worth setting up a completely separate account for the time you are there. Be aware that there will be a cost to you for implementing this option. Investigate this early as setting up an account can take time.

▶ Some systems will allow the use of a cell-phone as a modem or you can use a satellite phone or a BGAN satellite modem to access the Internet. These are often very expensive alternatives and the later two usually require at least a year's subscription as well as the purchase of the expensive phones and modems.

▶ Make sure that you can use the electricity where you will be and that you can be protected from it.[1] Most laptop transformers can be used with either 110v or 220v (with a plug adapter appropriate for the country). Make sure that your equipment can handle dual volt-

ages, but if it cannot, consider purchasing a larger transformer that can handle multiple electrical devices. It has been our experience that laptops and other battery driven devices that actually use a much lower voltage do well with 220 volts but many other pieces of equipment such as printers may not work well on the on transformed voltage. This may be because 110 volt equipment is 60 cycles and 220 volt is normally 50 cycles. Although voltage has been stepped down from 220 volt to 110 volt but it is still at 50 cycles. This change in frequency may interfere with the internal "clocks" necessary for the proper function of some electrical equipment. The small transformers found in many travel currency kits are not rugged and may burn out at the most inopportune time. They also allow only one thing to be plugged in at once. A more rugged one may be advantageous to have but have the disadvantage of being rather heavy. You might check with your host and see if they can purchase one for you in the country you are visiting. A multi-outlet strip for the appropriate voltage is often valuable (so your spouse doesn't unplug your computer to use his or her hairdryer!). It may be able to be combined with a surge protector. A high quality surge protector (in the appropriate voltage) is a necessary thing to take but again has the disadvantage of being hard to find in the average North American store if you need one for 220 volts. It may also be somewhat bulky to pack. We have had good luck with a small portable one (e.g. www.apc.com, Belkin and others) that fits between the transformer power cord and the transformer but it does have the disadvantage of only protecting the laptop and not any accessory devices. Make sure your surge protector also protects the telephone line. As an aside, we have made it a point to unplug anything not absolutely needed—surges and brown-outs (low voltage) are common in Third World countries and both are bad for your equipment. The inconvenience of remembering to be finicky enough to plug it in and take the plug out when you are done is much less than the inconvenience of not having the equipment when you need it because now it is a smoldering piece of useless junk!

▶ Consider an extra battery for your computer to take with you. The plane rides can be long and the reliability of power at the mission site may not be great. An extra charged battery can make the difference in being entertained and/or being effective if the power goes out. Some airlines now have power for laptops built into business class or first class seats, but these usually require a special adapter. If you are flying with one of those airlines in one of those nicer cabins (lucky you!), you may desire to buy those adapter(s) before you go. For those of you in much more primitive settings, a portable inverter device (transforming 12 volt input from automobile batteries to 110 volts) are relatively heavy but invaluable if power is really unreliable.

▶ Check with the missionaries to see if you need any special adapters to plug your standard telephone cord from your modem into the local telephone systems and find out if those adapters are available in the country.

▶ If you plan to communicate with a large number of people, make sure that you have your address and e-mail list printed out. You cannot always count on being able to count on being able to "cut and paste" the lists from one type of e-mail software to another. It is sometimes easier to work from the paper list than from your computer—and a computer crash will leave you unable to communicate if you rely on the computer alone. If you are able to keep your usual e-mail address, consider asking the people with whom you communicate to refrain from forwarding each and every cute or "meaningful" item, URL or picture that crosses their screen. With slow modems on some foreign servers, unreliable telephone lines and expensive connections, you may regret their thinking of you! Be sure they realize that despite your plans to have e-mail access, loss of service is painfully frequent and you may be out of touch for days or even weeks.

▶ Alternatively, most e-mail programs have a way to limit the size of the e-mail they will accept/download. This is definitely helpful. Ask your computer guru for help in setting this up.

▶ If you have a CD or DVD burner, take blank discs with you. They may be hard to find, and are usually expensive if you do. Plan to leave them if you don't use them—the missionaries will love you for it!

▶ Sometimes, depending on the project and the size of the files, we have found it worthwhile to take a flash drive with us to facilitate transfer of large files. Keep the flash drive on a lanyard to help prevent its loss.

▶ Buy a small set of headphones (ear buds are perhaps best unless you plan to use an Internet voice service where you would need ones with a microphone) that will fit your computer. Conditions may be cramped and it may prevent some grating of nerves when one of you wants to sleep.

▶ If you are taking a digital camera with you, don't forget to make sure your drivers have been installed on the laptop and the connecting cord that goes to your computer. While we are on the topic, don't forget the extra memory devices, battery chargers and/or extra batteries either. Make yourself familiar with the picture software, especially find how to "shrink" the pictures and to send the picture in one of the "condensed" formats, e.g. a .jpg format. A 40 kilobyte attachment is much more convenient than a 2 megapixel attachment and will give the folks at home a general idea. You can give them the high-resolution picture later.

As You Travel

▶ Keep your laptop with you at all times. To avoid problems with customs, make sure it is clearly marked as belonging to you and it is best if it appears "used". A photocopy of the sales receipt from its purchase may be wise if you know that the country you are entering is one with a reputation of being difficult or if your computer looks new. They may be concerned that you are trying to bring in a computer for someone within the country without paying duty on it.

▶ Many smaller foreign airlines are very fussy about the size and weight of carry-on baggage but we have found that if they want us to check our bags (which are of standard size to fit international regulations), they will usually be willing to forego that demand if we explain that it has our computer within and we don't want to be separated from it.

▶ Scan every file that enters your computer before you open it. Nine thousand miles from home is no time to have a virus wipe out your hard drive!

▶ Unplug it whenever possible—the best surge protection comes from a disconnected power and telephone line!

▶ Send us an e-mail and let us know how your trip is going and what the Lord is doing in your lives!

The three top factors in real estate are location, location, location. The best way to share your experience overseas is communicate, communicate,

communicate. E-mail is such a blessing for people on the mission field, both career and short-term because it allows rapid communication. You might be happiest if you discipline yourself to write some sort of newsletter at regular intervals. It saves you from writing everyone individual letters and especially if you are not journaling, it is a way to put down some vibrant memories. When you are old and gray, you will be glad you did. It is amazing how soon you can forget some experiences that at the time are so vibrant that you swear you never will.

Before you leave, compile a list of those who will be praying for you or those who have indicated that they would like to hear reports of your trip. Include non-believing friends and relatives if they want to hear—it can be a great witness to them. Include your family, friends and co-workers—one physician's office staff made the letters available to interested patients and this was a great testimony. Include missionaries where you have worked before. Keep your church informed. Realizing that not every one has e-mail, recruit a contact person who can serve to relay letters and e-mails to those who do not have e-mail. Even if you have to communicate only by surface mail, write to one person who then photocopies and mails them back out to your mailing list. It saves time and money for you. If you have to communicate by surface mail, remember that it is much quicker and cheaper to send letters from the US and Canada than from other countries. Take stamps and envelopes with you and send letters back to North America with people who are returning from the field.

When you write, tell of your experiences and what your reactions are. Send regular reports of what God is doing in your own life and in the ministry. Include requests for prayer and updates on God's provision—it is a ministry to those at home as well as a great exercise for you.

Bruce and Micky Steffes live in Linden, N.C. They are both natives of Lapeer, Michigan. Attending the same church there as children, they went to different Bible colleges for their first years of college but finished their undergraduate work at the University of Michigan—Flint College. Bruce subsequently graduated from the University of Michigan College Of Medicine and then trained in general surgery at the University of Florida. Since that time, he has been also awarded a Masters of Business Administration from the Fuqua School of Business at Duke University and was certified in tropical medicine by the American Society of Tropical Medicine and Hygiene.

As a surgeon and as an entrepreneur in Fayetteville, N.C, he underwent a personal and spiritual crisis that changed the focus of his life. He resigned from his practice in December, 1997. Micky had a similar experience in her life. They married in 1998 and their honeymoon was an around-the-world trip to war-torn and forgotten mission outpost. Since then, serving always as volunteers and with a focus upon supporting the true heroes in the trenches, Bruce and Micky (an accountant by training) have used their surgical, business and administrative skills in multiple hospitals and other missionary efforts in the developing world. Traveling an average of 40,000 to 70,000 miles a year in the air, they have spent the majority of each year as a short-term missionaries in Haiti, Belize, Guatemala, Brazil, Kenya, Uganda, Togo, Benin, Zambia, Sierra Leone, Liberia, Angola, Papua New Guinea, Afghanistan and Uzbekistan. They have also visited several other countries and medical works, now totally over 50 nations. They serve regularly with the Mercy Ships and World Medical Mission (the medical relief arm of Samaritan's Purse) doing short-term (up to seven month) stints at each place. Micky and Bruce have worked with two orphanages in Jinja, Uganda. He has worked with several other agencies and NGOs as a volunteer. In 2005, they moved to East Africa to develop a proposal for a $40M pediatric national referral hospital in East Africa, working on behalf of the First Lady of that country. Sadly, that project did not come to fruition.

Bruce is especially interested in medical education. An active member and assistant Financial Officer of the Continuing Medical and Dental Education Commission of the Christian Medical and Dental Association, he assists in their mission to bring current medical information to those serving on the front-lines in developing countries. In early 2006, he became the Chief Executive Officer of the Pan African Academy of Christian Surgeons (PAACS), a general surgical training program for African residents. PAACS is a rural-based health initiative and is a Commission of the Christian Medical and Dental Association. Seeking more ways to serve, he has taught resuscitation courses for trauma, pediatrics and advanced cardiac life support in the U.S. and East Africa. When in the U.S., Steffes the Surgeon-in-Residence at Methodist University Physician Assistant Program teaching anatomy, physiology and general surgery to PA students each fall. He is also associate professor in surgery at Loma Linda University and he is also a guest lecturer yearly at the West Virginia University Clinical Tropical Medicine and Traveler's Health Course. In 2009, he was named as one of the Distinguished Global Faculty of The University of Toledo. Steffes is a fellow of the American College of Surgeons, the West African College of Surgeons and the College of Surgery of East, Central and Southern Africa. He has been recognized for his work with PAACS with the 2008 International Medicine Award (from the Institute for International Medicine) and induction to the Medical Missions Hall of Fame, located at the University of Toledo in Ohio.

Micky has had her own ministry which has been intertwined with the challenges of raising and home-schooling an active young son while living out of suitcase. Her skills as an accountant have done much to improve various ministries, her skills as wife and mother have kept the family together and her skills as a listener have brought healing to many a missionary wife and single missionary.

In their efforts to mobilize interest, personnel and finances for medical missions, they are speakers in churches, service groups and missionary conferences here in the U.S. In aid of that effort, the Steffes' wrote the "Handbook for Short Term Medical Missionaries," published by ABWE (2002) and the first self-help book aimed largely at medical missionaries. When the book went out of print, it was revised, expanded and divided into two separate works. The first half became available in 2009 as "Medical Missions: Get Ready, Get Set, Go!" and this book completes the set.

INDEX

A

Adapters, electrical   126, 151, 307, 323
Address, giving yours out   203, 235
Affection, public displays of   207
AIDS (see HIV)   72, 73, 249
Airlines   34, 35, 36, 38, 39, 40, 107, 109, 110, 112, 121, 124, 136, 140, 145, 147, 157, 158, 159, 160, 167, 169, 323, 325
Airport departure tax   44, 154
Alcohol   68, 96, 146, 208, 233, 304
Altitude   68, 146, 163, 309
Altitude sickness   68, 303
   prevention of   68, 120, 303
   symptoms of   65, 68, 303
Altitude, changes during flight   146, 309
American culture, presuppositions underlying   204
American culture, time and punctuality   205
American traits, negative perceptions of   203
Amodiaquine   86, 88
Amoeba   65, 92, 96, 215, 220
Anti-malarials, (see Malaria, prophylaxis)   64, 73, 74, 75
Antiseptic cream   90, 171
Antiviral software   321
Ants   228
Apathy upon reentry   266, 268
Artemesin (artemether, artemisinin, artesunate)   88
Arrival at airport   141

Arrival in country   147, 148
Athlete's foot   95
Attitude   58, 134, 188, 205, 271
Audio CD   130, 134, 167, 308, 320
Automobile travel   69
Azithromycin   65, 91, 99

B

Babies
   backpacks   161, 162, 163
   bedding   165
   carriers   162, 167
   clothing   160, 161, 168, 302
   diapers (see Diapers)
   feeding, breast   83, 163, 171, 173
   feeding, formula   163, 166, 169, 170
   feeding, formula, use of boiled water   163, 164
   in flight   168, 169
   port-a-cots   162
   skycots   39
   sterilization of baby bottles   164, 220
   strollers   162, 163, 165
Baby carriers   162, 167
Backpacks   162, 163
Banned items, airlines   110, 121, 208
Bargaining   224, 229, 231
   determining the right price   230
   suggestions about   224, 231
   where it is appropriate   224, 231

G

Giardia lamblia   92, 215, 220
Gifts   20, 23, 114, 128, 129,
  131–134, 153, 183, 200–202,
  227, 228, 231, 232, 278, 298,
  306
  foods and seasonings   228
  for hosts   131, 202, 227
  for missionaries   128, 129,
    227
  for nationals   132–134
Goal-setting   3, 53, 74, 178, 194,
  196, 206, 269
Gospel, methods of sharing   6, 28,
  56, 133, 235, 250, 252, 253
Grocery shopping   224–226
Guest, acting as one   200, 213,
  237, 239
Guilt   24, 52, 200, 201, 234, 235,
  267, 275
Gum, chewing   124, 133, 146,
  166, 179, 211, 306

H

Hairdryer   322
Hand cleanser   118
Hand gestures   244
Hat   95, 117, 160, 176, 302
Hazardous materials   110
Headphones   167, 324
Healing, consistent with God's
  nature   288, 289, 328
Health insurance   42, 47, 50, 65,
  66, 137, 141
Health, children
  malaria prophylaxis   75, 80,
    170, 174
  pediatric health kit   171

  prevention of ear pain in plane
    146
  travelers' diarrhea   172, 174
  treatment of malaria   67, 87,
    88
  vaccinations   102–104,
    170–173
Heart disease   65
Hepatitis A   91, 103, 172, 216
Hepatitis B   103, 172
HIV
  avoidance of   70–72
  prophylaxis   70–72, 249
  prophylaxis, timing of
    70–72, 249
  risk of exposure classifications
    70–72, 249
  universal precautions   70
Home repair in your absence   50
Home security system   50
Homecoming (see also Reentry)
  274, 275
Homesickness   187, 192, 197
House lights   139
Household servants   200
Humor   134, 192–197, 229,
  245, 248
Hydrocortisone cream   90, 304

I

IAMAT   66
Ice cubes   221
Idiom   209, 243
If only   39
Immigration   35, 147, 147, 154
Immune globulin (immunoglobulin)
  91, 103, 104
Immunizations (see Vaccinations)
Influenza   77, 173
Insect repellent   78

R

Rabies 82, 93, 103
Racial issues 206
Radio 17, 125, 127, 184, 201
    short-wave 127, 307, 267,
        272
    two-way 125
Rainy seasons 106
Raising support
    aid from your church 19
    asking others 15–17
    children assisting 22
    employer's help 23
    follow-up contacts 21, 25
    letter requesting support 20
    list of potential donors 16,
        17
    matching grants 23
    news release 22
    patients 21, 22
    sample letter requesting
        support 297
    speaking to groups 21
Razor 110, 119, 124, 128, 303
Reaction of others to your trip
    190, 271, 273
Reading glasses 121, 302, 304
Recipes 222, 226, 227, 310
Reentry 266, 274, 275, 278
    apathy 266, 268
    avoiding problems in 274
    crisis of faith 276
    debriefing, by others 277,
        278, 280
    debriefing, self 277, 278,
        280
    family reaction to 275
    guilt feelings 267, 275
    individual variances 266,
        275

    maintaining effectiveness
        277
    need for counseling 274,
        276, 281
    reasons for difficulty 266,
        274
    why you came home 275
Refrigerator 26, 127, 140, 141,
    226, 228
Regrets 282
Rest 37, 68, 91
Returning home 89, 91, 268
    analysis of trip 277
    report to church 271
    report to support team 273
Reverse culture shock 263, 264
Rifaximin 65, 98, 99
Roaches 196, 228
Romans Road, gospel presentation
    257–262
Rotavirus 173, 216
Rubella 91, 103, 172

S

Safes, can type 125
Safety 8, 11, 39, 69, 85, 92, 94,
    158–160, 169, 179, 217, 225,
    235
    hotel room and 79, 94
    prevention of assault 69, 92,
        93
    spray for self-defense 93,
        110
    valuables 93, 94, 125, 150
Salmonella 96
Sample drugs 131
Sample letter for support 297
Sandals 14, 115, 302
Sandfleas 95
Sanitary napkins 101